Gender, Democracy and Inclusion in Northern Ireland

Women's Studies at York Series

General Editors: **Haleh Afshar** and **Mary Maynard**

Haleh Afshar
ISLAM AND FEMINISMS
An Iranian Case-Study
WOMEN AND EMPOWERMENT
Illustrations from the Third World (*editor*)
WOMEN IN THE MIDDLE EAST
Perceptions, Realities and Struggles for Liberation (*editor*)

Haleh Afshar and Stephanie Barrientos (*editors*)
WOMEN, GLOBALIZATION AND FRAGMENTATION IN THE DEVELOPING WORLD

Haleh Afshar and Carolyne Dennis (*editors*)
WOMEN AND ADJUSTMENT POLICIES IN THE THIRD WORLD

Judy Giles
WOMEN, IDENTITY AND PRIVATE LIFE IN BRITAIN, 1900–50

Mary Maynard and Joanna de Groot (*editors*)
WOMEN'S STUDIES IN THE 1990s
Doing Things Differently?

Haideh Moghissi
POPULISM AND FEMINISM IN IRAN
Women's Struggle in a Male-Defined Revolutionary Movement

Shirin M. Rai (*editor*)
INTERNATIONAL PERSPECTIVES ON GENDER AND DEMOCRATIZATION

Carmel Roulston and Celia Davies (*editors*)
GENDER, DEMOCRACY AND INCLUSION IN NORTHERN IRELAND

Women's Studies at York
Series Standing Order ISBN 0–333–71512–8
(*outside North America only*)

You can receive future titles in this series as they are published by placing a standing order. Please contact your bookseller or, in case of difficulty, write to us at the address below with your name and address, the title of the series and the ISBN quoted above.

Customer Services Department, Macmillan Distribution Ltd, Houndmills, Basingstoke, Hampshire RG21 6XS, England

Gender, Democracy and Inclusion in Northern Ireland

Edited by

Carmel Roulston
Senior Lecturer in Politics
University of Ulster

and

Celia Davies
Professor of Health Care
School of Health and Social Welfare
The Open University

palgrave

First published 2000 by
PALGRAVE
Houndmills, Basingstoke, Hampshire RG21 6XS and
175 Fifth Avenue, New York, N.Y. 10010
Companies and representatives throughout the world

PALGRAVE is the new global academic imprint of
St. Martin's Press LLC Scholarly and Reference Division and
Palgrave Publishers Ltd (formerly Macmillan Press Ltd).

Outside North America
ISBN 0–333–76065–4 hardback
ISBN 0–333–76066–2 paperback

In North America
ISBN 0–312–23361–2 hardback

This book is printed on paper suitable for recycling and
made from fully managed and sustained forest sources.

A catalogue record for this book is available
from the British Library.

Library of Congress Cataloging-in-Publication Data
Gender, democracy, and inclusion in Northern Ireland / edited by Carmel
Roulston and Celia Davies.
        p. cm.
    Includes bibliographical references and index.
    ISBN 0–312–23361–2 (cloth)
        1. Women—Northern Ireland—Social conditions. 2. Women in politics—Northern
    Ireland. 3. Women and democracy—Northern Ireland. 4. Civil society—Northern
    Ireland. I. Roulston, Carmel, 1950– II. Davies, Celia.

    HQ1599.N67 G46 2000
    305.42'09416—dc21
                                                              00–022308

10   9   8   7   6   5   4   3   2   1
09 08 07 06 05 04 03 02 01 00

Printed in Great Britain by Antony Rowe Ltd, Chippenham, Wiltshire

Contents

Preface and Acknowledgements

This book could not have been started without the financial support of the Economic and Social Research Council for a research project (R000236224) 'Democracy, Gender, and the Politics of Women's Inclusion: Case-Studies from Northern Ireland'. We would like to thank the Council for support and advice as project team members found new employment or were otherwise unable to continue. Our most heartfelt thanks go to the members of the groups and organisations which agreed to allow us to research them. They were welcoming, interested in us and our project, open and forthcoming and very tolerant of our shortcomings. We hope that as members of the Chrysalis Women's Centre, the Cornerstone Community and the Northern Ireland Public Services Alliance read these chapters they will feel that the time, and energy which they gave to us have not been wasted. Owing to the departure of one of our team, we did not have the resources to turn our report on the Workers Educational Association for Northern Ireland into a chapter which would have done justice to their organisation. The discussions we had and the practices we observed in the meetings and classes which they so generously allowed us to attend have informed our reflections on the theory and practice of democracy and we are very grateful to them for their support.

As editors, we owe a debt of gratitude to all the authors who have contributed to this book. We would particularly like to thank Margaret Whittock, the Research Officer on the ESRC project. Changing personal circumstances meant that she could not stay with us to the end, but the contributions she made to the fieldwork and to the thinking of the project in its formative stages are not adequately reflected in authorship of one chapter. Project team members Monica McWilliams and Eilish Rooney offered ideas, practical help and participation on fieldwork for the full duration of the project. Monica's growing involvement with the Northern Ireland Women's Coalition was charted in discussions at team meetings. We were pleased that she was able, with the help of Kate Fearon, to produce the lively account that forms Chapter 6 of this book. Eilish brought her knowledge of local activism and her involvement with the intellectual ideas central to the project to bear in offering a commentary that sets the case-studies in a wider perspective of nationalism and feminism in the unique setting of Northern Ireland. Cynthia Cockburn, at very short notice, agreed to join the project as the researcher on the trade union case-study. Her contribution was invaluable, and we are very grateful for her full participation in our discussions. When it was clear that the editors were hopelessly overstretched, Grainne McCoy agreed at a late stage to contribute an introductory overview for the book and reacted with good heart to the comments and criticisms we offered. Last but far from least, we wish to thank Lis Porter, who was a supportive and sympathetic commentator on our research project and who brought her scholarly knowledge to bear on the task of writing a chapter on participatory democracy with great enthusiasm and amazing speed. As this book was being written, Lis was preparing to return to work in Australia. Australia's gain is a considerable loss to our local academic community.

The project and this book were also greatly helped by the support and encouragement of colleagues in the University of Ulster and the Open University. Our respective heads of school and research coordinators have provided moral and financial support. We were also greatly helped by Morag Stark, who provided invaluable secretarial support for the ESRC project, and Rosemarie Bell, who worked with great speed and accuracy on the typing and formatting of this book. Both of them also gave us advice and encouragement. Our thanks go to them, and to Karen Brazier, our editor at Macmillan, who has been encouraging and helpful through many delays and changes to this book.

The responsibility for the book as a whole rests with the two editors. In pursuing the vision of the project that underpins the book and in our commitment to ensuring that the book as a whole is accessible to those without a background knowledge of Northern Ireland, we have been more active than is often usual in the editorial role. Without the forbearance of our contributors, as well as the help and support of many other people who sustained and encouraged us with their interest, this work would not have been completed. We thank them all.

CARMEL ROULSTON
CELIA DAVIES

Notes on the Contributors

Cynthia Cockburn is Research Professor in Sociology in City University London. Her best-known books include *Brothers: Male Dominance and Technological Change* (Pluto, Press, 1983), *Machinery of Dominance* (Pluto Press, 1985), *Two Track Training* (Macmillan, 1987) and *In the Way of Women* (Macmillan, 1991). More recently she has published an acclaimed book on gender identities in conflict societies, *The Space Between Us* (Zed Books, 1998), which includes studies of women working together across differences in Northern Ireland.

Celia Davies was formerly Professor of Women's Studies and founder and Director of the Centre for Research on Women at the University of Ulster, and is currently Professor of Health Care in the School of Health and Social Welfare at the Open University. She is author of *Gender and the Professional Predicament in Nursing* (Open University Press 1995). She also co-authored a range of reports and publications on women in Northern Ireland, including: *Who Cares? Child Care and Women's Lives on the Shankill* (1992), *School-age Mothers – Access to Education* (1996), *A Matter of Small Importance? Differences between Protestant and Catholic Women's Employment in the NI Labour Market* (1995).

Kate Fearon was formerly Deputy Director of Democratic Dialogue and at present is Political Aide to Northern Ireland Women's Coalition Northern Ireland Assembly members Monica McWilliams and Jane Morrice. Kate has completed a book (*Women's Work: The Story of the Northern Ireland Women's Coalition*), soon to be published by Blackstaff Press, Belfast. She was an active campaigner for the opening of the Brook Advisory Centre in Belfast and was a member of its management committee. Currently, she is on the steering committee of the Belfast based *Conflict Transformation Project.*

Grainne McCoy was a Community Development Officer with Belfast City Council from 1993 to 1995. Since then she has worked as a research officer, currently with the *Preparing for Post-Conflict Trust*, based in the Urban Institute of the University of Ulster. Grainne is also researching a PhD thesis, provisionally titled 'Women and Peace-Building: An International Study'.

Monica McWilliams is Professor of Women's Studies and until recently was also coordinator of postgraduate women's studies courses at the University of Ulster. She is co-author (with Joan McKiernan) of *Bringing it out in the Open: Domestic Violence in Northern Ireland* (HMSO, 1993). She was a co-founder of the NIWC, gained one of the two elected places at the 'peace talks' and was subsequently elected to the Northern Ireland Assembly. She has published an account (with Avila Kilmurray, in 1997) of the emergence of the Coalition for the *Irish Journal of Women's Studies*. She is currently much in demand for her NIWC experience for lectures in the USA.

Elisabeth Porter previously taught at the University of South Australia, the Flinders University of South Australia and, more recently, has been a Lecturer in Sociology at the University of Ulster. Her most recent book is *Feminist Perspectives on Ethics* (Longman, 1999) She has published extensively on feminist social, moral and political theory, including two other books: *Women and Moral Identity* (Allen & Unwin, 1991) and *Building Good Families in a Changing World* (Melbourne University Press, 1995).

Eilish Rooney is a Lecturer in community education at the University of Ulster. She works, writes and researches in the areas of feminism, politics and culture. She is a member of '*Women into Politics*' (which conducts educational programmes for women on politics and history in working-class areas of Belfast). She is a founder member of the West Belfast Women's Network and is a member of a cross-border, university accredited political education programme for women. She has published articles in books and journals and contributes to local media.

Carmel Roulston is Senior Lecturer in politics at the University of Ulster. Among her recent publications are 'The Women's Movement in Northern Ireland, 1975–97', in *Feminist Nationalisms* (edited by Lois A. West, Routledge, 1997), and 'Feminism and Post-Modernism', in *Contesting Politics* (edited by Yvonne Galligan and Rick Wilford, Westview Press, 1999).

Margaret Whittock has a PhD in sociology from Queen's University, Belfast. Following a period working as a research officer with the Centre for Research on Women at the University of Ulster, and as Development Officer for the 'Women into Trades and Non-Traditional Occupations' Project, she went to live in Istanbul, where she has been employed as editor of a magazine for the British community there.

Introduction

This book had its origins in a series of seminars on 'Women in Politics' which took place during 1994, sponsored by the Centre for Research on Women in the University of Ulster. With the twin aims of developing our skills as teachers on a postgraduate course in women's studies and of identifying priorities for research projects, a group of lecturers and researchers from various disciplines met to discuss recent feminist contributions to political theory. In the course of these discussions, we turned our attention to women in politics in Northern Ireland. We began to look at where women were to be found in political life and the significance of what they were doing and how. We could not have failed, of course, to be aware of the contributions of women to the remarkable network of community and voluntary groups which had been a striking feature of political life in Northern Ireland for more than twenty years. A combination of events and experiences led us to take another look at this complex web of women's activism from a fresh perspective.

The whole question of civil society in Northern Ireland, and the positive roles which civil society groups and organisations could play in a future, peaceful Northern Ireland had been raised by the Opsahl Commission, which had set out to hear the ideas of citizens about ending the conflict and creating a new society. The importance of women's work in community groups was particularly highlighted in the report of the Commission,[1] whose members were profoundly impressed by the carefully prepared and presented statements from groups and activists. A common theme in many such presentations was that the women saw their work as 'not political'. In fact, the evidence suggested, theirs was a new way of acting politically. It was, however, a form of political action which was not acknowledged or rewarded by those engaged in what was referred to as 'big-P politics'.

At the time we were meeting it had become apparent that the ground was being prepared for a new round of political talks on the future of Northern Ireland. Given the male-dominated leadership of the major political parties, it seemed likely that women's voices would not be heard in the process. In response, women from diverse backgrounds and perspectives were gathering at conferences and meetings to articulate women's concerns for the future. The ideas and arguments coming out of these conferences made it clear that there were new perspectives on gender and politics, inclusion and exclusion that deserved to be heard.[2] Some of what we were hearing resonated with the themes and debates coming from the academic feminist political theorists we had been reading. Their critiques of the structures and values underpinning representative liberal democracies, and their ideas about remodelling democracy, so that women would no longer be on the outside or at the margins, seemed very pertinent to the experiences of women in Northern Ireland at that time.

We set out to look at what women in a number of different settings were doing and how they were doing it, trying to connect the insights from feminist political theory with the knowledge and experiences of the activists. We wanted to see whether the experiences and reflections of women in their different organisations and campaigns could help to take forward some of the discussions in the literature about the public and the private, inclusion without assimilation, identity and difference. The women speaking at the conferences and to the Opsahl Commission had been working out how to make decisions democratically, under enormous pressures, with many conflicts over loyalties and priorities. We set ourselves the task of finding out what methods they had used and what values they had created which might help to solve the problem of making democracies include women. To begin with, we invited women with experience of working in the community sector, in voluntary organisations and in trades unions to come to a series of seminars where the issues and ideas from feminist political theory, and their relevance to women's political agendas in Northern Ireland were discussed. These busy women gave up several hours of their time to discuss the theory and practice of women's activism. With their help, we defined the questions we might ask and the issues we might explore with the organisations we were about to approach for permission to study their methods and their problems.

With funding from the Economic and Social Research Council, we embarked upon in-depth studies of four organisations: a trade union, a cross-community religious group, a voluntary sector adult-education provider and a community-based women's centre. Our aim was not to be 'representative', but to try to locate and explore different traditions of democracy and inclusion in groups and organisations drawn from these different sectors. The groups we approached welcomed us and gave us access to their meetings, classes and documents (see Appendix 2). Volunteers, paid workers and members alike talked to us at length and with great frankness about their hopes and visions, their problems and setbacks. The accounts in this book provide only a fraction of what we learned from our involvement with the men and women who have created the structures and practices described within it.

As the fluid and fraught political situation in Northern Ireland unfolded over the next two years, through cease-fires and the hope of dialogue to political intransigence and a return to violence, a new force emerged on the political scene. A group of women activists, some from the very groups with which we had become involved, frustrated at the continued exclusion of women's perspectives from the political scene, created a Women's Coalition to campaign in the elections for the Forum for Political Dialogue, membership of which had been made a prerequisite for admission to the All-Party Peace Talks. To the surprise of other political parties, the Coalition won enough votes to qualify for two seats at the table, one of them to be occupied by a member of our project team, Monica McWilliams. We considered that it was vital to include an account of this new venture, which complemented the themes and issues dealt with elsewhere in the project, giving them a particularly high-profile testing ground. The Women's Coalition takes its place in this book, in the company of the Chrysalis Women's Centre, the Cornerstone Community and a trade union, the Northern Ireland Public Service Alliance (NIPSA). In all of these settings, the members have made it their business to find ways of bringing women's distinctive and diverse voices and perspectives into decision-making structures and processes, while at the same time responding to the particular demands and challenges of the politics of national conflict in Northern Ireland.

The focus of this book is women and politics, but it is about dealing with gender differences – and in particular, overcoming the exclusion of women – in a context where women themselves have been deeply divided by culture, history and national identity, as well as by class, sexual orientation, able-bodiedness and age. This book does not provide an account of the 'Northern Ireland conflict'. It has, however, been written by women who have different understandings and experiences of and responses to that conflict. We hope that we have done justice to the diversity of opinion within our team, as well as within the groups and organisations whose idea and experiences we have presented here. Like the members of the groups and organisations described here, we ourselves have had, on occasions, literally 'agreed to disagree', accepting that we have different perspectives but keeping the discussions going and building common ground where we can.

Our original aim was to draw together theory and practice, to study our case-study groups in the light of new feminist political theory and to ask, in turn, how their experiences could help develop the theories. The organisation of the book reflects the plan of the original project. Part I sets the scene. The first chapter provides the reader with an outline of the context within which civil society organisations work in Northern Ireland and an introduction to the history of women's activism in the community. (Here, as throughout, the chronology given in Appendix 1 will be helpful to those unfamiliar with events in Northern Ireland.) Chapter 2 surveys some of the key tenets of the feminist political theory which provoked our investigation. How can women be included in political systems founded on a separation between the public and private spheres which itself works to exclude women? How can we avoid the danger of eliding the differences among women themselves? The importance of such questions is considered alongside a discussion of recent attempts to identify the values and processes which can allow the creation of democratic coalitions in which multiple allegiances and identities can be recognised.

Part II, the centrepiece of the book, contains the accounts of the case-studies, all of which draw upon the theories and ask some new and difficult questions for the theorists. Chapter 3 describes the Chrysalis Women's Centre. The metaphor of the butterfly growing and changing in the chrysalis reflects the aspirations and beliefs of this group of women. For them, the potential of individual women can be realised only with the support of a self-conscious collective, in which hierarchy is actively resisted. The chapter explores a number of attempts to create structures and processes to allow women to become active participants, self-confident in all their diverse identities. The Cornerstone interfaith community also resists hierarchies, and has experimented with inclusive structures. Chapter 4 examines this group's aspirations and the struggle of its members to foster a deep understanding of each other. We found the women in this group working to construct an identity as women which would not reduce or restrict their opportunities to participate. Chapter 5 describes a trade union which has reached a watershed.

Having amended its decision-making structures to give a strong voice to women, NIPSA was now dealing with the argument that equalities issues all be dealt with 'in one pot'. We had decided at the outset that the project would steer away from the theme of women's participation, or lack of it, in electoral politics.[3] We agreed, however, that the Northern Ireland Women's Coalition was a very special case of women's presence not their absence. Chapter 6 gives an account of its origins and development and raises some questions as to its significance for women in Northern Ireland and in other political contexts.

Part III contains two chapters which continue to raise questions and matters for debate. In Chapter 7, Elisabeth Porter explores in detail the dilemmas of creating a dialogue across individual and group differences. This chapter provides some normative evaluations of feminist deliberative democracy informed by the experiences of the case-studies. In Chapter 8, Eilish Rooney offers further reflections on the dilemmas of difference. In Northern Ireland, she points out, national identity has been overtly significant in political life; the 'abstract individual' has been less abstract than in the liberal democratic systems about which feminist political theorists have written (though interestingly not 'less abstract' in the ways that that theory calls for). She warns against attempts to incorporate women in ways which try to bracket or ignore the identities and inequalities which divide them.

When our original conversations took place, in 1994, Northern Ireland was anticipating – with hope and anxiety – cease-fires and political talks. Since then, we have experienced successive waves of hope and despair. Cease-fires started, then ended, then resumed again; political talks were stalled, then revived, then stalled again. At the beginning of April 1998, it looked as though the process would stall yet again; instead, on Good Friday, the Belfast Agreement was signed, and subsequently endorsed by overwhelming majorities in both parts of Ireland. As we write this, the differences left unresolved in that Agreement have surfaced again and we are back in a political stalemate, which it is clear will require more time, talks and goodwill to break. Despite the pessimism which this inevitably induces, it is clear that in many ways Northern Ireland has changed for the better and much of the credit for that change must go to the women and men in the groups and organisations whose hopes and fears, mistakes and insights are presented in this book.

Notes

1 See Andy Pollak (ed.) (1993) *A Citizen's Enquiry: The Opsahl Report for Northern Ireland*, Dublin: Lilliput Press.

2 One of these conferences was facilitated by the Centre for Research on Women (see Chapter 6 of this volume). For an account of others, see Bronagh Hinds (1999), 'Women Working for Peace in Northern Ireland', in Yvonne Galligan, Eilis Ward and Rick Wilford (eds) *Contesting Politics: Women in Ireland, North and South*, Boulder, CO: Westview Press: 109–29.

3 Our study was intended to complement the research project on women in formal and party politics carried out by colleagues at Queen's University, the results of which have been published in Robert Miller, Rick Wilford and Freda Donoghue (1996) *Women and Political Participation in Northern Ireland*, Aldershot: Avebury.

Part I
Context and Concepts

1
Women, Community and Politics in Northern Ireland

Grainne McCoy

To examine the relationships between women and politics in Northern Ireland is to reveal a somewhat contradictory state of affairs. As many researchers and commentators (for example, Roulston 1996, Wilford 1996) have observed, until recently women have been noticeably absent from the leadership structures of mainstream party politics. The presence of women, on the other hand, has also been a feature singled out for commentary (Morgan and Fraser 1994, Rooney and Woods 1995, Gray *et al.* 1997, Miller *et al.* 1996). Many hundreds of women contribute positively, and with enormous energy, to the social and political fabric of Northern Ireland at every level. For the most part, they are to be found in the hundreds of voluntary and community organisations through which the citizens of Northern Ireland attempt to compensate for the deficiencies of democratic politics and government in their region. Women have been described as the 'mainstay of community groups' (Pollak 1993:81), whose activities have helped to hold the society together through years of great adversity. Women's groups operate at many levels in the community in Northern Ireland. The scope of their activities is very wide, from campaigning on domestic violence to dealing with all the issues that affect their immediate neighbourhood. Yet the Equal Opportunities Commission for Northern Ireland expressed concern that 'the inequality and marginalization suffered by women in the economic, political and social spheres undermine their status as full citizens' (*ibid.*: 82).

This chapter attempts to introduce and explore some of the contradictions. Beginning with a survey of the under-representation of women in formal politics, it provides a description of women's community activism, with a brief account of its origins and an

3

outline of women's groups and networks. This activism is put in the context of the constraints and pressures facing women and women's groups in a society that is deeply divided by sectarianism and violent conflict and in which women's initiatives are constrained by lack of funding and resources.

Women in mainstream politics

To give an account of women in mainstream politics and government, it is necessary first to outline the distinctive features of the Northern Ireland political system. From 1921 until 1972, Northern Ireland was governed by a local parliament (at Stormont in Belfast) and cabinet, based on the so-called Westminster model of government, with, from 1929, a first-past-the-post electoral system, which gave the Unionist party a permanent majority. This parliament had considerable autonomy in domestic matters, supported by its own civil service. In 1972, the Stormont parliament was closed down, having been judged by the British government to have failed to control the civil disorder which had escalated from 1969. An unsuccessful attempt was made, in 1973–4, to restore devolved government to a new Assembly in which unionist parties would share executive powers with nationalists.[1] Apart from that brief experiment, there has been direct rule from Westminster, with the secretary of state and Northern Ireland Office ministers responsible for policy-making, using the mechanism of orders in council to introduce legislation. The Northern Ireland Office (NIO) has its own Westminster-based team of civil servants; there is also a separate Northern Ireland Civil Service (NICS), with six departments.

The abolition of the Stormont parliament was accompanied by a reform of local government. As a result, control over housing, education, libraries and social services was removed from local councils and placed in the hands of a housing executive and area boards, whose members were appointed or approved by the relevant minister or department. In this way, it was hoped, provision of statutory and important services would not be blighted by political or sectarian biases. There are, at present, 131 non-elected public bodies responsible for many aspects of policy-making (Heenan and Gray 1999:189). Twenty-six local councils, with very limited powers, were created. The councils' responsibilities are locally said to consist of little more than 'bins and burials'; since the 1970s, however, they have also been required to take responsibility for improving community relations and promoting community development, responsibilities which, as will be seen, have particular significance for women's participation. With a population of just over 1.5 million, and an electorate of 1.1 million, Northern Ireland has a lot of elected representatives, but suffers from a lack of democracy. In the electoral sphere, Northern Ireland has the 26 local councils, and returns 18 members of parliament to Westminster and three members to the European Parliament. In June 1996 a Forum for Political Dialogue with 110 elected members was created as part of the peace process. With the acceptance of the Belfast Agreement in the referendum of May 1998, a 108-member Northern Ireland Assembly was elected, replacing the Forum. At time of writing, the Assembly had not taken over control of policy because of a fundamental disagreement, principally between Sinn Féin and the Ulster Unionist party, over the exact timing of decommissioning of paramilitary weapons in the process of implementing the agreement. Direct rule continues.

Throughout its history Northern Ireland has elected few women to parliaments or local councils. In total 9 women (the majority of them in the dominant Unionist party) were elected to Stormont during its lifetime. There were never more than 4 women (out of 52 members of the Northern Ireland parliament) in any session, and only one ever became a minister. Only 3 women (2 unionists) have represented Northern Ireland seats at Westminster, the most recent being Bernadette Devlin (now McAliskey) who held a seat as a 'nationalist unity' representative from 1969 to 1974 (Galligan and Wilford 1999). There are currently no women among the 18 Westminster MPs, nor among the members of the European Parliament. 14 members (13 per cent) of the Northern Ireland Assembly are women, including 2 members of the Northern Ireland Women's Coalition. Of the 26 district councils, there are 3 with no women members at all and overall, approximately 15 per cent of council members are women (Roulston 1996). The picture is better in the public bodies, where women make up 24 per cent of appointed or nominated members. As Heenan and Gray (1999:189–91) point out, however, there are still 8 public bodies with no women members at all, and at the most influential (and salaried) levels of such bodies the percentage of women is much smaller.

In the political parties, a similar pyramid of power can be discerned. Among the party rank and file there are large numbers of women, but their proportion decreases further up the hierarchy.

Some of the larger political parties have, slowly, responded to pressure from women among their members and voters to improve the representation of women in their leadership structures. The nationalist Social-Democratic and Labour Party (SDLP) and Sinn Féin both have quotas for women on policy-making bodies and women's sections. The SDLP has 3 women among its 24 Assembly members, while Sinn Féin has 5 women in the Assembly out of a total of 18 members. The cross-community Alliance Party puts forward quite large numbers of women candidates; 1 of its 6 Assembly seats is held by a woman. In the largest of Northern Ireland's parties, the Ulster Unionist Party (UUP), 42 per cent of members are women. The UUP has had a women's council since 1911, and more recently has created a women's policy committee (Wilford and Galligan 1999:170). Only 2 of its 28 assembly members, however, are women; it has a poor record of putting women forward for election, as has the Democratic Unionist Party, which has 1 woman assembly member out of 20. On the whole, the nationalist parties are better at selecting women.

Since the closing down of the Stormont parliament, the local parties have had less influence over policy-making and administration, concentrating most of their attention on the 'constitutional future of Northern Ireland'. While they are represented on public bodies, and have access to civil servants in the NICS, the NIO and of course in European institutions, direct rule has brought about a situation in which ministers and civil servants can bypass the political parties. Business leaders, academics, trade union leaders and, on occasions, people with a record of pressure group activism or community politics are consulted about policy initiatives. Northern Ireland is a very small place, where it is relatively easy for people from government to have a wide range of contacts. There are opportunities for women, including some with a background in feminist campaigning, to make representations and have some influence, as Davies (1991:164) observed. Women's access to policy-making has been promoted and encouraged by the Equal Opportunities Commission for Northern Ireland (EOCNI). This was created in 1976 and has been exceptionally forceful and effective (Sales 1997) in campaigning for women's inclusion in decision-making at every level in Northern Ireland.[2] It would be inaccurate, nevertheless, to suggest that the policy-making structures of direct rule are regarded as ideal by women in Northern Ireland. Access for the majority of women (and other excluded groups) is very constrained (Cockburn 1998:58) and many feel that the processes lack transparency. Women's groups are also worried, however, by the prospect that devolved government would restore responsibility for policy-making to the local political parties, with their strong focus on sovereignty issues and their poor record in promoting women's inclusion.

Contradictions of community politics

Women have turned to grass-roots activism and community politics in order to have some influence over the policies that affect their families and themselves. This has not, by any means, been simple or straightforward. There are many difficulties which undermine the efforts of women in such groups, which they have sought to overcome by the creation of networks which exchange information and provide support. One source of difficulties has been the unstable policy framework within which groups and networks operate. Direct rule from Westminster has been interpreted by successive British governments as a 'temporary measure', which they have, in various initiatives, attempted to bring to an end. Responsibility for policy-making on certain issues has, as a consequence, shifted back and forth between different agencies and elected bodies. Two main strands of policy-making – community relations and community development – have affected and influenced grass roots activism.

Community relations policies were introduced by the Stormont government at the beginning of the current troubles in 1969, when a Ministry of Community Relations and a Community Relations Commission were created. The Commission began to adopt a policy of rooting the promotion of harmony across the political and sectarian divide in the social and economic regeneration of the poorest catholic and protestant communities. Its philosophy of 'community empowerment' brought it into conflict with the ministry (Fitzduff 1995:65). From 1975 until 1990, community relations policies were the responsibility of the Department of Education (NI), but in 1990 a higher priority for this area was signalled with the setting up of a Central Community Relations Unit (CCRU) within the NIO. This was accompanied by the creation of an independent, though government-funded, Community Relations Council (CRC). It is from the CRC that many community groups seek financial support for their activities.

Community development policy was also introduced by the Northern Ireland government in 1969 through the Social Needs

Act, which among other things supported community groups. Under direct rule, community development moved into the remit of local government with the passing of the Recreational and Youth Services (N.I.) Order in 1973. This instructed the 26 district councils to take on responsibility for the provision of recreation, social, physical and cultural activities. Only Belfast City Council and Craigavon Borough Council established (in 1976) separate community services sections. The others tucked the role of community work within their recreation and tourism departments. In 1991, local councils were also required to take on responsibilities for promoting good community relations; community relations officers were appointed by all 26 local authorities. So, there are different agencies, with different strategies for these two strands, which have influence over which grass-roots activities are supported and which not.

Inevitably, this situation produces a further difficulty for groups, that of locating financial and other resources to support their campaigns. Many sources of funding must be sought, and there are different and inconsistent criteria. Local government, within the remit of community development, has responsibility for stimulating public participation but, even had they the best will in the world, their budgets for social programmes have been small, with district councils stretching to include running costs of voluntary community centres and eventually women's centres. Funding for women's projects and development officer posts must compete with other programmes; in such competition, women's interests often come off worst. Belfast City Council, for example, employed a women's development officer for two years, 1983–5, only to drop this post from the agenda of the subcommittee of community services. Instead, a community relations programme that employed three officers, one responsible for women's issues, was introduced (after much debate). This brought an angry response from women's groups and centres in the city. They protested that this initiative was the outcome of a directive from central government to local government, intended to redirect funds from community development to community relations. The women pointed out that their work had made a considerable contribution to improving community relations, but argued that the criteria set for involvement in officially defined community relations programmes excluded women.

The community relations officers for Belfast facilitated a two-day workshop in which coordinators from women's centres participated, to analyse the criteria for funding programmes and projects under local government (district councils), central government (CCRU) and the Community Relations Council. In the discussions, representatives from women's groups and networks argued that projects which attracted funding tended to conform to a limited and rather middle-class image of promoting good community relations. Funding flowed to 'recreational' and tokenistic projects, for example 'putting Catholics and Protestants together on a trip to Butlins'. They also argued that established groups were favoured over newly emerging ones, and that no additional support was available for the administration of grants. Both of those factors made it difficult for women's groups to receive support. In short, it was hard to avoid the conclusion that all three programmes 'had criteria that excluded women from applying for any meaningful grant-aid' (Women's Support Network 1993:*passim*). The workshops recommended that women's groups should be consulted in future about community relations projects. They also suggested that the community relations department should cover a wider range of issues of specific relevance to women, and that funding for childcare be built into the budget of programmes. Both Belfast City Council and the Community Relations Council studied the recommendations and some liaison with women's groups was introduced.

Where funding has been made available, women have often developed the resources provided to the utmost. Belfast City Council Community Services Section, for example, currently directly manages 23 community centres. The participation of women is very high, not only in women's groups but also on management committees, voluntary work and membership of other mixed sex groups. Most of the community centres have established women's groups. In 1991, the community services officer for Belfast City Council found that 65 per cent of the council-run centres (22 in all) host women's groups, which offer a wide range of opportunities. Some have developed a great deal over the years, offering educational opportunities, which in turn have provided excellent employment opportunities for the women involved (Bowers 1991).

In the 1970s, as in the UK generally, priority was given to environmental improvement to enhance the living conditions of inner-city residents and to create a suitable physical infrastructure for industrial development. In Northern Ireland, this resulted in the creation of inner city task forces and action teams. Both were charged with the responsibility of coordinating government action and promoting public participation. They operated on budgets that allowed only modest exercises in positive action to include women. In addition, economic projects, rather than social projects, were of greater importance for the inner city task forces and action teams. Therefore, the investment in social development projects dropped from 50 per cent in 1980 to 42 per cent in 1984 (Morrissey and Gaffikin 1990:132). Women's groups once again slipped down the list of priority funding.

In the 1980s, the confusion around statutory funding bodies was further compounded by the creation of programmes such as the urban development corporations and enterprise zones. This led to rivalry between various government departments, each of which had a partial responsibility for delivery. In part because of the inter-departmental competition, marginalised groups were often avoided and sometimes ignored. A more successful programme launched by the Department of the Environment (a Northern Ireland civil service department) in 1988 was *Making Belfast Work*. Its aim was to stimulate greater economic activity in some of the depressed urban areas, by reinforcing local enterprise, improving the quality of the environment and equipping the people of these areas to compete successfully for available employment. This organisation was composed of seconded civil servants from mainstream statutory bodies and experienced professionals from public bodies such as the Youth Service and the Northern Ireland Housing Executive. Even though the focus was on West Belfast, all five Belfast-based women's centres have benefited, securing funding for specialist projects and in the case of Ballybeen and Shankill (through Belfast Action Teams) securing capital funding for purpose-built centres.

In common with other economically disadvantaged regions of the UK and Ireland, Northern Ireland has also attracted the attention of European policy-makers, which has brought benefits but also some conflicts. European initiatives to combat poverty and social exclusion brought funding and support which transformed loose networks and informally constituted groups into more structured organisations which had to have clear objectives and procedures. In the late 1980s, the European Poverty 3 programme provided the impetus for groups throughout Northern Ireland to set themselves on a more secure footing and to become more formally structured and potentially more influential. Northern Ireland has been designated as an Objective One region within Europe, that is to say it is defined as one of the most deprived regions. Within the remit of the Northern Ireland Single Programme Document which secured structural funding from Europe for the period 1994–9, Northern Ireland is deemed to be eligible for 75 per cent grant aid. Northern Ireland Civil Service departments have also provided funding through a variety of central and local structures which can be accessed by community groups. Since 1995, additional European funding, to assist in the development of a good social infrastructure on which a successful peace process could be established, has been made available through the European Peace and Reconciliation Fund.

As with local and central government, European policies contain both community development and community relations strands, and sometimes the emphasis shifts from one to the other without any consultation with the community sector. On occasions, a 'cross-community' requirement is built in as a criterion when projects are considered, especially under the European Peace and Reconciliation Fund. This ignores the dangers inherent for women in cross-community work and does not allow them the autonomy to decide when it is appropriate. It also implicitly discounts the benefits of 'single-community' work carried on by women's groups. As Sales (1997) and others have shown, this latter has been of great benefit to many women and is often regarded as an essential prerequisite for cross-community projects to be successful. Women's development has not always been given a high priority, even in the allocation of European funds. Taillon (1992:156) found that the European Commission's 'positive recognition of women as a disadvantaged group does not appear to be reflected in departmental administration of European money'. A major problem identified is the difficulty for women's groups of obtaining information about how European funding works and how to investigate the provision of matching funding by government.

Women in community politics

It has often been the work of women in groups which aim to promote non-violence and to counter prejudice and bigotry which has attracted a great deal of attention from outside Northern Ireland. There have been several peace initiatives and movements, which have always attracted many women in both communities, often leading to cross-community work (Jacobson 1997). From the Peace People and Women Together in the 1970s, to the more recent Community Dialogue formed in 1996, women have taken the first steps to form such movements and have devoted their energy and

commitment to keep them going. It does not detract from the contribution made by such initiatives to wonder whether the attention
they receive has been influenced by stereotyped images of women
as inherently peaceful, or to point out that they form only one
(important) part of women's participation in community movements.

Women have, in general, played a remarkable, though for many
years largely unacknowledged, part in community activism. The scale
and character of women's commitment to community politics was
influenced by 'the Troubles', with particular episodes, events and
policies producing and sometimes shaping organised responses. To
a great extent, however, community activism takes place within
the structure of 'parallel universes' (Galligan and Wilford 1999:168)
that characterises social life in Northern Ireland. Women (as well
as men) have often been mobilised in support of their national or
religious communities against actual or perceived threats or oppression. Women were centrally involved in the civil rights protests
over discrimination against Catholics by local councils and other
authorities. A key event was a protest over bias in housing allocation, when 40 young women submitted a petition to Dungannon
Council and 67 women proceeded to picket the council meeting a
few days later (Purdie 1990). The Northern Ireland Civil Rights
Association, established in 1967 to campaign against discrimination in law, policy and employment, also contained many women
among its members. As inter-communal violence escalated in the
early 1970s, the impact of security policies on predominantly working-
class Catholic communities brought a strong resistance which women
were to the fore in mobilising and sustaining. Women in Protestant areas were also drawn into community-based movements of
solidarity. In both communities, women were to the fore in the
creation of support groups for those imprisoned for paramilitary
violence and their families, as well as campaigns for special status
for such prisoners (Loughran 1986, Sales 1997).

The parallel universe pattern does not, however, encompass all
social and political engagement. Even during the worst years of
the Troubles, women in Northern Ireland organised actions for
improvements in social, welfare and environmental policies, often
motivated by concern for the health and well-being of their families
(Porter 1998). Groups of women displayed great imagination, cap-
turing attention despite having few resources. In 1971, for example,
an action group of women from the lower Ormeau Road in Belfast
led a cow into the city hall as part of a protest against the imple-

mentation in Northern Ireland of a Conservative government policy to end the provision of free school milk. The 1970s saw the emergence of many such local and often short-lived groups, as well as the development of larger campaigns and networks. Commentators have often noted the extent to which women from both the unionist and nationalist communities were trying to attract the attention of policy makers to a similar set of problems. Unemployment, poor provision of services, social exclusion and violence (from the security forces as well as paramilitaries) affected both communities.[3] These commonalities have not always resulted in united, cross-community movements of women, as Chapter 8 points out, although in spite of many obstacles some have been created.

As Sales (1997) and others have noted, there has been a stronger tradition of a community-based oppositional politics among the Catholic/nationalist population in Northern Ireland, because of its alienated relationship to the state. While voluntary organisations and pressure group activity has also had its place among the Protestant population, radical politics was more likely to take the form of trade unionism or left-wing or radical party politics. By the late 1980s, however, various influences had led to a reduction in this divergence, especially where women's involvement was concerned. A growing sense of alienation based on fear of betrayal by the British state among sections of the Protestant population, and the effects of Conservative government welfare policies on the fabric of social life, produced a new style of political engagement which brought more women into action. They too were demanding, among other things, better housing, education resources and fairer treatment for young people (Porter 1998).

There has been, since the 1970s, a feminist movement in Northern Ireland, which has been influential despite its relatively small support base. There were attempts, in the 1970s, to form a unified women's movement, which would give priority to gender over other aspects of identity. The Northern Ireland Women's Rights Movement (NIWRM), founded in 1975, was the largest such group. Their ideal of a cross-community movement of Catholic and Protestant women, as Eilish Rooney argues in Chapter 8, was regarded by other feminists as a denial and suppression of differences (Roulston 1997) and there were numerous splits and regroupings. In Northern Ireland feminists, like socialists, remained divided over the issue of nationalism.

Feminist groups generally attracted academic, professional and trade union women. As Cockburn (1998) and Miller *et al.* (1996) observe, it is certainly true that the majority of women involved in community politics were unlikely to identify themselves as feminists. Nonetheless, feminist ideas and insights have inspired campaigns about important issues which have changed policies and attitudes. The Northern Ireland Women's Aid Federation, which has gone from strength to strength, was founded at this time. Trade union campaigns for equal pay for women and to extend the Sex Discrimination Act to Northern Ireland have had long-term effects (Evason 1991). The EOCNI, as already noted, has been a most effective advocate on all women's issues and has forged links between the different strands of women's community politics. In a number of campaigns around certain key issues for women, these connections have made for more effective action.

Women's centres

The influence of feminist groups, and individuals working in the community development sector, can be seen in the growing pressure to channel resources to support women's grass-roots activism. From the late 1970s onwards, opening a women's centre was viewed by women in many types of campaigns and groups in Northern Ireland as an achievement in its own right and a necessary stage in the process of empowering women (Roulston 1996, Smyth 1995). The first women's centre was established by the NIWRM in central Belfast in 1980, with the support of funding secured by the women's community development officer of Belfast City Council. Locating in a 'neutral' area was intended to establish that this centre would be accessible by all women, regardless of religion or political allegiance. Its usefulness as place where women from working-class communities could go for meetings, advice or classes was in fact limited by its city-centre location, given the inadequacies of both public transport and childcare facilities. This centre was replaced (in 1985) by the Downtown Women's Centre, a resource base used by several women's networks for which they secured funding from various sources.

Women's groups in the largely segregated working-class areas of the city fought for funding to create centres closer to home. In Ballybeen, a working-class Protestant area of East Belfast, thanks to the efforts of a local community development worker, a women's centre was opened in 1983. A women's centre was opened in 1982, in the Catholic Falls Road area, and one on the Protestant Shankill Road in 1987. In 1987, women in the lower Ormeau area opened an advice centre with its own café, the Lamplighter, which aimed to draw in women from both communities. Hillary Clinton, famously, was served a cup of tea there during her visit in 1995, by Joyce McCartan, an inspirational leader of working-class women's fight against the system which ignored them. Centres have also been established in Derry, in 1981, and in smaller towns and some rural areas. With smaller populations and sometimes even less-secure funding, the women's centres outside Belfast have to try to provide facilities which will allow both Protestant and Catholic women to feel welcome.

Where funding has not become available for a women's centre, women have made use of community centres or council-run leisure centres as a base for their activities. Women's groups have been formed and are operating on a range of issues in all twenty-six district council areas. There continues to be little consistency in the funding of women's activities. As Taillon (1992) discovered, women's groups and centres have to apply to a number of different agencies and are not always made aware of the criteria according to which grants are awarded. In spite of these obstacles, the women's centres and groups have helped to facilitate women's projects and have allowed networks of support to be created which have on many occasions crossed the sectarian divide.

Women's networks

Since 1980, a complex web of organisations, which exchange information, share resources and offer solidarity to each other has been constructed by women activists in Northern Ireland. In Belfast, for example, women involved in tenants' associations, community education projects and other self-help groups began meeting occasionally to exchange ideas and pool information. This led to the establishment of the Women's Information Group (WIG) in 1980. This organisation has held monthly meetings across centres in Belfast for the last twenty years, scrupulously alternating between Protestant and Catholic areas. Meetings involving between 150 and 200 women from both sides of the divide have been convened throughout the entire period of the conflict to discuss problems prioritised by women in the various groups themselves. The issues have included health problems, rent rises, juvenile crime and environmental problems. Even after major incidents which heightened tension between the two communities, the meetings have continued to take place.

The Women's Support Network (WSN), based in the Downtown

Women's Centre in central Belfast, has also brought women together to campaign for better resources. An umbrella group, it is
based and operates primarily in Belfast, but has links with women's
organisations throughout Northern Ireland. The Network emerged
as a result of a decision in 1990 by Belfast City Council to with-
draw funding from the Falls Women's Centre, alleging that its
management team, key worker and many of those who used it were
well-known republicans. All the Belfast-based women's centres –
including those in predominantly Protestant areas – publicly accused the council of a sectarian decision. This was a courageous
act of solidarity, given the fact that women's groups and centres
have been treated with some suspicion by many politicians and
community 'leaders' in their areas. As the WIG had found, cross-
community contact among groups of women could often be sustained
only by working in a very quiet, low-profile way.

A group of women disturbed by the ignorance and condescen-
sion towards women displayed by many of the city councillors raised
some funding (from the EOCNI) for a survey of women's activism
in Northern Ireland. They found over two hundred groups of various sizes and with an array of policy ideas, but little coordination
or support. The next step was to secure resources for a few workers, a home and some equipment, and the Network was launched
with the aim of linking women's groups and providing support for
the coordinators and other paid workers in the women's centres.[4]

Most of the networks of support develop in this way. A setback
or act of violence provides a catalyst, which calls on women's in-
genuity or determination and out of this grows a set of contacts
which, with good luck or good timing, can win a small amount of
development funding from somewhere. The Shankill Women's Forum,
for example, was born out of the work of women to sustain that
community in the aftermath of an IRA bomb which was set off in
a crowded fish shop one Saturday afternoon in 1994. Similar initiatives have led to the establishment of the Rural Women's Network,
the Fermanagh Women's Network, the Training for Women Network and the Women's Education Project. One important source of
support for network-building has been the Workers Educational
Association, whose women's education branch has, since 1990, drawn
women into programmes which allow them to work out what they
need to do and how to get help to do it. The Irish Congress of
Trades Unions has a women's section which has also sponsored
empowerment programmes for women at the grass roots. A recent

development associated with the WSN and also based in the Downtown Women's Centre has been Women into Politics. This was launched in 1995 to develop women's political skills and encourage their participation in party politics. The mere mention of women in politics intimidated many working-class women, as the terrain of politics for the past thirty years has been held by men. Many women from different centres, nevertheless, have taken part in these courses, which are open to women interested in any of Northern Ireland's parties.

It is worth highlighting the fact that women are involved in many different community-based networks, often drawn into activism by the experiences of their families. Women who commence lobbying officials or representatives to improve the ways in which, say, the authorities deal with the perennial problem of 'joy-riding' will find themselves involved in a community youth policy forum, or (possibly and) in a pressure group to reform the criminal justice system. The women's networks have been an important factor in fostering and encouraging this participation. It is also important to remember that such participation may bring trouble and danger to women. For example, in 1997, a visit was paid by the then president of Ireland, Mary Robinson, to the Windsor Women's Centre in a predominantly Protestant area of Belfast. President Robinson had given enthusiastic support to women's activism throughout Ireland (Coulter 1993) and was also known to have a great deal of sympathy for unionist fears of being pressurised to accept Irish unity. The visit by the head of state of the Irish Republic was, nevertheless, greeted with hostility by some loyalist groups in the area and the Centre suffered a series of arson attacks. Again, the other women's centres rallied to support them in whatever way they could, though it was thought advisable that this support should be behind the scenes rather than very public.

Issues for women

The women's centres and networks exist because of the overwhelming problems which beset women in Northern Ireland's working class communities. Many women have come to see the problems and issues as inextricably linked, stemming from three major factors identified by Cynthia Cockburn (1998): political neglect, poverty and violence. Overcoming the first of these has been the inspiration for the involvement of the majority of women in community groups. Frustrated at the ignorance of and indifference to the economic and social problems of their communities shown by policy-makers, women have tried to find ways to make public these problems and possible solutions.

The issue which is constantly referred to in women's groups and centres is poverty, as Chapters 3 and 4 of this book indicate. The consequences for women and their families as a result of Northern Ireland's economic difficulties have been severe. In 1986, a report by the Northern Ireland Poverty Lobby (NIPL) emphasised the bleakness of the present situation for women living in poverty in Northern Ireland and argued that, if anything, the future promised to be even bleaker (NIPL 1986).

One source of poverty, which has not always been acknowledged (Davies and McLaughlin 1991), has been low pay and unemployment for women. This problem, in fact, appears to be getting worse in some respects. In 1973, women in Northern Ireland earned 63 per cent of male average earnings. In 1981 the figure had risen to 76 per cent, but by 1987 it had fallen back to 73.5 per cent. In 1998 the Northern Ireland Economic Council (NIEC) highlighted the problem of low pay among women, particularly for full-time workers. However, the most recent earnings survey suggests that the incidence of low pay, especially among women, has been underestimated. Furthermore, women are more likely than men to remain in low-paid jobs (NIEC 1998). In a report on long-term unemployment, Donnison (1995) acknowledged that female unemployment was difficult to quantify because very few unemployed married women are able to claim benefits in their own right. However, he estimates that there could be 20 000 women who are not considered to be economically active but who would offer themselves for work or training should the opportunity arise. With the support of the EOCNI, ICTU and trade unions such as UNISON and NIPSA, women have pushed for improvements in pay and employment conditions. Through women's groups and centres they have also responded by seeking out and creating education and training programmes. The Workers Educational Association (WEA 1996) has found that the majority of its students are women and it has had long waiting-lists for programmes such as Opportunities for Women Learning which it has mounted in association with women's centres and networks.

The violence in the streets of Northern Ireland has brought many women into the political arena to protest against actions by the paramilitaries and security forces, or to advocate more peaceful approaches to problems. Violence in the home has been equally pervasive and made much harder to deal with because of the political situation. Although the Women's Aid Federation has been successful in its efforts to transform police attitudes to and methods of dealing with domestic violence, it is not always easy for women in republican and some loyalist areas to call on the Royal Ulster Constabulary for assistance. Paramilitary, and wider community, disapproval of turning to the 'security forces' is reinforced by a reluctance on the part of the police to venture into certain areas of Northern Ireland in response to any calls for help, however desperate. This situation has led to calls for more creative responses to the problem, channelled through community health and social service providers (McWilliams and McKiernan 1993). Finding a solution to this problem looks likely to be a long-term process, in which women are already engaged.

A 'situated politics of everyday life'

Societies which have experienced violent conflict over ethnic differences or national identity have often been described as characterised by strongly traditional attitudes towards women's roles. There has certainly been evidence of conservatism in attitudes to social and moral issues in Northern Ireland, attitudes which many women themselves hold. A closer look reveals a more complex situation. Women are certainly closely identified with their families and accept the responsibility of sustaining them and acting for them (McLaughlin 1993). It is often the case that women are more active on behalf of their families and communities than they are in the cause of their own gender. This has led women into diverse and difficult campaigns throughout Northern Ireland. In the movement for integrated education, for example, we find women taking the first steps in many areas. Similarly, it is women who organise and sustain protests about heavy traffic near schools and playgrounds, opposition to hospital closures, victim support groups and resettlement of offender schemes. This has been described, by Elizabeth Porter (1998), as a 'situated politics of everyday life', in which women take action in spaces which are quite different from the terrain of traditional, mainstream politics. Using these distinctive spaces, she argues, has allowed women to create distinctive, more participatory and inclusive methods of working as well. Many women find it frustrating that this new style of organising has not yet had a sufficient impact on the mainstream of politics.

Over the last twenty-five years, women in Northern Ireland have been engaged in a three-pronged process of work and struggle. They have had, first, to concern themselves with the bread-and-butter issues – lobbying for better services, benefits and living conditions. Second, they have had to take account of the political stalemate and daily violence, which has often meant that women give priority to support for their own communities. Finally, they have occasionally had the space to consider what would be good for themselves as women, which has drawn many into support and self-help groups and projects. Giving priority to their needs as women has often had to be justified by reference to the contribution women can make to community regeneration or to the promotion of good community relations. Women are no longer content to accept that the priorities which they have identified as important do not seem to appear on the key policy-making agendas. They have now achieved greater acknowledgement for women's contribution today than there was even ten years ago. (We must not forget the role of such influential figures as Hillary Clinton, Mary Robinson and Mo Mowlam in bringing women's activism into the light of public attention.) The next priority for many is to bridge the gap between this women's politics of everyday life and the politics which goes on in public institutions. Bridging the gap is particularly difficult in Northern Ireland, given the way in which constitutional matters relegate other issues to secondary importance and lead to the valorising of a tough, uncompromising style of engagement.

May Blood, the chair of Shankill Women's Forum, addressing a meeting of the newly formed Northern Ireland Women's Coalition in May 1996, expressed women's continuing frustration with developments in the peace process. On one hand, women have been described by both men and women themselves as the 'backbone of their community' and the potential peacemakers who can leave their differences aside and talk to each other (Sales 1997:195). On the other hand, it is the very concerns on which women have found common cause which appear to be excluded from current debates in Northern Ireland. Women, celebrated as the peacemakers, have been largely absent from the peace process (Jacobson 1997, Sales 1997). During the political talks which resulted in the Belfast Agreement, and in the referendum and election campaigns which followed, as Chapter 6 shows, many women raised their voices to argue that a genuinely new politics would have to include women's concerns. Two key elements of the Agreement, discussed in Chapter 6, were a result of their pressure: the recognition of the importance of the inclusion of women in politics and the proposed introduction of a Civic Forum. The latter, many of whose members would be drawn from the community and voluntary sector, is intended to have an advisory role and some influence over the work of the Assembly. The Forum will be, among other thing, gender-balanced. Of course, it is assumed that members of the Forum, unlike those elected to the Assembly, will work unpaid and part-time, and they are likely to find their influence somewhat restricted. Through such an institution, however, the community politics sector would for the first time have a guaranteed input into the policy-making of a devolved government in Northern Ireland.[5] Women have started to have an impact on the agenda of mainstream politics, but there is still a long way to go. As one experienced participant in community politics argued (Hinds 1999:126):

> The energy experience and commitment exhibited by women will not be contained solely within traditional structures. Women have played and continue to play their part in the transformation of Northern Ireland and expect to reach beyond the traditional towards something more innovative and forward looking.

Notes

1 The power-sharing Executive created by this Assembly took part in a Conference at Sunningdale in Berkshire in December 1973. At the Conference a Council of Ireland, unwelcome to many unionists, was created. There was also a considerable loyalist opposition to and suspicion about power sharing. After many serious protests, including a major strike, the plan was abandoned. See Flackes and Elliot (1994).
2 In 1998, against opposition from women's groups and forums, NIO decided to create a new Equalities Commission which will have responsibility for ensuring that legislation outlawing discrimination on the grounds of religion, sex, race and disability will be effective. There have been concerns that this will lead to fewer resources being directed towards gender equality issues.
3 They were not affected equally by these problems; unemployment, for example, is higher among the Catholic than the Protestant community. For a discussion of its relative impact on Protestant and Catholic women see Davies *et al.* (1995).
4 See Cockburn (1998) for a detailed account of the Women's Support Network.

5   It is to be hoped, should the parties fail to create an Assembly in the forthcoming review, that the principle of having an advisory chamber to reflect 'civil society' will be retained in any future process.

References

Acheson, N. and Williamson, A. (eds) (1995) *Voluntary Action and Social Policy in Northern Ireland: Some contemporary themes and issues*, Aldershot: Avebury.

Aughey, A. and Morrow, D. (eds) (1996) *Northern Ireland Politics*, London: Longman.

Bowers, M. (1991) *Services and Provision for Women in Belfast funded by the Community Services Department of Belfast City Council*, MSc Thesis, Queens University Belfast.

Cockburn, C. (1998) *The Space Between Us: Negotiating Gender and National Identities in Conflict*, London: Zed Books.

Coulter, C. (1993) *The Hidden Traditions: Feminism, Women and Nationalism in Ireland*, Cork: Cork University Press.

Davies, C. (1991) 'Reforming the Agenda' in Davies and McLaughlin (1991) 153–165.

Davies, C. and McLaughlin, E. (eds) (1991) *Women, Employment and Social Policy in Northern Ireland: A Problem Postponed?*, Belfast: Policy Research Institute.

Davies, C., Heaton, Norma, Robinson, Gillian, and McWilliams, Monica (1995) *A Matter of Small Importance? Catholic and Protestant Women in the Northern Ireland Labour Market*, Belfast: Equal Opportunities Commission for Northern Ireland.

Donnison, D. (1995) *Long-term Unemployment in Northern Ireland: A Report*, Belfast: Northern Ireland Council for Voluntary Action.

Evason, E. (1991) *Against the Grain: the Contemporary Women's Movement in Northern Ireland*, Dublin: Attic Press.

Fitzduff, M. (1995) 'Managing Community Relations and Conflict: Voluntary Organisations and Government and the Search for Peace', in Acheson and Williamson, 63–83.

Flackes, W. D. and Elliot, S. (1994) *Northern Ireland: A Political Directory 1968–1993*, Belfast: Blackstaff.

Galligan, Y. and Wilford, R. (1999) 'Women's Political Representation in Ireland', in Galligan *et al.*, 130–48.

Galligan, Y., Ward, E. and Wilford, R. (eds) (1999) *Contesting Politics: Women in Ireland, North and South*, Boulder, CO: Westview Press.

Gray, A. M., Heenan, D. and Cousins, W. (1997) *An Examination of the System of Public Appointments in Northern Ireland*, Jordanstown: University of Ulster.

Heenan, D. and Gray, A. M. (1999) 'Women and Nominated Boards in Ireland', in Galligan *et al.*, 185–200.

Hinds, B. (1999) 'Women Working for Peace in Northern Ireland', in Galligan *et al.*, 109–29.

Jacobson, R. (1997) *Whose Peace Process? Women's Organisations and Political Settlement in Northern Ireland, 1996–1997*, University of Bradford: Peace Studies Papers.

Lovenduski, J. and Norris, P. (eds) (1996) *Women in Politics*, Oxford: Clarendon Press.

McLaughlin, E. (1993) 'Women and the Family in Northern Ireland: A Review', *Women's Studies International Forum*, 16(6), 553–68.

McWilliams, M. and McKiernan, J. (1993) *Bringing it Out in the Open: Domestic Violence in Northern Ireland*, Belfast: HMSO.

Miller, R. L., Wilford, R. and Donoghue, F. (1996) *Women and Political Participation in Northern Ireland*, Aldershot: Avebury.

Morgan, V. and Fraser, G. (1994) *The Company We Keep*, Coleraine: University of Ulster.

Morrissey, M. and Gaffikin, F. (1990) *Northern Ireland: the Thatcher Years*, London: Zed Books.

NIPL (1986) *A Life of Poverty*, Jordanstown, Social Policy Society and University of Ulster.

NIEC (1998) *Annual Report*, Belfast: Northern Ireland Economic Council.

Pollak, A. (ed.) (1993) *A Citizen's Enquiry: The Opsahl Report on Northern Ireland*, Dublin: Lilliput Press.

Porter, E. (1998) 'Identity, Location, Plurality: Women, Nationalism and Northern Ireland' in Wilford, R. and Miller, R. L. (1998): 36–61.

Purdie, R. (1990) *Politics in the Street: the origins of the Civil Rights Movement*, Belfast: Blackstaff.

Rooney, E. and Woods, M. (1995) *Women, Community and Politics in Northern Ireland: A Belfast Study*, Jordanstown: University of Ulster.

Roulston, C. (1996) 'Equal Opportunities for Women' in Aughey, A. and Morrow, D. (eds) (1996): 139–46.

Roulston, C. (1997) 'Women on the Margin; The Women's Movement in Northern Ireland' in West, L. (ed.) (1997): 45–58.

Sales, R. (1997) *Women Divided: Gender, Religion and Politics in Northern Ireland*, London: Routledge.

Smyth, M. (1995) 'Women, Peace, Community Relations and Voluntary Action' in Acheson and Williamson (eds): 145–60.

Taillon, R. (1992) *Grant Aided or Taken for Granted: A Study of Women's Voluntary Organisations in Northern Ireland*, Belfast: Women's Support Network.

WEA (1996) *Annual Report*, Belfast: Worker's Educational Association.

West, L. A. (ed.) (1997) *Feminist Nationalism*, New York, London: Routledge.

Wilford, R. (1996), 'Women and Politics in Northern Ireland' in Lovenduski, J. and Norris, P. (eds) (1996): 43–56.

Wilford, R. and Galligan, Y. (1999) 'Gender and Party Politics in Northern Ireland' in Galligan *et al.* (eds) (1999): 169–84.

Wilford, R. and Miller, R. L. (eds) (1998) *Women, Ethnicity and Nationalism: The Politics of Transition*, London: Routledge.

Women's Support Network (1993) *Response to the Community Relations Programme*, Belfast: Women's Support Network.

2
Democracy and the Challenge of Gender: New Visions, New Processes

Carmel Roulston

Democracy has always been a contested concept, among theorists as well as practitioners. From being considered a dangerous means of introducing 'mob rule' it has become the political system which most states claim to have adopted (Arblaster 1994). Nevertheless, debates about the fundamental values of democratic politics and the best ways of expressing them in institutions continue to absorb the attention of politicians, activists and writers. Political theory, from its very beginnings, has been fascinated by democracy, yet there continues to be confusion and disagreement about how it can be achieved and by what criteria a state or other institution can be judged to be democratic.

Political theory, however, like other social theories, has until relatively recently been produced almost exclusively by men (Beasley 1999). Feminist writers have argued that male theorists have incorporated the interests and perspectives of men into the founding principles of citizenship and democracy. The challenge from feminism has allowed new lines of argument to be opened about the values which underpin democracy and new visions to be created of what democracy might mean. In revealing the ways in which the structures and founding concepts of democracy have ignored or deliberately excluded women, feminist political theorists have been particularly inspired by the alternative structures which women have sometimes been able to put in practice.

This chapter will examine some of the key themes in recent feminist writing about citizenship, democracy, representation and difference. It will outline the principal critiques, which link the serious under-representation of women in the power structures of western liberal democracies to gender biases at the centre of the web of ideas and customs that make up our conception of 'the citizen'. It will also discuss the solutions which some feminist theorists have offered to the problems of creating democratic practices which can represent differences. In doing this, it will attempt to relate the ideas of the theorists to the experiences of the women in our case-studies in Northern Ireland and show how practice and theory can illuminate each other.

Unmasking 'the individual citizen'

Definitions tend to emphasise that democracy must be seen as both a set of ideals and values and a type of political system for collective decision-making founded upon those values (Beetham and Boyle 1995). The founding values contain the promise of inclusion – of a system which permits all citizens to share the power of making policies. Yet, in the creation of actual democratic polities, there has been an uneasy relationship between the ideal of inclusion and popular control and the principles and values of liberal philosophy. Clearly, certain liberal rights are essential. Democracy would not work well without liberalism's emphasis on freedom of speech and assembly, for example. Liberal thought also defends individual rights and attempts to limit the power of the state through the construction of separate 'public' and 'private' spheres. In practice, however, this can deny collective interests and serve to prevent public discussion of some serious abuses of power and privilege, as early radicals such as Mary Wollstonecroft and John Stuart Mill pointed out. The defence of liberal values, indeed, has often been the expression of the interests of elites, who feared the unbridled power of the masses. Inequalities, as David Beetham notes, can all too easily undermine the promise of democracy; and there have been repeated struggles over the social agenda necessary to make 'the principle of popular control by equal citizens properly effective' (1992:44).

Faced with liberalism's failure to address class inequality, many turned to socialism. When socialist states proved to be no more accommodating of democratic ideals than their liberal rivals, 'new left' movements emerged in the developed world, offering critiques of both systems. Whereas the 'old left' had located the source of inequalities in the economic sphere and viewed political institutions as responsible for their perpetuation, the new left saw power and dominance reproduced in every social, cultural, economic and political institution. Neither liberal representative nor state socialist collectivist forms of government, according to this viewpoint, were adequate to deliver democracy's radical promise of government by the people. To expose these unequal relationships and to overthrow the interlocking systems that produced them, a more 'participatory' form of democracy was proposed.[1] Second-wave feminist writers who were involved in or influenced by new left movements very much agreed with this discovery of politics as 'everywhere'. They were dissatisfied, however, by the absence of discussion of power inequalities between men and women, particularly in the home and the family.[2]

The slogan of second-wave radical feminism – 'the personal is political' – was intended literally to bring new left politics home, to challenge its neglect of gendered inequalities. For many radical and socialist feminists, the effect of this slogan was twofold. It challenged in a more fundamental way the accepted tradition of a divide between the public world of politics and government and the private sphere of home, family and intimate relations. It also undermined the accepted notion of the distinctiveness of the business of public politics. For many feminists the formal arena of parties and governments was just another part of the patriarchal order, and one which was so masculine that it was best avoided altogether. Rejecting both formal 'mainstream' politics and the methods of organisation of the left, feminists developed their own style of participatory democracy (Phillips 1991), which was more inclusive and less hierarchical. The almost universal absence of women from political leadership, and the concomitant lack of interest in how policies affected women, was, however, challenged by some activists and theorists. In political theory, Susan Moller Okin's (1979) landmark text critically examined the strong split underlying classic theories of liberal democracy between a public sphere of collective action and a private home and family sphere. Okin's studies of political philosophy revealed implicit, and sometimes explicit, gendering of these two worlds, with women excluded from the public *because of* their strong association with the private. In a later study (1989), Okin pointed out that, in fact, men's public power meant they could dominate both worlds. The secrecy surrounding the family and the ignoring of gender differences in the construction of the image of 'the citizen' meant that this domination had been disguised.

The business of politics, it emerged, was arranged on the assumption that those who carried it on had no domestic duties or work to absorb any of their energies. Justice in the public sphere required public interest in the injustices of the private sphere. Even a radical theorist like Rawls (1973) could produce a theory of justice which did not take account of the fundamental injustice at the heart of male–female relationships.

Calling for the dissolution of *all* distinction between public and private was not welcomed by all feminists. For some feminist political theorists,[3] the radical feminist attempt to dissolve the boundary contained a dangerous threat to the autonomy and privacy of family life. Increasingly, however, feminist writers have wanted to take a closer look at this boundary, and at the individual whose liberties have been protected by it. In a series of influential publications, Carole Pateman (1986, 1989, 1992) has argued that although modern societies no longer dispute the eligibility of women for full citizenship, women have been admitted to a citizenship defined in male terms. The 'individual' of early liberal political theory, around whom the meaning of citizenship had been built, turns out to be the male head of the household (Brennan and Pateman, 1979). Women, especially married women with children, fitted, and continue to fit, badly into liberal ideas of citizenship. Pateman also (1986) drew attention to the 'patriarchal' meanings attached to the public and private spheres and to the separation and opposition between them. In modern welfare societies, the boundary between public and private is discussed in terms of the state and the economy. The domestic sphere remains invisible, and because of this, formally equal rights are not enough. Such rights are undermined by women's subordination in the private sphere. Women's limited inclusion into the public sphere, furthermore, means that private subordination can be renewed and reinforced by law and custom (Pateman 1989).

Women, as Pateman and others have argued, have been treated as citizens who just happen to be women. In practice, this results in the suppression of the female and the dominance of male identities in liberal democratic polities. In our legal institutions and political culture, Pateman argues, we work with conceptions of individuals as 'owners' of their bodies. Underlying these conceptions is a notion of the mind and the body as separate, the former controlling the latter (Pateman 1989). This is a masculine interpretation of identity; by abstracting from the 'embodiment' of human ways of being, we are refusing to acknowledge the differences between men and women, setting our standards according to the needs and interests of men.[4] The conclusion Pateman draws is that citizenship needs to be recognised as different for men and women. An open acknowledgement of this 'differentiated citizenship' might at least allow the particularity of women to be reflected in the public sphere.

As we shall see, these conclusions have provoked considerable debate. It would be fair to say, however, that most feminists take as their starting-point the key themes already outlined. They stress the need to question the boundary between public and private spheres, the masculine identity of the liberal citizen and the assumption that conferring citizenship on women would make them equal citizens. Different feminists have constructed different visions and strategies from these starting-points.

Representing women

The starting-point for many feminists concerned with democracy has been the limited effectiveness of winning formal political rights for women. In country after country, with few exceptions, the absence of women from legislatures,[5] governments and political party leaderships led to the same conclusion. Liberal democracy appeared to be incapable of representing women.

Observing that women were often as interested and willing to take part in politics as men, writers such as Pippa Norris (1987) and Vicki Randall (1987) began to look for explanations. They detected a complex set of processes whereby ideologies about gender and leadership, selection processes and electoral systems frequently combined to ensure that few women reach the most influential positions in the apparently open contests for power in liberal democracies. As their analyses became more detailed and sophisticated (Lovenduski and Norris 1993), they revealed that achieving equality or parity of representation of women in parliaments, cabinets and executives would be no simple matter. Although there are large numbers of women active as rank-and-file party members or in grassroots organisations, it remains rare for women to become leaders of parties, or candidates, or to be promoted to the cabinet or the front bench once elected. The obstacles in the way of women are to some extent the result of simple bias. Women are also impeded by the acceptance as normal in the political sphere of working

conditions and procedures which assume both the absence of de-
pendants in need of care and the existence of some domestic support
for the person who steps into that sphere. Women, it seems, do
not fit comfortably into mainstream politics as presently organised,
and there are no guarantees that the women who manage to
make their way into parliaments and governments will be able –
or willing – to act in ways significantly different from their male
colleagues.

Disillusionment among feminists with the system of representative democracy was produced not only by its failure to include
women but also by the limited scope it offered for genuine and
wider participation. Politics seemed to have become a technocratic
business, carried on by elites, from which the mass of the population was excluded by lack of information and loss of confidence
that the problems of the majority of people would be addressed. In
the 1970s, as noted above, feminist groups in many parts of the
world experimented with direct, participatory forms of democratic
engagement. These had a number of attractive aspects. They were
seen as more inclusive, more likely to produce consensus and therefore
a sense of shared ownership of decisions and less likely to lead to
hierarchies and unfair distributions of power. They allowed the women
involved to identify and name the problems and issues which most
mattered to them, and to invent new strategies for dealing with
them. They also revealed that processes can be as important to
participants as outcomes; winning or losing on an issue matters
less where there is a sense of fairness, of having learned something, of every option having been considered. Furthermore, taking
part in such movements allowed participants to feel a sense of
empowerment; even where they did not attain their goals, they
could often feel positive about having taken part (Phillips 1991,
Mansbridge 1983). There were, of course, disadvantages. While the
practices devised by these groups – encouragement of everyone to
speak, rotation of duties and responsibilities, refusal to have leaders
– generated excitement and enthusiasm, it proved to be difficult
for the groups themselves to sustain them over time, let alone to
extend them into wider arenas of decision-making. As Phillips observes (1991), such intensity and commitment were very demanding
of time and energy, of which most women do not have a surplus.
It was also the case that the groups themselves did not remain free
from hierarchies or abuses of power (Freeman 1989), but rather
that these were more difficult to detect and challenge.

In many countries where women's principal form of political participation is through small, locally based, participatory groups, it is noticeable that this does not by any means improve women's representation in formal political institutions. It has been difficult to create bridges from the grassroots movements to the centres of government. As Chapter 1 has argued, even in the exceptional circumstances of direct rule in Northern Ireland, women's groups were permitted a very limited amount of access to policy-makers. That this form of participation continues to attract so many women, despite the problems, raises some questions which participants in the case-studies in Part II try to answer. Is this a particularly 'womanly' form of organising and engaging? If so, are efforts to 'feminise' mainstream politics likely to have only limited benefits? Is there a democratic system which can include women, address their interests and ideas and engage their enthusiasm as these groups appear to?

The 'difference' debates

The unmasking of the masculine person under the cloak of the abstract, supposedly ungendered citizen was accompanied by a feminist critique of the 'abstract universalism' (Phillips 1992) of western social and political theory in general. This tendency, according to feminists, arises when values, traditions and viewpoints associated with men are taken as 'the standard or rational/sensible/proper, universally applicable view' (Beasley 1999:10). So, the principles and rules surrounding political life reflected men's experiences and concerns and devalued women. The belief, for example, that rational discussion necessarily precludes emotion,[6] or that an objective perspective, detached from personal involvement with an issue can be attained – these are founded in a male world of independent individuals who 'forget' their connections to nature and the body.

That politics was imbued with such beliefs seemed to be borne out by the evidence (Randall 1987, Lovenduski and Norris 1993) that even when women broke through into the political world, women's issues and concerns remained marginalised. How could equality be attained for women when the concepts and practices of equality exclude women's experiences and identities? For some, the answer lay in celebrating and highlighting women's differences from men, while arguing for new forms of citizenship and new rules for the public sphere. Jean Bethke Elshtain, in an early and influential text in the liberal feminist tradition (1981), argued that even feminists themselves have undervalued the importance of women's maternal roles and the powers which women enjoy within the family. Elshtain aspires to an ethical polity which can incorporate the cooperative, nurturing, altruistic values which we seek in our intimate private relationships. Following a similar thread, Carol Gilligan (1983) proposed that a feminine 'ethic of care' was needed to balance the masculine 'ethic of justice'. Sara Ruddick (1989) also wants to see the public sphere become imbued by the attitudes and values which women bring to mothering, but which, she argues, men can also acquire. In the peace movement and in other forms of politics of resistance – the Madres de la Plaza de Mayo[7] for example – women have already brought transformations through actions inspired by these values. Pateman, too, while arguing for strategies to change the political meaning of sexual difference, and accepting that motherhood will 'no longer fill women's lives', nevertheless argues that 'motherhood and citizenship are intimately linked' (1992:29). Increasingly, however, such ideas created some dilemmas for feminist writers. On the one hand, it appeared that women would have to become like men in order to enter the public world of politics and power. On the other hand, stressing the differences between women and men might doom women forever to a 'lesser' form of citizenship. While many feminist theorists and activists could accept the logic of some or all of the arguments outlined above, the analysis seemed to present women with impossible goals: be better than men and make the world a better place. There seemed no obvious strategy that women in politics could use here and now to make liberal democracy function better. The celebration of women's essential difference seemed to accept the state of affairs whereby the majority of women in politics had to choose between always dealing with 'women's issues', or completely avoiding them in the hope of a successful career.

These debates among feminist writers became even more challenging when feminists themselves were accused of 'false universalism'. The celebration of women's difference was founded on a version of 'womanliness' which reflected the image of white, middle-class European heterosexual women. Lesbians, black, third-world and working-class women and women with disabilities all argued that the experiences and aspirations of white, middle-class women were being assumed to stand for those of all women. Attempts to make feminism more 'inclusive' appeared to replicate the pattern of women's admission into the world of politics. 'Norms' of womanliness had been established, to which 'other' women must conform, while the unequal power relationships between some women and others were supposed not to matter (Anthias and Yuval-Davis 1983, Collins 1990). Coinciding with and reinforcing post-modern critiques of feminism (Nicholson 1994, Coole 1993), these challenges were dismaying, in so far as they seemed to undermine one of the core elements of the case for women's inclusion into politics: that women had perspectives and concerns which required their presence. In the longer term, however, as the next section indicates, the challenge of difference brought responses from feminist writers which have been both creative and innovative.

A new politics of difference

Thinking through the implications of difference and diversity for democracy and for women has led feminist political theory to engage with other schools of thought which have also been concerned with citizenship, participation and the link between civil society and political institutions. In particular, Anne Phillips, Iris Marion Young and Chantal Mouffe have drawn from the civic republican, communitarian and deliberative schools to find some new approaches to democracy and difference.

A central theme which has emerged has been that of whether conceptions of 'a common good' can survive in diverse, multi-cultural societies. Acceptance of difference, Anne Phillips observes, was one of the core values of liberalism. As societies became manifestly more heterogeneous, no single version of the common good could prevail, so democratic mechanisms to choose between different programmes and rules about tolerance were brought into being. In this version, however, difference has been interpreted 'as difference in opinions and beliefs, and the resulting emphasis on the politics of ideas has proved inadequate to the problems of political exclusion' (1995:6). This point is echoed by Judith Squires (1996:622), who points out that

> certain differences have always been acknowledged by liberal democratic systems – yet these have been differences of interest and ideology rather than of identity . . . The issue of which differences are to matter politically has always been particularly sensitive.

Such suppression of differences has been defended on the grounds that it will allow the emergence of policies which are for 'the common good'. Feminists are sceptical of such promises, but Iris Young, for example (1990a:114) accepts that there have been positive aspirations contained in the original vision:

> An ideal of universal citizenship has driven the emancipatory momentum of modern political life...Whatever the social or group differences among citizens, whatever their inequalities of wealth, status, and power in the everyday activities of civil societies, citizenship gives everyone the same status as peers in the political public.

Some recent advocates of a revival of democracy[8] have tried to recover the emancipatory ideal by redefining the meaning of citizenship. Democracy, in these theories, should involve the transcendence of different interests and perspectives into a common vision, which will be forged through argument and open debate in strongly participatory democratic institutions. The citizen has not only the right but also an obligation to participate in politics. The intention of these 'civic republican' or 'communitarian' theorists is to challenge liberal ideas about the individual citizen. The liberal vision is viewed as offering an overly 'thin' concept of citizenship in which passive, self-interested individuals protect their narrow set of values and interests against the state and each other. For many such theorists, however, it is still essential to draw a clear dividing line between the public sphere, which concerns matters of general importance, and a private sphere, which includes particular interest and affiliation. Political participation is defined as relating to the needs of the society as a whole.

Many feminists, perhaps most notably Pateman (1992), have argued that the civic-republican vision, like the liberal one, is based on a masculine identity, which derives directly from the hero-soldier tradition. Others, most notably Mary Dietz (1992), see it as capable of extension to include women. Iris Young argues that, first, the ideal of an impartial general interest is a myth:

> In a society where some groups are privileged while others are oppressed, insisting that as citizens persons should leave behind their particular affiliations and experiences to adopt a general point of view, serves only to reinforce that privilege, for the perspectives of the privileged will tend to dominate this unified public, marginalizing or silencing those of other groups. (1990:120)

Attempts to realise the original, emancipatory ideal by excluded or oppressed groups, she argues, have proved disappointing or frustrating. The extension of 'equal citizenship' has not led to social justice or equality. In the modern definition of citizenship, as Young and others have noted, 'the idea that citizenship is the same for all' has been 'translated into the requirement that all citizens be the same' (1990:118). This is because, Young argues, the ideals and meanings attached to citizenship in modern political communities are responsible for inequalities and exclusions. Far from accepting that group differences can be transcended by conducting public life as if they did not exist, she wants to argue for a concept of *differentiated citizenship*, which will be instrumental in allowing participation and inclusion for all.

Young accepts that the objective of those who advocate strong democracy and responsible citizenship is to move away from the present model of interest-group pluralism, where policy-making has become privatised and fragmented, taking the form of backroom deals where the wishes of the mighty prevail. By identifying *all* particularity with such definitions of interest, however, they perpetuate a model of citizenship which refuses to acknowledge the processes of exclusion that can characterise democratic discussion and bargaining. For Young, achieving equality requires the creation of 'institutionalized means for the explicit recognition and representation of oppressed groups'. Such group representation is 'the best antidote to self-deceiving self-interest masked as an impartial or general interest' (*ibid.*: 121).

How, in practical terms, can such representation be achieved? For Young, the inequalities in modern societies, and the exclusion and subordination inherent in all our practices and institutions, can only be counteracted by facilitating and encouraging the oppressed to organise and articulate their needs, interests and values. Justice is not only a matter of redistributing resources, but also of recognising identities. What Young proposes might be viewed as a variant on consociational theories of democracy (Lijphart 1977), which attempt to find ways of making liberal democracy work in states divided by ethnicity, language or religion. Northern Ireland has been one testing ground for consociationalism. Whereas consociational theories stress elite accommodation, Young is suggesting that governments and states should create mechanisms which would allow all oppressed or minority groups to meet, discuss and formulate policy. They would have the right to be consulted on policy proposals which affect their group, including rights to veto legislation. Young envisages that a plurality of groups (which could be self-identifying but would have to show evidence of disadvantage and/or exclusion) could come into existence and fade away, and would have members who belong to more than one group. Young does not intend that groups should be closed, or that they should be an obstacle to the emergence of solidarity across the boundaries of difference; but such 'transcendences' can come only through the processes of groups' self-definition.

Although many feminist writers share Young's reservations about impartiality and the common good, there are some, who, while broadly sympathetic, have identified some difficulties with her approach. Judith Squires (1996), for example, points out that the question as to which institution or agent has the authority to decide which groups are to be represented or refused recognition raises yet more practical problems of power and domination. Anne Phillips, who has worked through all these testing questions about women, difference and democracy in a series of publications, offers some serious objections. Phillips accepts that Young's arguments about the need to rethink traditional models of participation are overwhelming, yet worries about some of the implications of this approach. The biggest danger of group or gender-based citizenship is that classes, genders and ethnic groups are not homogeneous. How is conflict and difference within them to be represented? Who defines the membership of groups and how are key characteristics to be established? Furthermore, she worries about the limitations this would impose on members of particular groups:

> No-one (I imagine) would want to flee the abstractions of an undifferentiated humanity only to end up in its opposite; no one would favour the kind of politics in which people were elected to speak only for their own group identity or interest, and never asked to address any wider concerns. Even setting aside what we would lose in terms of competing notions of the common good, such a development could mean shoring up communal boundaries and tensions, which could be as oppressive as any universal norm. (Phillips 1993:118)

Phillips admits that she finds herself torn between the need for a radical improvement of liberal democracy and the anxiety that we may lose its benefits. Feminists, she argues, have more to fear from some of the alternatives to liberal democracy and may wish to make its defence a priority. Phillips reminds us of the power of the state; the advance that liberalism represented was that it recognised the need to protect individual rights and freedoms, to set limits to the powers of any political institution. She does, nonetheless, accept the need for improvement, which may consist of balancing the interests of groups against those of 'the individual'. Phillips is committed to a politics of change, by which people can begin to transcend their group identities and construct solidarities not based on self-interest. Precisely how this will be done, what measures or procedures will be appropriate, she suggests, cannot be decided in advance, in isolation from politics and political mobilisation.

In a recent study of the problems of representation (1995), Phillips attempts to discuss the problem in terms of a contrast between the 'politics of ideas', whereby citizens in liberal democracies are assumed to choose representatives on the basis of their views and programmes, and the 'politics of presence', which requires that representatives have shared experiences or identities with the communities on whose behalf they act. In the end, it is a combination of these two principles that Phillips sees as offering the best hope for achieving a more radical and responsive system of democracy:

> While the politics of ideas is an inadequate vehicle for dealing with political exclusion, there is little to be gained by simply switching to a politics of presence . . . Taken in isolation, the weaknesses of the one are as dramatic as the failings of the other. (pp. 24–5)

Phillips identifies two problems. The first is that shared experience is not an 'adequate guarantee of fair representation' in the absence of mechanisms of accountability. Second, it is easier to see that some groups have been excluded than to be sure of 'the difference that inclusion brings about' (p. 52). As she puts it, 'representation is a muddle' at present. We expect politicians to be accountable and to come up with good ideas. If, however, we attempt to tie the choice of politicians too closely to identity groups we may limit their autonomy to come up with good answers to unforeseen problems. Some of these reservations stem from Phillips's attraction to the ideals of 'deliberative democracy', which she shares with Young. Deliberative theorists[9] also want to reject liberal ideas of citizenship and democracy, above all the conception of the citizen as an autonomous individual capable of identifying and expressing his interests in isolation from others. Deliberative theorists acknowledge the diversity of modern societies, but they aspire to a version of politics that goes beyond a mere aggregation of interests. They favour instead a process of unfettered, open, public debate through which new, previously unexplored ideas and problems can emerge.[10] Pre-existing positions and preferences might – should – be changed in the course of open and public debate. Politics would cease to be a zero-sum game of winners and losers (as it has been for so long in Northern Ireland) and become an arena where accommodations should be the norm rather than the exception.

In an important move, Phillips resists the dichotomy between the deliberative ideal and the 'politics of presence'. On the contrary, she argues that open-ended discussion might make attention to who is present more rather than less important. If the rules of accountability are to be so relaxed as to let representatives have a great deal of autonomy, then it is important that all groups feel that someone is there who will know what the implications of certain policies may be for their lives and well-being. Even with this protection, Phillips feels that some deliberative theorists do not take enough account of the problem that a culture of deliberation might privilege some participants over others. Those with a particular background, culture and interests, in other words, an already privileged group, will have the advantage. Phillips acknowledges the attractiveness of the deliberative ideal, for one of the problems of modern government is the fact that certain aims and ideas are never permitted to be part of the policy agenda in the first place. This limits the value of accountability; what if there are policies which you might support but which no one is even offering you the opportunity to think about? On the other hand, given the hierarchies of interests in modern societies, it is important that certain groups have their needs addressed and their interests protected. As she puts it, both 'advocates' and 'deliberators' are essential in modern democracies.

In the end, Phillips argues, resolving the problem of representing difference becomes a political question, to be settled in different ways in different situations. 'The case for a different system of representation depends on historically specific analysis of the existing arrangements for representation and the existing conditions of political exclusion' (1995:43).

This rather pragmatic approach to resolving the problems of

difference is echoed by Chantal Mouffe, who tries to fuse civic-republican and liberal traditions into a radical politics of solidarity. Mouffe has been influenced by post-modern and post-structuralist 'deconstructions' of fixed, essential identities and oppositions; however, she accepts the realities of inequalities and subordination. The role of dominant institutions of various types, including the state, is at the foreground of Mouffe's discussions of politics and citizenship. One central aspect is her attempt to show how a feminist politics remains possible even if the 'essentialist' conceptualisation of women as a coherent group, the subject of a social or political movement, is flawed. Mouffe has pointed to the ways in which our identities are constructed for us, by political and other agencies. Like some post-modern feminists, she stresses the fluidity of gender and other identities and the different ways in which these identities interact with each other.

> Many feminists believe that, without seeing women as a coherent identity, we cannot ground the possibility of a feminist political movement in which women could unite as women in order to formulate and pursue specific feminist aims. Contrary to that view, I will argue that, for those feminists who are committed to a radical and democratic politics, the deconstruction of essential identities should be seen as the necessary condition for an understanding of the variety of social relations where the principles of liberty and equality should apply . . . The 'identity' of (such a) multiple and contradictory subject is . . . always contingent and precarious, temporarily fixed at the intersection of . . . subject positions and dependent on specific forms of identification. (1992b:371–2)

Like Phillips, then, Mouffe hopes for the transcendence and solidarity promised in democratic theories, but accepts that there will be a constant redefining of the ideals to be pursued. Unlike those feminists who argue for the incorporation of 'feminine' values into the model of democratic politics, or those liberal feminists who believe that a set of reforms can confer equal citizenship upon women without challenging the existing liberal model of politics and citizenship, Mouffe proposes a conception of politics which accepts the inevitability of diversity, antagonism and conflict. She tries to reinstate the notion of a common good, without reifying it as some civic republicans do, by arguing that it must be founded upon the acceptance of politico-ethical principles such as tolerance, justice and equality. Young's group politics, from Mouffe's perspective, is still too essentialist, leading to a fixity of positions; Young's model might be viewed as the first stage of a process leading to the construction of a 'common political identity' where, presumably, no one would regard identities and interests as permanent or inevitable.

Mouffe argues that accepting the lack of fixed, pre-given identities and positions means that the content and links between categories such as 'women', 'working-class', 'black' and so on can and must be constantly renegotiated and redefined. Mouffe sees the possibility of 'a truly different conception of what it means to be a citizen and to act as a member of a democratic political community' (1993:377), where it is possible to imagine, for example, that sexual difference would not have any pertinent significance in many cases. The public/private distinction would not be abolished, but renegotiated and always subject to challenges, while the minimal liberal definition of 'rights' would be expanded and our identities would never be reduced to one single position of class, race, nation or gender.

This imagining of new meanings for citizenship has been followed up by several feminist writers. In a recent work, Ruth Lister (1997) aspires to new conceptions of citizenship based upon the principle of 'differentiated universalism'. This implies changing the gendered meanings attached to the public and private spheres, incorporating the values of care into the image of the citizen, and using the levers of public policy to achieve a fairer division of domestic labour. Above all, the concept should be cleaned of all connotations of worth based on autonomy and independence, the fictions which render women's work invisible. Citizenship should remind us, says Uma Narayan (1997:65), that we have 'a collective as well as an individual stake in the decency and humaneness of our policies and public arrangements'.

What the writers outlined above – and many other feminist theorists – have in common is their desire to reinstate democratic politics as an activity which is distinctive, which must be carried on according to established rules and procedures. They want feminists to accept that politics can be an activity in which radical change can come about. They are also aware that, as presently conducted, mainstream politics has not offered much to women. To mainstream theorists they are arguing that identities cannot simply be suppressed in the public sphere. To other feminists they are suggesting that identities can be created and changed through action in the public sphere and that feminist politics must be open to such renegotiations. All of these writers consistently remind us about other identities, exclusions, oppressions and resistances. Women will engage in politics in many guises, and any feminist design for citizenship and democracy must take this fact into account.

Towards coalition politics

The challenges from women who have felt unrepresented by second-wave feminism and the insights of post-structuralism, post-modernism and theories of difference have resulted in the emergence of new ideas about the possibilities for feminist strategies and activism in the 1990s. Even without fully agreeing with post-modern rejections of the uncertainty of any truth claims or the instability of subjects, individual or collective, many feminist writers concede that we can no longer think of women as a coherent, unified group sharing common interests.

The idea of the coalition has recurred in many forms in recent feminist political writings, in response to the multiplicity of identities and the diversity among women. Again, it must be stressed that this does not imply that it is no longer possible to identify and resist gender inequalities, but rather that we can no longer take as given that all women experience the same exclusions or injustices, or that they will have the same priorities. Where even the meaning of 'women', let alone their needs or interests, remains to be defined or produced in action, a process of debate and negotiation appears to be called for. Inevitably, there can be no outcomes taken for granted in advance, no guarantees that the result will be agreement. This will be a genuinely open-ended process, which may or may not be successful, depending upon specific contexts and circumstances. This warning of 'no guarantees' is echoed in Anne Phillips's (1995) acceptance that efforts to find a means of overcoming exclusion and representing difference will always be 'a shot in the dark', to be settled in different ways according to the demands of different situations.

Nira Yuval-Davis (1997), too, welcomes any feminist politics that recognises differences and inequalities among women, but warns of the dangers of founding coalitions on a politics of identity which simply displaces essentialism and homogenisation from women as a whole to particular groups and communities. She argues that multiculturalism, whether feminist or not, has often been based on a 'belief in the inherent reconcilability and limited boundaries of interest among those who are disadvantaged and discriminated against' (p. 128). Such positions can allow fundamentalist, sexist and even racist leaderships to come to the fore in marginalised and oppressed communities. A coalition, by contrast, must be negotiated around principles, otherwise there will be a collapse into complete relativism. Solidarity is by no means assured, but has to be achieved. The outcome may well be unlike what was originally hoped for by any of the participants.

Yuval-Davis argues for an openness and pragmatism about feminist politics and methods of organisation, so that women can adapt in ways they believe most appropriate. She ends her examination of gender and nation with a discussion of one methodology for dealing with differences among women, namely 'transversal politics'. This is an initiative which has come from Italian feminists working with women from conflicting national groups. In this process, women enter into dialogue with a commitment to try to uncover a fair solution to the conflict which divides them. They are all rooted in a particular community, but make no claim to represent it, or even any particular subgroup within it. In the process, they aspire to learn about and respect the situations of women from the 'other' community.[11] Both 'rootedness' and the capacity to 'shift' are regarded as equally important if all are genuinely to learn about their differences.

'Transversal' signifies that the underlying principle must be that of dialogue. It is neither universal – which claims to be inclusive, but in practice becomes exclusive – nor relativist – which assumes that no common understanding can be reached. A transversal dialogue opens with the important expectation that neither community is homogeneous; alliances and shared values may be achieved across this broad division. Again, there are no guarantees of success. There may be strong pressures and interests which impede or make impossible reconciliation. The starting-point of transversal politics – that one can learn about different perspectives without abandoning one's own identity – offers the possibility of empowerment and inclusion, without the likelihood of reproducing national and racial stereotypes. Some differences, may, however, be irreconcilable. And as Ruth Lister points out (1997:82), not all subordinated groups may find it possible to use the methodology of dialogue in the first place, because their survival may depend upon defending particular positions.

On the surface, it may appear that there is nothing essentially or exclusively feminist about transversalism. This could also be said about some of the solutions to difference argued for by Iris Young, Anne Phillips and Chantal Mouffe. It is no accident, however, that they have been produced by feminist writers. The values, insights and concepts they contain have been developed in the context of certain kinds of feminist practice and theory. Yuval-Davis (1997:130) argues, for example, that transversal politics has specific benefits for women, who have often been victims in situations where exclusionary community identities have been constructed in the male image. Versions of transversal politics could be used in other cases where difference has become an obstacle, not necessarily always where there is violent conflict. Such a politics is likely always to depend upon other factors – cultural, economic, political, legal – for its potential to be realised. In our present world, where acknowledging the claims for recognition of differences has become an essential part of our idea of justice, it would seem that some such methodology will be an essential part of any politics. Above all, it is founded upon the idea that negotiating coalitions across differences require rules and procedures, but that these in turn are subject to review and negotiation.

A transversal politics of coalitions has clear implications for the vision of citizenship to provide the basis for any new models of democracy. With its emphasis on dialogue across difference and the search for commonalities, it allows for the expression of allegiance to identities and communities, but avoids fixing people for ever in particular positions. It leaves scope for protection of the individual, but this is an individual who is located within the context of relationships to others. It remains important to represent women and their interests, but this will be achieved through processes which allow women, in all their diversity, to define the issues and interests and to decide on which have priority.

Making links

Many feminist readers of this chapter may want to argue that adopting the complex and subtle concepts and strategies described above will still leave women outside the mainstream where real power and influence are wielded. Just when feminists have come to accept that it is worthwhile to attempt to break into the male-dominated world of state institutions, it seems we are returning to the partici-patory model of women's activism in civil society. The point is, however, that while women can make, and have made, their way into these institutions this has not by itself brought the changes in policy or practice that most feminists have sought. If women are to make a difference to politics in democratic states, then their access will have to be accompanied by changes in the structures and processes of the key institutions.

A consensus has begun to emerge that to create a polity that is 'woman-friendly' (Jones 1990), more inclusive and responsive to a greater variety of identities and interests, women will need to be active at all levels of decision-making, from governments to grass-roots groups. Bridges will have to be built to link these levels. For this to be effective, states will also need to invest in educational and self-development programmes (Narayan 1997) which will allow the present 'outsiders' to learn about the levers of power. Frameworks can be created which will allow pressures from the ever-expanding range of civil society organisations to be felt at the centre – second chambers, social forums, for example.

It is increasingly clear that no single model of democracy works at all times and for all type of organisations (Jones 1990), but ques-tions still remain about whether and in what ways the best combinations can be devised and generalised. There are many ques-tions, too, about the methods by which 'different' differences can be acknowledged in any societies. Is it possible to create structures and processes which allow for many forms of oppression and ex-clusion to be addressed at once, or will some divisions capture the attention, pushing others into the shadows? All of the case-studies in Part II throw some light upon these tricky problems. All of them, in different ways, provide examples of new ways of making deci-sions democratically without excluding emotion, diversity or the problems of everyday life. What lessons can be drawn from femi-nist theory, and what challenges remain, is the subject of Part III.

Notes

1 See Mansbridge (1983) for a fascinating discussion of participatory democ-racy in theory and practice.
2 Juliet Mitchell's groundbreaking essay (1966) is an excellent example of a feminist critique of the new left.

3 Most notably, Jean Bethke Elshtain. See especially *Public Man, Private Woman* (1981), which supports Okin's perception of the gendered nature of this divide, but which argues against its dissolution in the interests of (among other considerations) sustaining a distinction between these two different kinds of human activity.

4 The accepted version of contracts, for instance, is that a free, voluntary agreement among individuals can justify whatever those individuals may choose to do. This has been used to justify prostitution, incorporating the assumption that the bodily differences between the male and female parties to that 'contract' are irrelevant, a fiction which in Pateman's view glosses over the inequality of such interactions.

5 The stark pictures of under-representation which we find in Northern Ireland today may be an extreme case, but it is not unique, and improvements are being achieved slowly. In the Republic of Ireland, women hold 12.5 per cent of seats in the Dáil. In the UK, women held 9.2 per cent of seats in the 1992 parliament; as a result of a Labour Party policy to give preference to women candidates in safe seats, this became 18 per cent in 1997. However, this policy has been declared unlawful and in the absence of a radical change in the electoral system, this figure is likely to represent a peak. Italy has 8 per cent of women in its parliament, Germany, 20 per cent.

6 The men and women of the interfaith community described in Chapter 4 are particularly concerned to accept expressions of emotion in their discussions.

7 This was a group of women whose children, or other relatives, had been abducted by the military regime in Argentina in the 1970s. The Madres began to assemble in public places, quietly and with great dignity demanding information about the fate of the 'disappeared'. See Georgina Waylen (1998) for a discussion of this movement.

8 I am thinking of both civic-republican and communitarian schools of political theory. See Kymlicka (1995).

9 Jurgen Habermas is the best-known exponent of deliberative democracy. Seyla Benhabib (1994) has developed a version inflected by feminism.

10 I am indebted to Noel O'Sullivan who explained deliberative (and other) conceptions of the political in a lecture in the University of Ulster. The text was later published and provides an interesting account of many theorists. See O'Sullivan (1997).

11 The NI Woman's Coalition (Chapter 6) provides a remarkable example of transversal politics. So, too, I believe do some of the negotiations within the trade union discussed in Chapter 5.

References

Anthias, F. and Yuval-Davis, N. (1983) 'Contextualising Feminism: Gender, Ethnic and Class Divisions', *Feminist Review*, 15, 67–75.

Arblaster, A. (1994) *Democracy*, Buckingham: Open University Press.

Barrett, M. and Phillips, A. (eds) (1992) *Destablizing Theory: Contemporary Feminist Debates*, Cambridge: Polity Press.

Beasley, C. (1999) *What is Feminism? An Introduction to Feminist Theory*, London: Sage.

Beetham, D. (1992) 'Liberal Democracy and the Limits of Democratization', *Political Studies*, XL, Special Issue, 40–53.

Beetham, D. and Boyle, K. (1995) *Introducing Democracy*, Cambridge: Polity Press.

Benhabib, S. (1994) 'Deliberative Rationality and Models of Democratic Legitimacy', *Constellations*, 1(1), 26–52.

Bock, G. and James, S. (eds) (1992) *Beyond Equality and Difference: Citizenship, Feminist Politics and Female Subjectivity*, London: Routledge.

Brennan, T. and Pateman, C. (1979) 'Mere Auxiliaries to the Commonwealth: Women and the Origins of Liberalism', *Philosophical Quarterly*, 27(2), 183–200.

Butler, J. and Scott J. (eds) (1992) *Feminists Theorize the Political*, London, New York: Routledge.

Charles, N. and Huntjens, H. (eds) (1998) *Gender, Ethnicity and Political Ideologies*, London: Routledge.

Collins, P. H. (1990) *Black Feminist Thought*, Boston: Unwin Hyman.

Coole, D. (1993) *Women in Political Theory*, Hemel Hempstead: Harvester Wheatsheaf.

Dietz, M. (1992) 'Context is All: Feminism and Theories of Citizenship', in Chantal Mouffe (ed.) 1992(a), 63–85.

Elshtain, J. B. (1981) *Public Man, Private Woman: Women in Social and Political Thought*, Princeton, NJ: Princeton University Press.

Freeman, J. (1989) 'Feminist Organisations and Activities from Suffrage to Women's Liberation', in Freeman, 541–55.

Freeman, J. (1989) *Women and Feminist Perspectives*, Mountainview: Mayfield Press.

Gilligan, C. (1983) *In a Different Voice: Psychological Theory and Women's Development*, Cambridge, MA: Harvard University Press.

Jones, K. B. (1990) 'Citizenship in a Woman-Friendly Polity', *Signs*, 15(4), 781–812.

Kymlicka, W. (1995) *Contemporary Political Philosophy: An Introduction*, Oxford University Press.

Lijphart, A. (1997) *Democracy in Plural Societies: A Comparative Exploration*, New Haven, CN: Yale University Press.

Lister, R. (1997) *Citizenship: Feminist Perspectives*, London: Macmillan.

Lovenduski, J. and Norris, P. (eds) (1993) *Gender and Party Politics*, London: Sage.

Mansbridge, Jane (1983) *Beyond Adversary, Democracy*, Chicago, ILL: University of Chicago Press.

Mitchell, J. (1966) 'Women: The Longest Revolution', *New Left Review*, 40, 11–37.

Mouffe, C. (ed) (1992a) *Dimensions of Radical Democracy*, London: Verso.

Mouffe, C. (1992b) 'Feminism, Citizenship and Radical Democratic Politics', in Butler and Scott, 369–384.

Mouffe, C. (1993) *The Return of the Political*, London: Macmillan.

Narayan, U. (1997) 'Towards a Feminist Vision of Citizenship: Rethinking the Implications of Dignity, Political Participation and Nationality', in Shanley and Narayan, 48–67.

Nicholson, L. (1994) 'Feminism and the Politics of Postmodernism', in Wicke and Ferguson, 69–85.

Norris, P. (1987) *Politics and Sexual Equality: The Comparative Position of Women in Western Democracies*, Brighton: Harvester.

Okin, S. M. (1979) *Women in Western Political Thought*, Princeton, NJ: Princeton University Press.

Okin, S. M. (1989) *Justice, Gender and the Family*, New York: Basic Books.

O'Sullivan, Noel (1997) 'Difference and the Concept of the Political in Contemporary Political Philosophy', *Political Studies*, 45(4) 739–54.

Pateman, C. (1986) 'The Theoretical Subversiveness of Feminism', in Pateman and Gross, 1–12.

Pateman, C. and Gross, E. (eds) (1986) *Feminist Challenges and Political Theory*, London: Allen & Unwin.

Pateman, C. (1989) *The Disorder of Women*, Cambridge: Polity Press.

Pateman, C. (1992) 'Equality, Difference, Subordination: The Politics of Motherhood and Women's Citizenship', in Bock and James, 17–31.

Phillips, A. (1991) *Engendering Democracy*, Cambridge: Polity Press.

Phillips, A. (1992) 'Universal Pretensions in Political Thought', in Barrett and Phillips, 10–30.

Phillips, A. (1993) *Democracy and Difference*, Cambridge: Polity Press.

Phillips, A. (1995) *The Politics of Presence*, Oxford: Clarendon Press.

Randall, V. (1987) *Women and Politics, An International Perspective*, Basingstoke: Macmillan.

Rawls, J. (1973) *A Theory of Justice*, Oxford: Clarendon Press.

Ruddick, S. (1989) *Maternal Thinking: Towards a Politics of Peace*, Boston: Beacon Press.

Squires, J. (1996) 'Liberal Constitutionalism, Identity and Difference', *Political Studies*, XLIV, Special Issue, 620–34.

Shanley, M. L. and Narayan, U. (eds) (1997) *Reconstructing Political Theory*, Cambridge: Polity Press.

Waylen, G. (1998) 'Women's Activism, Authoritarianism and Democratisation in Chile' in Charles and Huntjens, 146–87.

Wicke, J. and Ferguson, M. (1994) *Feminism and Postmodernism*, Durham, NC: Duke University Press.

Young, I. M. (1990a) *'Throwing Like a Girl' and Other Essays in Feminist Philosophy and Social Theory*, Bloomington, Indiana University Press.

Young, I. M. (1990b) 'Polity and Group Difference', in Young (1990a) 114–137.

Yuval-Davis, N. (1997) *Gender and Nation*, London: Sage.

Part II
Democratic Practice in Action

3

'We are these Women . . .':
Self-Conscious Structures for
a Women's Centre

Carmel Roulston and Margaret Whittock

The story of Chrysalis Women's Centre provides an account of women's activism which might have been found in many parts of Northern Ireland in the 1980s and 1990s. As Chapter 1 of this book has indicated, during those years a vibrant network of working-class women's groups was created. Women could be found working in diffuse networks of grass-roots campaigns and self-help or support groups, many which had been created to oppose or ameliorate the effects of unemployment and loss of publicly funded services. These groups and networks have required constant struggle to sustain them against seemingly overwhelming obstacles: limited resources, lack of childcare and poor access to transport, the pressures and tensions of working in the midst of violent civil conflict. When funding can be achieved for a centre which can be used as a base for women's activism, the returns for all the efforts invested are increased many times over, though, of course, securing the continuation of funding then presents a new set of challenges. The groups of women who have created the centre also have to invent structures and procedures which will allow it to be used fairly, productively and to the best possible effect for women and their families and communities.

While they have many features in common, women's centres may have rather different origins (Cockburn 1998:62), and have been adapted to the circumstances of their localities. The setting for the women's centre we studied is Brownlow, part of Craigavon borough some forty miles south of Belfast.[1] Craigavon was created in the 1960s to provide a residential area which would relieve pressure on Belfast and as part of a plan for industrial development in the south and west of Northern Ireland. By the 1980s, the development was running into trouble. Most of the firms attracted there by generous grants had moved away, leaving people who had moved from Belfast, Derry and elsewhere stranded in a rather sprawling series of partially completed housing developments. The new borough was located in a reasonably prosperous part of the countryside, and drew together with the new development some older towns and villages (including Portadown, now notorious for the bitter conflicts over Orange marches). Inadequate local transport, limited shopping facilities, badly lit streets and deserted open spaces have made this an unfriendly environment for everyone.

Brownlow was developed as the new centre of Craigavon. New housing and a civic centre were created, and inward investment strategies did bring some new employment for a time. The fact that the area has great potential – the pleasant surrounding countryside makes this a fine place to live if you have a job and a car – adds to the frustration felt by many of its residents. One of the women in Chrysalis described the Brownlow area as being like 'the inner city in the country'. The new housing developments have meant that Catholics and Protestants are more likely to live in mixed housing areas than is usual elsewhere in Northern Ireland. One of these more mixed areas is Burnside, where the women's centre is to be found. This area is also home to many ethnic minority communities, some of whom have been the victims of almost unnoticed and often violent racism (Hainsworth 1998).

Brownlow Community Trust (BCT) had been set up in the 1980s to mobilise local pressure groups to campaign for regeneration of the area. The trust allocated some of its £2.2 million budget to projects aiming to encourage women to overcome obstacles to their full participation in community life and to obtain training, employment and educational opportunities (BCT 1992). Almost as soon as this money became available, women in the Brownlow area began to campaign for a centre, even with the awareness that this would be the start of a long and difficult process, with many setbacks involved. They were aware that women's centres in other areas had been vulnerable to reductions in funding and, in some cases, had been the object of the hostility of some local politicians and paramilitary groups (Jacobson 1997). Women's groups had learned in the 1980s, as Chapter 1 indicates, that there is little consistency in the funding of women's activities of any sort in Northern Ireland. The grants awarded are usually comparatively small; it is not clear which agencies are responsible for providing them and there is a lack of transparency in the criteria for making awards (Taillon 1992). Some funding bodies require that the group undertake some 'cross-community' or reconciliation activities if they are to satisfy the criteria, which can undermine the ability of groups and centres to provide the much-needed safe space for women. Nevertheless, winning support for projects, particularly those which provide resources, has represented an advance for women's organisations which is widely felt to have been worth the risks and problems they have entailed.

The unique features of this story are to be found in the next stage, in the telling of what this particular group of distinctive, capable, imaginative women made of their centre in the somewhat untypical setting of a rather run-down, unsuccessful new town set in the middle of Northern Ireland's countryside.

First steps and setbacks

Economic decline and its effects are to the forefront in the minds of women in the area. Asked about the major challenge for them, women in Chrysalis gave similar responses:

> Poverty – very much so. We're now coming into our third generation – the unemployment is dreadful.

Many women in the area also experience a sense of isolation as a result of having moved away from extended family networks. This is compounded by the poor provision of childcare, which is missed especially given that lone parents – the majority of whom are women – make up 20 per cent of the local population. This was the major problem for some, as one woman commented:

> I think it would be the isolation. Getting stuck in the house, just meeting family, but not getting out to talk to people.

In this area, a large percentage of women have no formal qualifications and there are few employment opportunities apart from badly paid part-time jobs. From the 1970s, community groups with both self-help and campaigning orientations began to appear, hampered by lack of funding and the relative invisibility of some of those whose needs were being identified.

In 1990, after a series of meetings attended by voluntary groups and representatives of statutory agencies, the Women's Forum was created. The origins and role of the Forum are described by Claire McCann, who was later to become the chairperson of the Chrysalis Women's Centre:

> What happened was a group of women came together and started to meet in what was called a resource centre. That group basically came together because [BCT] had received European money . . . and had employed a Women's Project worker. . . . So the Women's Forum came together to talk really and also to direct her work.

At a meeting in 1991, the Women's Forum discovered that BCT had been offered the lease of a building formerly used as a family centre by the Craigavon and Banbridge Area Health and Social Services Trust.[2] BCT invited women's groups to present ideas about the possible use of this building as a women's centre, and also circulated a letter to local residents asking for their ideas. Initially there was some friction over the proposal; a group called the Craigavon Women's Network argued that the Women's Forum did not adequately reflect the needs of local women and nominated themselves as better suited to develop the proposed centre.

In the end, a public meeting was called to discuss the various options and proposals. This allowed the airing of grievances and suspicions, and resulted in BCT agreeing to take over the building and to convene a planning group representing women's organisations, which would make decisions the future. Eventually, the Centre would be handed over to what would become a Centre users' committee.

Over the next few months, the planning group and the Women's Forum held several meetings. These had the result of the Women's Forum becoming a more focused campaigning group, with a representative elected to the management committee of BCT. Plans were put on hold, however, when the health trust was obliged to delay handing over the Centre. A car bomb whose primary target was the local police station also destroyed a school, some shops and the local health centre, which was then temporarily relocated in the Burnside building.

It was not until December 1992 that the Centre was handed over to the planning group. By this time some plans had been made for its use, including a decision that two BCT workers (one of whom was the women's officer) would be based in the building. At an inaugural general meeting, one priority identified was to make the Centre more appealing to women. Before its temporary use as a health centre, it had been a family centre, where 'problem families' were sent for advice, counselling and therapy. A certain stigma had thus become attached to the place, and it became important to ensure that associations with the previous use were broken. Dropping the name 'Burnside' was suggested, and the inaugural meeting then discussed other options. In the end 'Chrysalis' was chosen. It was a deliberate and highly significant choice, as Theresa Watson (who later became Centre co-ordinator) explained:

> because of the whole meaning behind the name – the idea of an in-between stage between the caterpillar and the butterfly . . . this could be considered almost a dormant stage but it's not. It's actually when it's inside that the caterpillar is changing into a butterfly and is going to emerge as a butterfly. So we liked this idea of a protective space – a safe space for women to grow. So we chose the name Chrysalis.

At the same meeting, a users' policy was initiated and a constitution drafted, with the help of the Northern Ireland Council for Voluntary Action. A committee which consisted of representatives from local women's groups – a maximum of two from each group to avoid any perceived unfairness or suggestions of bigger groups taking over – was set up to manage the Centre until a user group committee could emerge. And so the Chrysalis Women's Centre was created, with optimism and wariness perhaps equally balanced against each other in its first days.

The much-desired Centre had some promising and some not-so-promising features. It is set in a row of houses in Burnside estate, close to one of the roundabouts on Craigavon's complex ring-road system. The estate, built in the 1970s, and managed by the Northern Ireland Housing Executive,[3] has a run-down appearance but includes houses of quite a good standard. It is reasonably accessible from other local housing areas. So the Centre has a favourable position from the point of view of potential users. Four houses have been knocked together, and Chrysalis occupies the bottom

floor, with the upper storeys used for social service training programmes. Chrysalis has been planning to annex some of this further
space in due course. A large, L-shaped room at the back had been
added for a crèche and was also used for meetings in the evenings.
Having four linked ground floors is not ideal in terms of how the
space can be used; the corridors are narrow and there are limits on
how much any one room can be extended. One of the ground-
floor areas contains a large kitchen and dining room, however, where
a great deal of informal meeting, conferring and other activities
take place. It is also used for cookery classes, demonstrations and a
lunchtime cafeteria which has proved popular.

The smaller rooms are used as offices and reading rooms and for
teaching and studying. The doors between offices and other rooms
are usually open; some outside doors and windows are covered with
grilles to keep out thieves and vandals. The workers would prefer
not to have the grilles, as they cut down the light, but local youths
have on several occasions attacked the Centre and stolen equipment and money. The rooms have been decorated to create a friendly
and warm atmosphere, with pictures of locally found butterflies in
each room marking out the different spaces and uses. A lot of work
has gone into making the Centre into a pleasant, welcoming place
in which women will feel comfortable. The evidence from interviews with and comments by some women using the Centre suggests
that this has been successful, with many repeating the theme that
Chrysalis is 'like a home from home'. Some described it as better
than home, as it offers space dedicated to the women's interests
and preferences, something often not readily available in the family home.

In the first months after its opening, the Chrysalis committee
decided to initiate a young women's group and an after-school club.
A subcommittee to look into childcare issues was formed, a community café was opened and a series of classes for women was
begun. BCT around this time came back to the Centre to suggest
that it should adopt a development strategy to increase the level of
activity and encourage more women to use it. The Trust, of course,
has an obligation to show that it is spending money on worthwhile projects that will meet the objectives of the funding agencies.
The planning committee in Chrysalis has additional commitments,
however. Minutes of discussions over the early months reveal a
desire to create and sustain a sense of ownership and control among
the women building the Centre. Out of these discussions came an

impulse to give Chrysalis a clear set of purposes and policies with which women in the area could identify.

Building an identity

The importance of creating an authentic relationship between the Centre and the community is one of the key themes that runs through documents and the interviews with women using and working in the Centre. Reference to 'local women' recurred in conversations and interviews and in accounts of relationships with BCT. The Trust itself identified building the actions of local women and facilitating their empowerment as priorities. Workers and volunteers frequently described their ambitions for the Centre in terms of representing and empowering women in the area, supporting them in finding a voice and being listened to. Theresa commented:

> All the statistics say we are a very poor and powerless community. Well, we may have no money, and we may have a lot of lone parents, but we don't have to be powerless. Our organisation definitely provides a voice for women at grass-roots level. Women are very, very powerful and they don't realise it. If they are empowered they can do so much – they can get changes ... But they need to feel empowered to do that, they need to take back their own power. And I feel that's what the Centre does for women – they claim back their own power.

Chrysalis took this a step further. A central concern was to forge an integrated identity between the women working in and managing the Centre and the local community of women. This is most graphically reflected in an anecdote about the visit paid to Chrysalis in November 1994 by Lady Mayhew, wife of the then secretary of state. On her departure, she expressed her admiration: 'Oh, it's wonderful work you are doing with these women,' only to receive the reply from Claire:

> Lady Mayhew, we *are* these women. We live on benefits, Theresa and Jackie [the salaried workers] lived on benefits, I still live on benefits. We are these women and that's what makes a difference.

The Centre workers and participants all sought inclusiveness and a non-hierarchical method of work which would allow Chrysalis to be what women in the area wanted, and to work the way they wanted it to work.

The development plan, which the Centre committee drafted in 1994, was intended to foster this bond between Chrysalis and its constituency. It was agreed, for example, that the Centre needed at least one paid worker, and funding for a coordinator post was sought. Almost immediately it was established that a local woman with local knowledge and experience should be given this post. Making this a priority was based on the belief that a local coordinator would symbolise the empowerment of local women that the Centre was expected to encourage and would increase local control over the Centre.

The development plan also proposed raising the commitment to childcare by creating a proper crèche and finding the money to appoint a childcare coordinator. Providing childcare and also laundry facilities was in answer to direct expressions of local need and was also part of an attempt to promote inclusion. By the time Lady Mayhew came to visit, the new workers – both women who had been involved with the Centre from the first meetings – had been in post for several months, a new committee had been elected and the laundry room had been installed. (Lady Mayhew was performing the opening ceremony.) Another the longer-term plan under way was the creation of an education programme within the Centre; without the crèche, participation would have been very difficult for most women with young children. The laundry room was important for at least two reasons. Not only was it used by women with families feeling the effects of the abolition of social security grants for household equipment, but it was also relevant for women from the travelling community whose local 'stopping sites' had virtually no amenities.

The education programme was informed by the aims of satisfying local needs and nurturing local capacities. By the time we came to visit the centre, the programme had expanded, becoming quite ambitious and very popular with women from the entire Craigavon area and beyond. The underpinning philosophy was summarised in an interview by the coordinator, Theresa Watson:

> This area has a lot of poverty and a great number of people who work here are professionals from outside. It's very devaluing of the people who live here and the skills within the community . . . So we want to value the skills of local women. The people who teach develop and grow, as well as those who are taught.

By the time of the second annual general meeting (AGM) in June 1995, the development plan was being steadily implemented. A wide range of courses was established, as many as possible drawing on the talents of women involved in creating the Centre and of other women living in the area. A local open learning centre had been drawn in to assist with accreditation of some of the courses, and the number of women coming to classes was increasing. The childcare project was developing as well, with four part-time workers whose funding came from the local unemployed workers' centre. The childcare coordinator had also started a club for primary school children and had taken responsibility for the young women's group. Some of the Centre's running cost budget was also set side to pay the wages of a part-time cleaner, a worker vital to making the crèche acceptable and to the smooth running of other activities, such as the cookery lessons and what became known as Fahra's Fabulous Asian Café. The growing confidence of the Centre committee can be seen in two proposals discussed at this AGM; one was to take over the lease of the building from BCT, while the other was to change the constitution in relation to election of committee members. On this latter issue, instead of local groups nominating committee members, it was proposed that women using the Centre be elected as individuals at the AGM. This was intended to make the committee more reflective of the many users who were not active in other groups or who might not be nominated by them. Only two years into its existence, the Chrysalis Centre was being shaped into a distinctive 'little polity' (Cockburn 1998), which was creating structures to help it run more effectively. Chrysalis was finding its own style and approach to managing problems and making policies.

Diversity, decision-making and empowerment

Some feminist theorists have been wary of claims to authenticity and inclusiveness based on community or locality (Phelan 1996; Yuval-Davis 1997). The major questions which have to be asked are 'Who defines the people or groups to be included?', and 'Which are the groups or individuals who find that they have not been counted in as part of the community?' As the experiences of second-wave feminism have shown, being among the relatively powerless does not prevent a group or community from acting to oppress others. Building inclusive, democratic structures requires not only awareness of the existence of different groups and interests but also practices that encourage participation by different groups and the expression of different identities.

Diversity

The Chrysalis Centre tries to be open to all women in the Craigavon area and beyond. In our observations, everyone who came making enquiries, offering help or seeking it, or simply looking for a sympathetic place for some food and company, was welcomed. That some groups were specifically invited with deliberate efforts being made to make them comfortable does not detract from the openness and warmth with which everyone is greeted. The stated priorities for the Centre are to provide support and encouragement for women on low incomes living without the benefit of many resources in the Brownlow area. That global category encompasses great diversity: of religion and political allegiance, of culture and ethnicity and of age, marital status, able-bodiedness and sexual orientation.

Chrysalis makes a special effort to offer support to mothers (and their children), and attempts to attract and support single and married mothers from every group in the area. Sensitivity is shown to those women who might have difficulty in availing of the resources offered. For example, some Islamic women indicated that their families might object to their coming to the Centre when men might be working as tutors, so arrangements were made to have the Centre women-only at certain times.

In interviews, some members of the committee worried that inclusiveness was still an aim rather than a reality. They acknowledged that although the immediate neighbourhood is 'mixed', there are relatively smaller numbers of Protestant women coming to the Centre. In its literature and publicity we found this to be a Centre which orientates itself towards heterosexual women, with a strong emphasis on women as mothers – though in interviews and conversations we found no evidence of prejudice against lesbian women. This would be difficult issue to deal with given the constraints of working within a fairly conservative environment, where the withdrawal of local support could be very serious indeed. More positively, we found the Centre to be open and welcoming and the committee members to be aware that informal customs and ways of working might develop which could make some women feel excluded.

Chrysalis aims to be not only inclusive in the sense of making all women feel welcome, but to promote a sense of ownership through participatory and democratic practices so that all who use and work in the Centre can play a part in deciding what it does and how. The objectives which the members of the Centre committee have set themselves are to encourage women to influence the policies and practices of the Centre and to develop planning, leadership and negotiation skills side by side with their aromatherapy and creative writing. These goals are not easy to attain; two key methods have been developed in order to bring them closer. First, there is a strong emphasis placed on the importance of *process* side by side with structure, and second, the education programmes are expected to foster the building of self-esteem and the confidence to participate.

Decision-making processes

Achieving democratic and inclusive decision-making is no easy task in any circumstances. There are factors in the circumstances in which grass-roots movements operate which make such an achievement all the more difficult for them.[4] It is, for a start, often not very clear who is included in the constituency of such a movement; that is, there may be questions about who the group is accountable to and to what extent accountability can be built into the decision-making structures of the group. In the case of Chrysalis, as we have seen, three constituencies were identified: women in the area, individual Centre users and groups which needed to use the Centre for their activities. By 1995, there were also workers and volunteers in the Centre whose interests had to be considered. When it has several objectives, as tends to be the case with women's groups, this problem can be compounded. In order to ensure wide consultation, radical groups often combine direct or participatory methods with representative procedures, but without clear rules as to which procedure is used when this can lead to decisions being challenged and grievances building up.[5] The structures and the rules which govern them have to be created from the beginning but have to incorporate some element of flexibility so that they can be adapted to changing circumstances. And of course, none of this takes place in a vacuum. Apart from the resource constraints and a generally hostile environment, there are also competing discourses (Ferreé and Martin 1995) about the group's ethos and purposes which can lead to continual questioning and review.[6]

The management committee of Chrysalis consists of fourteen members, who are invited to join it by the chairperson and coordinator. The committee and the chairperson are approved at an AGM to which workers, volunteers, users and local groups were invited. The committee includes two *ex officio* members who represent the funders and the borough council and some who have been suggested by key user groups in the Centre. It would be accurate to say that this committee is selected rather than elected, but it is also fair to say that this process is quite transparent. Anyone who wanted to be included in the committee could approach the chairperson or be nominated at the AGM; in general, the problem has been one of persuading people to accept the invitation rather than turning people away. The committee meets once a month and manages to get through a large agenda. Meetings are businesslike yet relaxed; everyone sits in a circle and members bring cups of coffee. Minutes are taken and summaries of key decisions are given to ensure that everyone is clear about what is happening. The management committee elects the usual officers plus coordinators for specific projects, such as education and childcare. The committee and coordinators are supported by a number of subcommittees: development and employment, funding, childcare and publicity. The purpose of the subcommittees is twofold: to delegate business to people with particular skills and interests so that the management committee can run more effectively, and also to bring in as many users and volunteers as possible into policy-making.

The consensus of opinion about this structure voiced in interviews was that this meant that Chrysalis was not run by a 'little clique' and that it made access to influence in the Centre more open. Women did not feel that they had to be able to commit an unmanageable amount of time in order to play a part in running the Centre. This was often contrasted with the experience of other community groups and centres where influence was shared less equally. Accessibility and sharing of influence are also promoted by encouraging women who are unable to join committees, to make suggestions about improvements and initiatives. Everyone is told, quite frequently, that the coordinator and committee members welcome comments and that suggestions will be brought to the management committee. Most of the committee members are to be found at least twice a week in the Centre, whether carrying on some business or simply visiting. Ideas for new developments can also come forward at the Monday Club. This is an open forum for discussion, where members can raise any issue which they consider of importance. There are also other occasions which the workers and committee members use to solicit opinion, to respond to questions and to float ideas about the Centre and its projects.

As well as these formal and informal channels of communication, there are also planned occasions for reflection on how the structures are working. Some months before our study began, the management committee had been on a residential weekend during which they had worked on a number of issues. They wanted to make the committee more effective, while remaining responsive. They also wanted to come up with ideas about expansion, drawing in wider groups of women and meeting their needs. One outcome of the residential was to develop some training for members of the management committee, in order to develop the individual skills of members and to share experience and expertise.

With the advice and support of two consultants, experienced in women's education and women's community activism, and who had facilitated the residential, a new course entitled 'Managing Community Groups' was devised and accredited by the Open College Network. When the course was drawn up, it was decided that it should be open to other Centre users and workers. The 'Managing Community Groups' course resulted in the production of a handbook which could be used, among other things, for induction of future management committee members.

Describing the course, Theresa outlined a vision of Chrysalis which was shared by most of those we talked to:

> We believe that there are a lot of people at the top – decision-makers – who don't understand the processes that happen with women – how women learn and pass on skills, and support each other. We have women at the top who are equally guilty of this – they become token men. Our type of learning is hard to quantify and it's not acknowledged or valued high up. Women empower each other by sharing their talents and gifts and that needs to be recognised. If you're looking at how women make changes in society and looking at top political structures – we don't want to be like those women at the top. This is the wholesome way to work. But how do we move from this to making changes, so that this is valued?

Empowerment in education

No one at Chrysalis made any claims to have found the answer to Theresa's final question. Many of the women we talked to, however, believed that the process started by giving women the confidence to value themselves, which is what the various education programmes aimed to do. The 'Managing Community Groups' course draws on the philosophy about education for women which Chrysalis has adopted. This is based upon the idea that courses should be constructed around the needs of the women who take them, that they should help to build self-confidence and that they should incorporate, in structure, content and methods, the experiences of the women themselves. In this, Chrysalis was assisted by a lecturer from the local further education college, who was developing adult education programmes also accredited through the Open College Network. He was keen to see traditional 'hobby' classes – jewellery making, creative writing, flower arranging – taken seriously. This could be done by offering credits for the learning work completed in them. He was also interested in trying out new ways of teaching and assessing adult classes, which incorporated the skills and knowledge adult learners bring to them. With his advice and participation, the workers and volunteers began to introduce a series of courses, some accredited, some not.

A few examples indicate the ways in which the education work linked into the wider purposes of the Centre. A course called 'Women the Peacemakers' opened up dialogues among women from different political and religious backgrounds and introduced some themes from feminist theology. An aromatherapy course proved very popular, but there were difficulties finding tutors who could come at convenient times. Theresa wondered why some of the women who had taken basic courses did not go further and become tutors. The problem was not only that some of the women lacked confidence but also that the available advanced courses were structured in such a way that they required attendance over several weeks at awkward times. After some persuasion and negotiation, a structure was worked out which met the demands of the course and the needs of the students. There is a strong commitment to using local women as tutors, which influences the shape of classes and promotes self-confidence among the women. One described how she was nagged by Claire and Theresa to offer an Italian cookery class; the endeavour was so successful that she was considering setting up a small catering business.

One particularly notable example emerged from the group of women who wanted Chrysalis to enter the annual raft race in the nearby lakes. They did not want to be patronised by other entrants as their raft slowly sank, so they decided to ask for some construction training at the local college. They negotiated a suitable set of classes, which met their needs. As a result, they managed to build one of the few rafts to stay afloat in the event. In this and the other examples, the courses resulted not only in completion of a programme of learning and the related increase in confidence for the students, but also some additional benefit to the Centre. There was now a raft which was safe enough to use again.

What came across in interviews with volunteers, workers, users and committee members – and is exemplified in the quotation from Theresa above – was the extent to which women in Chrysalis identified the *process* of participation as having a value independent of any benefits of the activities themselves. This emphasis on process led us to wonder about outcomes. Was it possible that some conflicts of interest or ideas might be blurred, or that some interests might not get equal expression or attention? Stressing that process is important might allow some people to get decisions made their way more often than others.

Sources of conflict

Although the overwhelming impression of the Centre was of cooperation, satisfaction and goodwill, we did uncover some conflicts, not all of which could be resolved to everyone's satisfaction. In a Centre where the standard of the crèche and the frequent availability of child-minding facilities was excellent by comparison with other groups, we were surprised to find that childcare policy had given rise to a major debate. The childcare coordinator was dissatisfied with how this part of the Centre's work was handled. In her view, childcare was seen exclusively in relation to other activities – the convenience to mothers being foremost – rather than as an important project in itself. Not enough of the Centre's resources were being devoted, she argued, to facilities and projects for the children's needs. After some discussion around this, a review of childcare was conducted with an external facilitator. It resulted in more time and money being given to this area of work. Most of those we spoke to were happy about this; some reported feeling ashamed when they realised how little thought had previously gone into the children's separate interests. Some felt that the balance had now gone too far and worried that it implied that women had to justify satisfying their needs by proving that the children were well looked after. But everyone we spoke to felt that the decision had been reached in a fair way and many reported that they had learned something through the process of the review.

Allocating resources in a Centre with limited funding is likely to be a source of dispute within the management committee, or between the committee and other users. In Chrysalis, as in other groups, applying for financial support gives rise to a seemingly endless and tedious round of writing grant applications, evaluations and reports. Many of the salaries and projects depend on support from more than one charitable foundation or statutory body.[7] We found no one who voiced serious disagreement with any of the priorities for spending; frustration about inability to undertake any project was attributed to the powers which controlled the flow of money to community initiatives. There was more discussion about the decisions about attracting income than about spending it. Theresa, supported by other committee members, argued very strongly against accepting funding for projects which might conflict with the strong emphasis on collective learning and empowerment through participation. So, every source of funding for education programmes and every invitation to become involved in joint projects was examined in detail and rejected if it did not fit with the values and the vision. Although this was recognised to be a very risky strategy, and some women wondered whether an occasional compromise would really do any harm, we found no actual opposition to it. At the time, in fact, the Centre was managing, not without difficulty and hard work, to fund as many activities as it could cope with, so this strong line was a source of pride for the women in the Centre. There was also intense collective involvement in a series of campaigns to have a bigger, purpose-built women's centre in the area. This was sparking a lot of discussion about what women really deserved and how they might get their hands on at least some of the money for it.

The main sources of opposition to resource attraction and allocation decisions that we found were among volunteers in the Centre. Voluntary work by dozens of women – tutoring, secretarial, maintenance – is essential to the continued existence of Chrysalis. This unpaid labour is very publicly acknowledged within the Centre and in its publications; it is described as central to the process of building local ownership of Chrysalis. In its dealings with external agencies and policy-makers continual reference is made to the lack of recognition and support for the contribution which voluntary work has made to community development. The voluntary workers are well represented in the committees and are included in reviews and residential weekends. Most of those we spoke to were keen to point out that they felt they had benefited a great deal from the experience of volunteer work. Some discovered abilities they had been unaware of, others found it revived their previous work skills. New opportunities had opened for some as a result of working in Chrysalis; they had gained access to further training and, as ever, had become more self-confident. But, some volunteers felt that the recognition was limited and that more efforts could – and should – be devoted to finding money to support paid workers. A few resented supervision or criticism of their work; in turn, some on the management committee articulated difficulties in dealing with one or two volunteers who responded badly to being told their work had not matched up to the high standards set by the Centre. Again, however, these disagreements and grievances were in the open; most of those we spoke to agreed that there was no inhibition on raising problems nor any sense of pressure to avoid expressing disagreement.

The informal, face-to-face process did not appear to stifle or inhibit expressions of opposition to the decisions taken by the management committee or the coordinators. This did not mean that everyone had equal influence over decisions or policies, but no one attempted to make such a claim. The coordinators and a few key individuals clearly had a great deal of influence, about which they were quite forthcoming. This was generally accepted as good leadership, exercised in an inclusive and specifically feminist manner. If anything, this was seen as another example of the Chrysalis team expressing the values of the Centre, rather than dominating the policy-making.

Wider horizons

The choice of the name Chrysalis, as noted earlier, was a very deliberate one, the aspirations of the Centre being encapsulated in the metaphor of the butterfly in the chrysalis. One woman, now a student, described the experience of being involved as having let her recover 'the woman I used to be', before marriage and motherhood had left her feeling undermined and powerless. Many women, however, expressed frustration that making the breakthrough into decision-making outside Chrysalis still appears difficult and even risky. One of the next steps which was frequently discussed was that of achieving more control over the conditions within which the Centre works, using whatever resources are available to shift the balance of power a little more in the direction of women. In a recent attempt to achieve more influence over external conditions, the management committee recently decided to join a community partnership which aims to develop an integrated approach for community action and to make the best use of available resources. The issues so far identified as important include the lack of facilities for young people, good-quality childcare, and support for parents. There were also demands for better programmes to encourage women to take up vocational training and employment. It is hoped that the partnership will enable the women from the Centre to influence a wider range of issues in the local community and to negotiate and engage in dialogue with those representing other interests. This may allow the women to express their sense of having needs and concerns in common with other groups, rather than having a single identity as women the expression of which brings them into conflict with other groups. This step has not been without its problems, however. The structures of other organisations do not easily harmonise with the Centre's style of work, and some of the agencies it works with have more status and influence. The Centre workers and volunteers expressed the opinion that they were being *permitted* to take part as representatives of women, that there was a limited and circumscribed place already prepared for them. Within the Centre, participation in this initiative is kept under review so that it does not lead to any departure from the agreed aspirations and priorities of the Centre. Some members have worries about 'losing what we've got here', while acknowledging that they may have little choice about pursuing the partnership goal. The Centre's representatives on any wider policy-making bodies often demand changes in the style of management and leadership of those bodies, towards greater inclusiveness and a sensitivity towards the need for less experienced participants to learn how things are done.

The value which is placed on what the Centre workers and users feel they have achieved is very high; to lose it would certainly be a serious blow. A strong sense of empowerment and growing confidence is expressed by many women:

> We're becoming more skilled at making the most of the chances that are there. We're definitely moving more into developing

those skills – to be able to talk in bigger arenas – or to be able to make demands in bigger arenas.

The changes which will be necessary if they are to achieve the influence in those 'bigger arenas' are not entirely within the capacity of the Centre's members to control. Many writers have pointed to the constraints upon grass-roots community activism. Cochrane (1986:73), for example, argues that when grass-roots activity attracts large-scale support it tends to be absorbed into mainstream politics, thus diluting radical demands; 'the initial strengths associated with community politics as a separate or autonomous area seem condemned to disappear'. In Northern Ireland at present, however, mainstream politics seems unlikely to absorb the concerns of women in the community and women activists at the grassroots are very reluctant to enter what is an extremely adversarial world. The peace process ultimately may result in the transformation of the sectarian and conflictual styles which mark political life.[8] The NI Women's Coalition, as Chapter 6 argues, has to some extent brought the grassroots experiences of women into the mainstream. Chrysalis, in common with other women's centres, certainly operates as a strong advocate for women within its local area and, given the opportunity, would press for women's concerns to be heard in as many policy-making arenas as possible. Advocacy on behalf of women, as Chapter 1 has argued, has been made possible to some extent by European funding and also under the consultation processes which existed under direct rule in Northern Ireland.

Like other community groups, Chrysalis was wondering whether devolved government in Northern Ireland was going to lead to reduced access to policy-makers. Their hope of a future system which would include them and accommodate their ideals of engagement through mutual learning and support seems far from being realised. The women in this Centre, however, were not enthusiastic about the notion that their ways of working could be a model for other groups. Others, they argued, should work out what they needed and develop processes that would work for them. Chrysalis, nonetheless, has a radical vision of creating democratic structures and processes to ensure inclusion and participation and one which respects diversity and difference. The key elements, however, were a willingness to be flexible and a commitment to inclusion of all perspectives and ideas. Through the processes described in this chapter, the women in the Centre have enjoyed the 'transformative' experience of 'meetings, discussions, talk' (Phillips 1993:113) which feminist theorists have outlined in more abstract terms. The secretary to the management committee, Frances Gentle, put into words just what that meant for her and for others:

> Coming here has definitely given me confidence ... I've been away to conferences in Scotland and I could never have done that, would never have dreamed of it. Not just me but other women coming here are more confident ... We're really now starting to get out of ourselves – we've started going to plays – and we'd never have dreamed of doing anything like that before – we'd always have thought that was for a different kind of person than us.

Notes

1 Fieldwork was carried out between dates October 1995 and March 1996. While both authors were involved, in the early stages, Margaret Whittock carried out most of the interviews and was responsible for most of the observations.
2 In Northern Ireland, health and social service provision are integrated.
3 The Northern Ireland Housing Executive was created in 1970, as part of the reform of local government discussed in Chapter 1.
4 Carole Mueller (1995:269–70) identifies some of the problems: 'Regardless of ideology, most small groups handle their internal affairs through informal understandings that are developed out of the common experiences of group members. Given enough time and stability of membership, such organisations usually develop a division of labour, leadership and accepted procedures for making decisions that help them to survive. When small group structure is coupled with an ideology of participatory democracy that encourages a mistrust of tradition and makes claims for the equality of all members experiences and skills, survival becomes considerably more problematic.'
5 Mansbridge's fascinating and detailed study of democracy in grass-roots groups (1983) gives many examples of such difficulties.
6 Iannello (1992) gives an interesting account of decision-making in organisations which have an ideological commitment to removing hierarchical structures.
7 The Centre coordinator's salary of £15 000 p.a. is, for example, funded 50 per cent by the Health and Social Services Trust; 25 per cent by the Joseph Rowntree Trust; 25 per cent by the Northern Ireland Voluntary Trust. The childcare coordinator's salary of £12 400 (it was hoped originally to have these two salaries equal) is funded 50 per cent by the Health and Social Services Trust, 50 per cent by Children in Need. The 'Managing Community Groups' course was supported by an award of £4000 from the Charities Aid Foundation, while the Community Relations Council and Craigavon Borough Council supported the Women the Peacemakers course.

8 At time of writing the peace process had been stalled for some months over the issue of whether the executive could be put in place before paramilitary arms decommissioning had begun.

References

Brownlow Community Trust (1992) *Progress Through Partnership: An interim Report*, Craigavon: Brownlow Community Trust.

Cochrane, A. (1986) 'Community Politics and Democracy', in Held and Pollit. 17–37.

Cockburn, C. (1998) *The Space Between Us: Negotiating Gender and National Identities in Conflict*, London: Zed Books.

Ferreé, M. M. and Martin, P. Y. (eds.) (1995) *Feminist Organizations*, Philadelphia: Temple University Press.

Hainsworth, P. (ed.) (1998) *Divided Society: Ethnic Minorities and Racism in Northern Ireland*, London: Pluto.

Held, D. and Pollitt, C. (eds) (1986) *New Forms of Democracy*, London: Sage.

Hirschmann, N. and Di Stefano, C. (eds) (1996) *Revisioning the Political*, Boulder, CO: Westview Press.

Iannello, K. P. (1992) *Decisions Without Hierarchy: Feminist Interventions in Organisation Theory*, London: Routledge.

Jacobson, R. (1997) *Whose Peace Process? Women's Organisations and Political Settlement in Northern Ireland 1996–1997*, University of Bradford: Peace Studies Papers.

Lister, R. (1994) 'Social Policy in a Divided Community reflections on the Opsahl Report', *Irish Journal of Sociology* (4), 27–50.

Mansbridge, J. (1983) *Beyond Adversary Democracy*, Chicago: University of Chicago Press.

Mueller, C. (1995) 'The Organisational Basis of Conflict in Contemporary Organisation', in Ferreé and Martin, 263–75.

Phelan, S. (1996) 'All the Comforts of Home: The Genealogy of Community', in Hirschmann and Di Stefano, 235–50.

Phillips, A. (1993) *Democracy and Difference*, Cambridge: Polity Press.

Taillon, R. (1992) *Grant Aided or Taken for Granted? A Study of Women's Voluntary Organisations in Northern Ireland*, Women's Support Network: Belfast.

Yuval-Davis, N. (1997) *Gender and Nation*, London and New Delhi: Sage.

4

'Equal in the Sight of the Lord': A Religious Reconciliation Group

Carmel Roulston

The Cornerstone Community is to be found on the upper Springfield Road, one of the main arteries that runs through West Belfast. This group of Christian men and women, whose primary aims are to work for and to act as a witness to reconciliation between Catholics and Protestants, selected this location after a great deal of thought. West Belfast is often described as a nationalist area, but although its population is predominantly Catholic, and its MP is the Sinn Féin leader Gerry Adams, there are also substantial numbers of Protestants living there.[1] Springfield Road in fact runs between the Protestant Shankill and Catholic Falls districts and is therefore what has become known as an 'interface area', a point of confrontation between working-class neighbourhoods marked by sectarian violence and tension. A few yards away from Cornerstone's home, you can see part of a high wall with large metal gates. The wall marks what became known – without any real intent of irony – as 'the peace line'. The walls were built in the 1970s and 1980s to protect residents on each side from sectarian attacks from the other side. The gates were opened in the mornings – sometimes with security forces staying on guard – and were shut fast in the early evenings to deny easy access to paramilitaries. Over the years, the walls were made higher and higher to block provocative taunting, missiles and petrol bombs. Protection, and a certain peace of mind, were provided at the expense of an apparently permanent, vivid reminder of the risks of trusting anyone from the other side.

The peace line and its barriers run through working-class and deprived areas, primarily in North and West Belfast. They do not – cannot – prevent outbreaks of sectarian violence, nor can they extend to every part of the city where Catholic and Protestant confront each other while going about their daily business. The building of these physical barriers was a clear indicator that violence in the area had reached intolerable levels. The alternative would have been population movement. This happened frequently in the early years of the Troubles, when large-scale evacuations of people from 'mixed' areas took place, leaving only a few places where Protestants and Catholics continued to live side by side.[2] During the 1970s an estimated 40 per cent of households in the upper Springfield district were forced to move because of the Troubles. This left a deep sectarian bitterness on both sides.

The area has also suffered over the years from acute social deprivation which has both contributed to and been made more severe by the political disorders. Poverty dominates the lives of many families and effectively excludes them socially, politically and culturally from the mainstream (Lister 1994:34). Unemployment is high in the area – indeed, recent figures indicate that while the unemployment rate has decreased in Northern Ireland, it has slightly increased in inner West Belfast, the area which includes the upper Springfield Road.[3] An upsurge in loyalist paramilitary violence which occurred in the months before the cease-fires were declared in 1994 was fuelled, it has been argued, 'by the growing poverty and sense of alienation and powerlessness experienced by Protestant working-class communities and especially the young men in them' (Lister 1994:33). And of course, as many commentators have observed, in this area of Belfast, where the two communities meet, such characteristics are not peculiar to one section of the community alone. Unemployment is much higher among Catholic males, but many studies have pointed to the extent to which poverty cuts across the religious divide; the gap between the 'haves' and 'have-nots' within the Catholic and Protestant communities being greater than the inequality between the communities (Borooah *et al.* 1993).

The men and women of Cornerstone chose this depressing landmark of Belfast's divisions precisely to prove that if Catholics and Protestants could live and work together here then it would be possible anywhere. In the eyes of the group, the walls of the peace line were both a sad reality and a metaphor for division. Their work was to create 'openings' in the metaphorical walls, to support any peaceful contacts which had survived the pressures of violence and sectarianism, and to attend to the spiritual – bearing witness to the 'true church'. One of the group, Noreen Christian, outlined the mission:

[T]o be there as a Protestant/Catholic grouping, living together, to understand each other on the human level. So that the struggle within ourselves of living together is the struggle of the people living around us. The struggle of accepting otherness.

Our case-study was concerned more with the secular than the spiritual, though we too had hopes of finding inspiration for the future. A community-based religious group was of particular interest because, although churches and religious groups in Northern Ireland contain high numbers of women, there has been relatively little research on their gender politics.

The case-study was carried by two researchers over a period of seven months. We attended formal and informal events in the community, interviewed both past and present members. We also took part in a retreat and review of the work of the community which was arranged during the period of the fieldwork.[4] We wished to explore how this group reached decisions about how to put ideals into practice, how differences within the group were resolved and whether their methods included any recognition of gender differences and inequalities. We wanted to study both the contribution such a group would make to renewing democracy in Northern Ireland and also how it could cope with gender differences within its own structures – whether and how leadership by women, for example, could be accommodated. Our preliminary enquiries revealed that Cornerstone contained slightly more women than men and that two of its three salaried workers were women. Much of the inspiration and energy in the early days of the Community had come from women and its first residents and leader had all been women. Would a group like this differ from the standard pattern to be found in churches, where women predominate among the laity but authority and leadership rest with a male hierarchy?

Origins and history

While the majority of commentators would agree that the Northern Ireland conflict is fundamentally about national identity and statehood (Whyte, 1990), not primarily about religion, it is clear that there are religious aspects to it, not least because the nationalist/unionist cleavage coincides with a Catholic/Protestant cleavage. The major Christian churches are woven tightly into the social fabric of Northern Ireland. The structure of education means that the majority of children are educated in schools which are predominantly Catholic or Protestant. Only a small minority of people marry someone from the 'other' religion (Love 1995:27). Intimidation and fear have driven great numbers of people to live among 'their own', reluctantly in many cases. Understandably then, the opportunities for inter-communal activity are often quite limited (Acheson and Williamson 1995b:3).

The roles played by the major Christian churches both in exacerbating the conflict and in attempts to resolve it have increasingly come under scrutiny. Until recently, as Morrow *et al.* (1991) point out, Northern Ireland's churches have not regarded intercommunity relationships as matters for specific programmes of action, and have rarely 'produced proposals for new initiatives which involve congregations and parishes at a systematic level'. These authors suggest that little evidence can be found that parishes and congregations have engaged in serious debate on the function of the churches in intercommunity relationships. Neither clergy nor laity, it is claimed, have sought to open up such discussions – discussions which could – and arguably should – contribute to the evolving democratic process in Northern Ireland. This is particularly important given the fact that nearly everybody in Northern Ireland has connections with one or other church in some capacity. Even non-church people come into contact with churches through a variety of social and recreational activities and by meeting church people through membership of outside groups, such as charitable organisations (Morrow *et al.* 1991:22).

Yet if we accept that the churches' record on cross-community work, until recently, has not been impressive, we must acknowledge that some of the individuals and groups most committed to promoting dialogue and reconciliation have come from within them. Even before the reoccurrence of serious intercommunal violence in 1969, there were a few such groups, the best known being the Corrymeela Community, which was created in 1965 to promote understanding among the different Christian denominations in the province (Love 1995; see also Morrow *et al.* 1991). The escalation of violence with its serious sectarian dimensions brought into existence many more groups – usually quite small and locally based – which attempted through direct and indirect means to counteract hatred, suspicion, prejudice and intolerance between Catholics and Protestants.

The Cornerstone Community was formally created in 1982, as

the outcome of a process of dialogue and prayer which had been going on for several years. In December, 1977, approximately sixty members from Christian Life communities in Dublin and Belfast attended a retreat in Northern Ireland. These communities were small groups of about eight Catholics who had been meeting regularly in order to 'deepen their Christian lives together, making use of the Spiritual Exercises of St Ignatius, and staying close to scripture'. One of the women who had initiated the meetings – Mary Grant, a member of the Little Sisters of Charity – invited a Methodist minister from Belfast to join them, bringing members of his and other congregations.

On this occasion, those present were asked to consider two questions: 'What are your favourite texts?' and: 'Why have you come along to the retreat?' This exercise was conducted in mixed groups (in terms of religion) of ten and on its completion everyone came together for a communal meal. The similarities of purpose, belief and inspiration which were revealed surprised some of those present, as one of the Methodists disclosed in an interview:

> Here was something quite unexpected by the Shankill people, most of whom had the fixed idea that no Catholic could be a believer . . . There were Catholics here who really knew the Lord Jesus, and had put their lives in his hands! And over the weeks afterwards this was the fact that was referred to time and time again, in wonder and joy!

Late in the following year, a group of about a dozen men and women, from both Catholic and Protestant backgrounds began to meet fortnightly at Clonard Monastery in Belfast. These meetings continued for nearly four years. Sister Mary Grant kept the group together and with others planned the programmes for meetings. During this time, they examined the various doctrines of the four churches they represented – Roman Catholic, Anglican, Methodist and Presbyterian. They also prayed together and sometimes met for various social activities. Not only did this increase their understanding of each other's doctrinal positions; they also found that more and more they were, as they describe it, 'growing together in the Lord'.

This burgeoning relationship was severely tested by the hunger strikes by republican prisoners in 1981.[5] By any standards, this was a traumatic period in the history of the Troubles, centred on an

issue which those involved in the group saw differently. Protestants regarded the fact that young men should die in this way for
some dream as an outrage, while for some of the Catholics, this
was an act of heroic sacrifice. In one interview, it was said that
two of the men in the community almost 'came to blows' over
this issue. In the end they agreed to disagree.

In spite of this setback, some members of the group were beginning to feel that more progress could be made to consolidate what
had already been achieved, by taking some kind of public stand.
They were aware of the implications that such a stand could have
in Northern Ireland, for, as Sam Burch, a Methodist minister, observed at the time:

> Any such public stand would require a deep, unshakable convic-
> tion that we are at one in Him, for it would clearly mean facing
> criticism and misunderstanding, if nothing worse . . .[6]

The group was in those early days drawn together by a strong sense
of shared spiritual experience and of having a divinely ordained
mission to break down the barriers between the churches. Their
reflections and exchanges brought feelings that they were being
directed towards Christian unity work in the Shankill–Falls area.
During an evangelical mission in Shankill Methodist Church, people
were asked to come forward and dedicate themselves to this work.
Quite a number did so, though as one member noted: ' . . . we
know that this would be madness and like Gideon in my weakness, I would need many proofs . . . before I could take part in such
a thing'.

Over the next year, the group received private donations from a
charitable trust (contacted by the minister who had come to hold
the mission), which bought two houses on the upper Springfield
Road. This was to be the home, for indefinite periods of time, of
some of the Community's members, who would always include both
Catholics and Protestants, as an act of witness against residential
segregation in the area. The houses would also be used for spiritual
activities for the Community and other people in the surrounding
districts. In December 1982 the Community took possession of the
two three-storey houses, and the first three residents, two Catholic
nuns from the Little Sisters of Charity, Mary Grant and Gladys
Hayward, and Hazel Dickson, a Methodist, moved in. According to
those interviewed, there was no conscious decision taken to have

all women move in at first. It did not necessarily guarantee a kind reception from potentially suspicious neighbours; a group of nuns from Mother Theresa's order who had attempted to set up a community on the Falls Road a few years previously had been made to feel quite unwelcome.

The main strategic decisions were to have a religious mix and initially to do little more than let some churches and groups in the area know, in a quiet way, about the venture. Members of the community would take part in inter-denominational acts of worship, something which would be viewed as scandalous and outrageous by many believers from all faiths in Northern Ireland. Members would, however, remain loyal to their original Churches while striving to transform them. The original project was to bring the message of Christian unity, actual and potential, to congregations both in the immediate neighbourhood and further afield, which might include the world outside Ireland.

Organising and acting

Cornerstone, then, had been formally in existence for almost thirteen years at the time we first visited in the autumn of 1995. Changes had taken place: in personnel, in methods of work and in the nature of the group's interactions with the people in the immediate area. Some things remained constant, however. The community was still small, although it had a vastly enlarged network of sympathetic and associated groups and organisations. At the time of our study, there were 16 full members of the community, 9 of whom were women. There were 9 Protestant and 7 Catholic members. Many belonged to other organisations or communities actively engaged in community development, peace-building or religious life. There were a further 5 'heart members' – former members or strong supporters, who want to be involved but do not have the time for regular meetings. There were 3 salaried workers, 2 of whom were women. The director (a salaried post) and treasurer were men, a position unchanged since 1984, and the secretary and house leader were women. There were also volunteers, usually young people who had come from the US or Europe to help with specific projects, some of whom became full members.

To fund its work, the community receives donations and grants from many sources. Among other things, 90 per cent of the salaries of the core workers are funded by the Community Relations

Council,[7] while charities and trusts provide the balance of the funding. Records have to be kept and evidence provided about how Cornerstone has made use of its various grants. Decisions have to be made about priorities and projects. Someone has to take responsibility for the form-filling, and the core workers – the director, the youth and community worker, and the family and development worker – require some kind of direction.

The annual general meeting (which heart members and others can attend, without voting rights) sets broad priorities and discusses difficult ethical issues (such as whether it would be right to apply for National Lottery funding, given the strong opposition to gambling among many members). The AGM elects an executive committee, not much smaller than the AGM, which meets monthly and is responsible for running the community and its projects from week to week. Provision has been made for emergency general meetings and there is also a commitment to hold a regular review of how the community is working. This is like a retreat, with a lot of self-critical reflection on whether and how Cornerstone is fulfilling its original purposes. Our 'outsiders' view was incorporated into the review in 1997, when we presented a report, conducted seminars, facilitated discussions and reflected with the Community on every aspect of its work. Supplementing these structures are opportunities for raising any kinds of matters at the weekly prayer meetings, in the regular acts of worship or in one of the weekly discussion meetings. The latter cover a wide range of topics and issues, and people from outside the community are invited to participate. Finally, there are frequent Community meals at which conversations about anything which has been debated are carried on.

The two interconnected houses are home for some of the members and volunteers, a workplace for others and the centre of activities for all the members and many others associated with the Community. This is central to the ethos of Cornerstone, but it produces work and issues of various kinds which need resolution; for example, who is responsible for inviting visitors to stay. For a small group, the Community is engaged in a wide range of activities, one initiative seeming to grow out of another and emerging into a complex web of projects and commitments. Although there was much overlap, we identified three broad strands of undertakings: spiritual, theological and practical engagement with churches and other religious groups; community-based development and reconciliation work; and broader peace, justice and human rights campaigning.

Members of the Community are all involved or associated with other projects and campaigns, some of which link back into Cornerstone's work. Sam Burch (a founder member) and Tom Hannon (the director) were very involved with Corrymeela at the time of our study, for example. Noreen Christian is a member of another similar community – Currach – in the area. Because Currach was becoming formally linked with Cornerstone in a joint project, sometimes Noreen was at meetings as a member of one Community or the other or sometimes both. It was a struggle to untangle all the connections at times, though Cornerstone's members seemed to have few problems in keeping clear who they were and what they were doing. This clarity, however, was the product of the frequent meetings and continual deliberation about the ethos and the work.

During the review in which we participated, such deliberation was very visible. Some members wanted to pause and reappraise directions in the light of their original purposes. There were concerns about what seemed to be a switch in emphasis from the tasks associated with bringing the Christian faithful together in favour of development work in the upper Springfield area. The Community by this point had become a major provider of support for local grass-roots campaigns and enterprises and was itself creating some innovative programmes for women and young people. Caroline Foster, the youth worker, with the help of the young volunteers and local workers, was hoping to launch a programme for young teenagers who were not responsive to the idea of a formal youth club. Bridie Cotter, the family development worker, was coordinating with Currach to establish classes and events for women in the area. Both were clear about the need for such services, focusing on the severe problems of the area. As Bridie put it:

> There's really nothing in the area – absolutely nothing in this big stretch. A lot of poverty and people feeling very bad about it. [*One woman told me*] I hope you are going to do something about this because we feel that we've really been forgotten about here – so it's people not being listened to.

Caroline remarked that the sense of alienation affected the children and teenagers in a way common, she felt, in a working-class area. 'For me working with the younger ones – it's building up their confidence, spreading their horizons.'

Woven through all these and other programmes (the lunch clubs for pensioners, the homework clubs, the neighbourhood festivals, the environmental campaigns) was the thread of cross-community links. Keeping this thread in the weave has often required patient mediation and negotiation with many local groups. Contacts were also built up with political parties and pressure groups in the area. Cornerstone tried to facilitate dialogue between them, and between opposing groups such as the Orange lodges and residents' groups. And Cornerstone has made itself available to support cross-community initiatives such as the Mid-Springfield Community Association (MISCA). This group had been set up as a result of efforts by two women residents in one of the few 'mixed' housing estates in the area to ensure that Catholic and Protestant families could remain living reasonably safely in proximity to each other.

Out of all of this development and support work, Cornerstone had drawn closer to the Currach Community and the Springfield Road Methodist Church, which had become a 'community church', opening its doors to youth and community groups. In the Community's newsletter, *Cornerstone Contact* (Winter 1995: *passim*), Noreen Christian described the relationship between these three groupings as 'an interesting triangle of opportunity for the promotion of peace and understanding amongst peoples'. The article continues:

> Over the past two years together we have found that a joint approach to the needs of the area in which we find ourselves has produced some very positive results and in the process we have found many similarities with one another . . . We are happy to display a 'doctrine of difference' over those areas in which Christians can disagree and yet still work together on a number of issues.

By the time of the Review, this 'triangle' had been expanded to include the MISCA, in a network called Forthspring. The four groups were discussing possible projects which could be managed jointly. Some within Cornerstone were worried that this might change the nature of their group irrevocably; this topic took up a lot of time in meetings and conversations. Where would they find the time for all the other business which they thought important? And would they have sufficient autonomy to decide on ethical issues, on priorities and on how to approach problems?

Ways of working

Cornerstone has hoped to retain a space for emotion, spontaneity and inspiration in their discussions about their activities. As a collective of people trying to achieve dialogue and understanding, they feel they must work in consensual ways; as a group performing public roles with the assistance of public funding, they are obliged to adopt arrangements which satisfy the demands of public auditing and scrutiny. Members appear to feel that the structures require explanation, even apology. There is a high priority placed on maintaining a less formal, more intimate atmosphere by most of the members. As one founder member, now a Heart Member, commented:

> I think it would lose something of itself if it were more structured. I can understand people getting frustrated with it but I think it suited the people who were there at the time – the informality. I think if it were too efficient you could get a bit cold.

Conflict within Cornerstone

Over the years, however, the Community had come to accept that this informal and intimate style could have disadvantages. Their doubts originated in an experience of a serious conflict which had disrupted the Community's life in its first few years, and which was frequently referred to in interviews and discussions. The absence of clear procedures for resolving disputes had, according to some members, allowed this one to get out of control. The conflict arose when Mary Grant, one of the original founders of the community, began to diverge in her thinking from the other members. In her view, the gradual introduction of policies aimed at social justice was an understandable but misguided move. She had become committed to more individually targeted counselling, healing and other therapeutic practices. The other founder members felt that Mary was rushing into untried projects, perhaps as part of a process of transformations in her own ideas about theology, spirituality and her relationship with the Catholic church. They worried that the wrong impression might be given as to what was going on in the house. No one was sure of how to handle the situation, which deteriorated into hostility.

Discussion as to how to resolve matters had dragged on for two years, with personal relations deteriorating to the point where Mary

Grant and some new colleagues occupied one part of the house, carrying on their work in isolation from the others. All of those involved recount this as a series of miserable and confusing experiences.[8]

In interviews, various members made clear their sense of disappointment with the way the dispute got out of hand, searching for explanations. Were they 'naive', 'inexperienced', 'too nice'? They expressed quite openly their awareness that this episode conflicted with their aim of finding ways of resolving differences, without having to resort to coercion, even the coercion inherent in voting and then closing down discussion.

Unfortunate episodes with unsuitable visitors, volunteers and candidates for membership likewise caused problems. They brought the introduction of procedures for application to join and admission to the Community. Again, formality was apologised for and tempered with the softening touch of personal knowledge and affection. Generally speaking it would seem that 'new' members have been well known to the Community for some time – by, for example, attending regular prayer meetings at Cornerstone. And, if they do not put themselves forward, but are thought of as being suitable, they may be invited to join by existing members. Norma Dodds (secretary for the Community) told us:

> We would attempt to go through the process [*she laughs*] – but what normally happens – I'm thinking of the last two members . . . they had actually been members of the Thursday prayer group for years so they were well known to everyone in the community. The community knew them – they knew the community – they knew the process so they knew what they were letting themselves in for – and so there wasn't such a formal shepherding – we dreamt up those things in case we ever need a safeguard.

There had also been a decision to have even more tightly applied criteria as a result of one or two unhappy incidents with volunteers. They are now required to visit Cornerstone for a short period following application, not just to allow the Community to assess their suitability, but also to see if they feel that they will personally fit into the community. There is then a protracted induction into the Community, which means that rules and safeguards will be needed less. It also means, of course, that there is a tendency to homogeneity in the membership; conflicts are avoided by drawing into the inner group people who share values, beliefs and norms of behaviour. This may produce the risk described by Shane Phelan (1996) of rejecting diversity rather than welcoming and dealing with it. On the other hand, negotiating membership and procedures in a radical group of any sort, as Carole Mueller (1995) points out, is always fraught with difficulties. In an environment which is hostile to its goals, as Mansbridge (1996:131) argues, some protection may be vital to survival for a group like Cornerstone.

With all their best efforts, conflict had not entirely been banished. There were, first, tensions between the live-in and live-out members of the community. This could work either way, with some live-out members complaining that certain items of information would be known to those 'in the house' but might not be passed on to those in the 'outer circle'. Conversely, those living in sometimes complained that they had not been made aware of unexpected guests or visitors. The domestic labour in the house was shared fairly among residents and non-residents, but this still left a lot of management and organising for Isabel Hunter, the house leader. Second, as we have seen, not everyone was sure about the new directions in which the community was headed. Some people were irked by the protracted discussions and wanted a more 'business-like' approach. The formally constituted committees would meet at appointed times, but meetings could be open-ended and reconvened, and voting on important issues is rare. Where there was disagreement, decisions could be postponed for further reflection, talk and prayer. This could amount to a veto on some decisions.

Emotions

One of the ways in which the Community tried to limit the potential effects of conflicts was by creating a high level of trust and understanding among members. Built into the processes described here are opportunities to disclose past experiences and problems which will allow members to know about the influences and perspectives that have shaped their colleagues' present approaches to life and work. At some Wednesday meetings, for example, members 'tell their stories' to each other. This is fairly open-ended; members can focus on painful events, significant people, life problems which are unresolved. All the members and former members we talked to found this to be a positive and rewarding practice, though some confessed to finding it an ordeal. One member recalled:

I remember sitting out on the front step and saying, no way am I doing this. I thought, these people haven't lived – they don't know what life's about. A lot of them in the clergy and quite sheltered like. But the person who told their story before me had had a very painful . . . even more painful and more shocking things than me. And I thought I'm judging people wrong. [After I'd told my story] people came over and hugged me. I found them very supportive – that would have been in my first year.

The stories do not always lead to discussion, though on one occasion during our study an intense and emotional conversation about sharing the Eucharist in each other's churches followed a member's account of working for Christian unity in the 1960s. During this discussion, differences between Protestant and Catholic members and between men and women emerged. Protestant members explained their 'hurt' at the fact that they could not take part in the Eucharist in Catholic churches; Catholic men regretfully acknowledged that change on this was not imminent. All the women, however, suggested that these were man-made rules, and where it gave no offence people should give themselves permission to share the sacrament with any other willing congregation. This discussion was not intended to lead to any policy changes or practical proposals of any kind; it was supposed to allow the members to understand each other better by listening to each other's experiences. There was no pressure to come to any conclusion or even to sum up what had been said. The topic could be taken up again at a new starting-point.

As an outsider, I was moved by the intensity of the feelings expressed and by the way in which they could be shared with heat but not rancour. I found myself, however, thinking of ways in which such discussions could be more 'purposeful'. For the Community, on the other hand, as I became aware at the annual review, the talking was an end in itself, a communal and religious event, which could be repeated many times, and whose effects would be to produce a fuller, shared understanding of the issues and each other. These practices did contribute to a sense of trust and security within the group. The belief in the possibility of perfect transparency and perfect understanding, however, as Iris Young (1991:235) points out, may become exclusive and tyrannical.

The 'tyranny of structurelessness'

In an early meeting with us, one of the members commented that the Community was anxious to avoid 'the tyranny of structurelessness', a problem which he presumed we might understand from our experiences in the women's movement (Freeman 1984). There seemed to be two sets of aspirations to be kept in balance. The Community wanted the safeguards of formal procedures but also the inclusiveness which warmth and informality could bring. Informality was valued because it was viewed as conducive to consensual decision-making, which in turn was regarded as likely to enhance trust and inclusion.

In a similar fashion, members wanted to be respectful of differences, but also to eliminate the salience of differences through learning about and from each other. In Chrysalis, the concern with structures and processes centred around the aim of empowering and including women who would otherwise be kept at the margins. In Cornerstone, a mixed organisation, we wanted to know whether the balancing of formal and informal methods of working allowed gender inequalities to be addressed, bringing women into the centre of decision-making.

Women, femininity and leadership in Cornerstone

Churches and religious movements have, in recent years, felt the influence of feminism both in doctrinal and organisational matters. Within Cornerstone, inequalities between men and women in various spheres are openly discussed and addressed. The women members come from a diversity of religious backgrounds, including Catholic, Church of Ireland, Presbyterian and Methodist, and were aware of the problems for women within these various churches, and of the progress that has been made by them in recent years. Both men and women in the Community saw the status of women in the major churches as problematic; they also revealed that Cornerstone had not always been free such problems. One of the women commented:

> I would say now that some of the men have had to have help with their concept of women – but they are open to learning which is the main thing for us.

One of the men acknowledged that some learning had been – and perhaps still was – required:

They [women] are taken account of – and more so within the last few years. [One of the men], unwittingly, because he is very gracious, would at times use very gender-specific phrases and sayings. [A female community member] took him on a few times and he has really grown from that. He's much more sensitive and aware of what he does and says. I mean it was done in a kind of humorous way. But it has been an issue and we have addressed it on a number of occasions.

While the issues about gender had been introduced by women, there were no clear male female divisions on these questions. One of the women returned to our questions, which she had been thinking about. 'I've been thinking this over and I really can't see that any difference is made [between women and men]. I think we all have the same standing – male and female.' She took the view, shared by some of the men, that differences might indeed be advantageous and in no way threaten equality. As one man put it: 'I think in some cases the women are more equipped to do the bereavement work . . . there's obvious differences there between the gifts of the male and the female.' Some of the men sought to specify the differences and challenge the values placed upon them. One commented:

Maybe we men try to express ourselves more analytically – which is given greater credence or greater value in certain circles than the more intuitive levels of understanding [which he attributed to women].

Another argued that the women's calmer, empathetic approach meant that they were very good at work such as bereavement visiting (for which some of the men also took responsibility). He attributed the welcoming and friendly atmosphere in the Community to the house leader and other women:

People like Isabel had a sort of calming influence there. Some women played leadership roles and some domestic roles and that would have been Isabel's thing. Perhaps more than anyone else she's been a continuity in the heart of the Community.

But some of the women expressed frustration with this. One said:

We had to highlight the whole thing of language – and the perception that there are certain things that women do and don't do. We had to say that that's not always the case and women need to be included here or whatever . . . I think we've heightened awareness but I still think there's a lot to be learned by the menfolk. I think that there's a certain willingness in their heads that they know that it's important and they're willing to accept it at that head level. But I think that at a feeling level, they accept it to some degree, but they struggle with knowing what the hell it is about. So the awareness has been heightened but the understanding isn't always there.

There were many indications that gender issues had been brought into discussions about many aspects of the Community's work. In relation to ideas about spirituality, there had been study and reflection as to whether the images of divinity with which Christian groups are imbued have been derived from masculine experiences and identities. If so, what kind of divinity could encompass women's ways of being? This on occasions led into – inconclusive – discussions about women's different relationships to their bodies and to questions about whether the very concept of spirituality was too abstract. In this area, there was no simple male–female division; both men and women had given thought to feminist theology, and the group had invited feminist theologians to talk and worship.

Incorporating women also has its place in the political mediations in which Cornerstone was involved. In its political dialogue work, Cornerstone tried to encourage loyalist and republican parties to bring women activists along to meetings, to ensure that the atmosphere would be less tense and more likely to be productive. There were mixed opinions as to what were the benefits or outcomes of women's presence in dialogues with the parties. Some of the Cornerstone women commented that they felt they had to be quite forceful in order to ensure that they were listened to; sometimes, one said, she had had to raise her voice to the point where she became aware of sounding quite angry in order to be heard. Being heard, evidently was worth the effort for another woman:

I think it's very important that we [women] let our voice be heard. I think because we're in touch with what's maybe happening on the ground level we're inclined to stay there. And we need to take every opportunity to be around where things are being said and where things are being heard.

One of the men involved in these talks thought that women's participation had been helpful by bringing in a different way of looking at things:

> I value enormously the perspective... [*pause*] ... not a perspective... I would say on the whole women look at things in a slightly more considered way, they wouldn't be so quick to react to things.

A visit by the representatives of the Orange Order to Cornerstone's Wednesday meeting, to take one example, revealed no straightforward pattern of male and female roles in Cornerstone. Having listened to what the two visitors had to say, mainly about the problem of contested parade routes,[9] Cornerstone members responded. This was not, however, a symmetrical exchange of positions; Cornerstone were offering questions, responses and reflections as concerned individuals, rather than as a group with policies worked out in advance. So, the speakers from the Orange Order were being asked to engage in an open-ended exchange, rather than to defend their positions. The Cornerstone women felt strong enough to open the discussion with questions about the limited range of roles for women in the Orange Order. Was their maleness both a sign and a cause of an aggressive approach which might exacerbate conflicts with those who opposed them? To say that this came as a surprise to the guests would be an understatement. In that encounter, the Cornerstone women who spoke were more openly critical of the Orange Order, and more assertive in suggesting ways in which the Order could accommodate residents' groups, whereas the men were more tentative in their comments and questions.

In their community development and social justice work, Cornerstone paid particular attention to women's groups and women in the local area. In part, this is encouraged by funding bodies, who evaluate whether activities are sufficiently inclusive of women. It has also been motivated by the belief that involving and including women can lead to more stable and successful communities, by drawing upon women's supposed greater altruism. Certain groups of women – young women or single mothers, for example – are seen as having needs which require special attention. The women who were trying to set up MISCA, for example, were quietly but directly approached and offered resources and support. Assistance is offered to groups trying to get funding for women's education or child-care facilities. Both male and female Cornerstone members acknowledged that they embarked upon such initiatives with pre-conceived ideas about what women in the area needed: mother and toddler groups, child-care education, assertiveness training. Over the years they have adapted to accommodate local women's own ideas about what they want; time free from families and children, time to sit and chat to other women over crafts or coffee, advice about debt, benefits, legal problems. Most of this development work with women in the area is the responsibility of women members of Cornerstone, though not all the women are involved in it, some having other tasks.

As we pursued the members, following up comments and ideas, we found that for the most part the women seemed to enjoy ex-tended discussions about gender and women's roles. The men, on the other hand, were reluctant to be too forthcoming on this sub-ject. Some expressed a concern that they would be found wanting in some way, but also worries that if they offered suggestions for change they would seem to be limiting the women's autonomy. This seemed to be another area where balancing acts were going on. Men in Cornerstone enjoyed the mix of domestic and formal and the chance to go beyond the limits of traditional roles and hierarchies, but did not want to usurp what they saw as women's essential difference. The women, in general, wanted gender differ-ences to be important sometimes, but not always. They did not want to be limited to any specific definition of femininity.[10] None of the women saw themselves as pursuing a politics of gender equality within the Community. When asked whether men and women were competing for power within the Community, one woman summed up the general feeling:

> Power? No. No, not power, as you would know power. That's not really true. For group attention, yes.

As in Chrysalis, Cornerstone women seemed to want to have the capacity to influence and change policies and attitudes, but with-out using methods of domination. They valued strength, but saw it being exerted in collective efforts with their male colleagues, a collective in which they would be equal in their diverse ways of being feminine. This was still something to strive for, not yet a reality.

Power, its uses and abuses became a central theme of our discussions in the review. The women and men in Cornerstone work in the hope that the power of faith will move mountains; in this case, the mountains of prejudice, anger, bitterness and injustice that fuel violence, hatred and division in our society. Unlike many strongly religious people (especially in Northern Ireland) they do not concentrate upon the power to judge and punish the evil-doer, but rather on the generation of forgiveness, trust and reconciliation. Like the other groups we studied, Cornerstone want to bring about radical change, but find it more difficult to think of themselves as having to exercise power in order to achieve this. In part, this stems from awareness that they have advantages which might allow them to dominate, as one member acknowledged: 'You're aware that you can dominate (a) as a male, (b) as an intellectual and (c) as a clergyman.' Once again they began to seem torn between using their resources and education to bring about change and the fear that they might gain unfair advantage from them.

Living their ideals

Cornerstone has attempted to live out their ideals, choosing to locate themselves in one of the least welcoming parts of Belfast in order to make a difference. They do not want to be 'a place apart where people go from their own settings', but feel a need 'to be inserted into the community, to feel what was going on'. Achieving the goals of respecting and transcending difference, they argued, required them to identify very publicly with their fellow citizens. The elaborate efforts to reach consensus within the Community are a way of working out in practice new ways of taking decisions without using domination. The methods can be seen as a form of deliberative democracy, and one which answers some of the criticisms of this approach made by socialists and feminists (Phillips 1995, Fraser 1997). This is a deliberative process which allows for vetoes and which recognises inequality and hidden exclusion.

There is much to be learned from the ways in which Cornerstone members have built their Community. They have created an environment in which difference is welcomed, rather than perceived as disruptive or threatening. By being open about painful events and experiences they have learned how to expose hidden sources of inequality and oppression. Their closeness to each other has not prevented them from being aware of the interests and needs of individuals and groups who do not share their beliefs and values. They have learned how to listen to and learn from the community groups with which they work. They have also devised structures and methods which allow them to change and develop, to undertake new ventures which carry considerable risks. Their methods have some things in common with the feminist tradition which attempts to replace 'power over' with 'power to' and to incorporate empathy, understanding and connection into the practices of making choices and decisions (Mansbridge 1996:131).

It is important to keep these lessons in perspective. The Community could only come into being after a long process of preparation; there is a strong sense of common purpose which underpins the tolerance, respect and patience of its members. The time-scale with which they are working is almost unlimited, so they can absorb some setbacks and difficulties, unlike other groups and governments. Community members themselves are conscious of the gap between their present achievements and what they hoped to bring about in Northern Ireland and elsewhere. They are also aware of the contradictions in their debates and reflections on gender differences. They are prepared to try to use these tensions creatively, working for future change. Sam Burch summarised their perspective:

[I]t's a long slog – slow stuff – there's years of learning how to relate and to understand each other.

Notes

1 In Cornerstone's immediate neighbourhood, 71.3 per cent of the population are Catholic, 5.7 per cent Presbyterian, 11.1 per cent Church of Ireland, 1.8 per cent Methodist, 2.6 per cent other denominations, 1.6 per cent no religion, 6.5 per cent not stated.

2 The 1991 census shows that residential segregation of the Catholic and Protestant communities has increased to the point where only 7 per cent of the population live in areas where there are similar numbers of Catholics and Protestants.

3 Within some areas, namely the Falls and Whiterock, male unemployment is approaching 60 per cent. 1991 Census data reveal that the number potentially entering the labour market in this area greatly exceeds the number leaving. Between 1991 and 2001, approximately 3000 people will have reached retirement age in the Inner West, but almost 6000 young people may enter the labour market. Within the Upper Springfield and Whiterock wards this will present more of a problem,

as these wards have relatively higher numbers of 6 to 15-year-olds. Of those unemployed, 58 per cent are classified as long-term unemployed.

4   Although the chapter is single-authored, the early part of the fieldwork was carried out jointly with Margaret Whittock, and her contribution to the analysis is gratefully acknowledged. For more on methods see Appendix 2.

5   On 1 March 1981, republican prisoners went on hunger strike, as the final escalation of a long and bitter campaign to have their status as political prisoners (removed as part of a normalisation policy pursued by the 1974–6 Labour government) restored. 10 prisoners fasted to death before a compromise was reached and the hunger strikes ended on 3 October. No one who lived through those months in Northern Ireland remained unaffected by the suffering of the prisoners and their families, though as with every other issue opinion is divided as to who was more to blame for the situation, in this case the republican leadership or Mrs Thatcher's government. Love (1995) describes members of Corrymeela as having been similarly divided over the campaign.

6   The sources for this sketch of the origins of the community are a memoir written for the community by Sam Burch, some private letters and interviews. Unless otherwise stated, the quotes come from the memoir.

7   In 1990 an independent though government-funded agency, the Community Relations Council (CRC), was created to undertake the 'pre-political' work of building cross-community understanding thought to be required as a basis for the emergence of any solution to the NI problem. The Council was the successor to various initiatives to promote good community relations which were introduced from 1969 onwards. As Fitzduff (1995) observes, the CRC attempted to introduce a more radical approach, which took into account broader issues of social exclusion. See also Bloomfield (1997) for a comprehensive discussion of peacemaking strategies in Northern Ireland.

8   Events, as they unfolded, are briefly documented in the minutes of executive committee meetings. An entry of 11 September 1986 reads: 'Mary should be informed in writing that the Community had asked her to vacate both rooms as soon as possible and before the 10 October, 1986.' However, the situation was finally resolved only after resort to law and an appeal to the trust which owned the property.

9   This meeting took place in the spring of 1996, at a time when protest groups all over Northern Ireland were opposing the continuation of parades along 'traditional' routes which went through predominantly Catholic areas. Cornerstone members were becoming drawn into mediation between local Orange lodges and residents.

10 A researcher who has considerable expertise in feminist theology and the issues of importance to Christian women offered some reflections from her perspective on gender issues: '[W]e operate along oppositional lines all the time in the way we construct gender (i.e. deal with and maybe even create difference) and they in turn perpetuate the particular construction of gender that mitigates against women.' (Fran Porter, personal communication to the author.)

References

Acheson, N. and Williamson, A. (1995a) *Voluntary action in Northern Ireland: Some Contemporary Themes and Issues*, Aldershot: Avebury.

Acheson, N. and Williamson, A. (1995b) 'Introduction', in Acheson and Williamson (1995a), 1–10.

Bloomfield, David (1997) *Peacemaking Strategies in Northern Ireland: Building Complementarity in Conflict Management Theory*, Basingstoke: Macmillan.

Borooah, V., McKee, P., Heaton, N. and Collins, G. (1993) *Catholic–Protestant Income Difference in Northern Ireland, Social Policy Research Findings*, York: Joseph Rowntree Foundation.

Calhoun, C. (ed.) (1992) *Habermas and the Public Sphere*, Cambridge, MA: MIT Press.

Ferreé, Myra M. and Martin, P. Y. (eds) (1995) *Feminist Organizations*, Philadelphia: Temple University Press.

Fitzduff, Mari (1995) 'Managing Community Relations and Conflict: Voluntary Organisations and Government and the Search for Peace', in Acheson and Williamson (1995a), 63–83.

Fraser, Nancy (1992) 'Rethinking the Public Sphere: A Contribution to the Critique of Actually Existing Democracy', in Calhoun. 109–42.

Freeman, J. (1984) *The Tyranny of Structurelessness*, London: Darkstar/Rebel Press.

Hirschmann, N. and Di Stefano, C. (eds) (1996) *Revisioning the Political*, Boulder: Westview Press.

Lister, Ruth (1994) 'Social Policy in a Divided Community: Reflections on the Opsahl Report', *Irish Journal of Sociology*, 4, 27–50.

Love, Mervyn T. (1995) *Peacebuilding Through Reconciliation in Northern Ireland*, Aldershot: Avebury.

Mansbridge, Jane (1996) 'Reconstructing Democracy', in Hirschmann, N. and Di Stefano, C. (eds) 1996, 117–39.

Morrow, Duncan (1995) 'Rebuilding the Democratic Process', in Williamson, A. (ed.), *Beyond Violence: The role of Voluntary and Community Action in Building a Sustainable Peace in Northern Ireland*, Belfast: Community Relations Council, 59–61.

Morrow, Duncan; Birrell, D., Greer, J. and O'Keeffe, T. (1991) *The Churches and Inter-Community Relations*, Coleraine: Centre for the Study of Conflict, University of Ulster.

Mueller, Carol (1995) 'The Organisational Basis of Conflict in Contemporary Feminism', in Ferreé and Martin, 263–75.

Phelan, Shane (1996) 'All the Comforts of Home: The Genealogy of Community', in Hirschmann, N. and Di Stefano, D. (eds) (1996), 235–50.

Phillips, A. (1995) *The Politics of Presence*, Oxford: Clarendon Press.

Whyte, J. (1990) *Interpreting Northern Ireland*, Oxford: Clarendon Press.

Young, I. M. (1991) *Justice and the Politics of Difference*, Princeton, NJ: Princeton University Press.

5
'Wide Awake to Women': Gender and Other Disturbances in a Trade Union

Cynthia Cockburn

The union that generously opened itself to our research was the Northern Ireland Public Service Alliance (NIPSA). It has just short of 36 000 members, of whom 61 per cent are women. The membership is mainly white-collar workers, comprising administrative, executive, professional, clerical and technical employees in the civil service (55 per cent) and the public service (45 per cent).[1] The Alliance is the product of a series of amalgamations over the course of the twentieth century of smaller and more specific unions organising in the public sector. It took its present form in 1978.

NIPSA is one of only three trade unions that are entirely local to Northern Ireland. The other unions with which it cooperates in the Irish Congress of Trade Unions (ICTU) are mainly regional elements of much larger unions based in Britain or the Republic of Ireland. NIPSA take pride in smallness, stressing the advantage this offers of ready access by the individual member to officials. 'Where else can you pick up the phone and get the general secretary on the line?' they say. Setting about this study, I approached NIPSA with a head full of questions organised around the straightforward notion of gender equity.[2] But of course this was like pulling a book from a badly stacked shelf. A landslide of other equality issues tumbled out with it. Religion, class, political opinion, sector, locality, age, marital status, dis/ability, colour, race, ethnicity, nationality, sexuality – they lay in a heap round my ankles. The research has been a process of making meaning and order of the ways in which NIPSA themselves try to make meaning and order out of this clamour of voices and the cross-cutting needs. Certainly sex/gender furnishes one important dimension of 'difference'.[3] But what other axes of differentiation are significant for the union's work, and how does sex/gender relate to them? Are these differences all of a kind – social matters of group belonging? Or are some of them solid matters of mere contingency, like where I happen to live or work? Or slippery matters of opinion and belief? Or several things at once? Can one strategy fix democracy for women as women, and for women as all the other things they are (along with men)?

NIPSA's constitution does not employ the term 'democracy'. But this is the clear import of its objectives, particularly those that commit it to 'represent, protect and promote the interests of its members' and 'to promote equal opportunities for all members' (NIPSA 1996a:5). An organisation like this is in a dilemma. It must subordinate differences enough to hold together an operational *alliance* between groups who conceive of themselves as having different interests, sometimes even opposed ones. At the same time, it must ensure enough expression of tendentially divergent interests to satisfy each member's sense of their complex identity and concerns. How has the organisation responded to this problem to date? In other words what *kind* of a democracy is this trade union within which women are looking for their place? What is current thinking about the future of 'equality' and 'democracy'?

I carried out the research in the first three months of 1997. Extensive documentation was provided by NIPSA and 18 unstructured but thematic interviews were held with a range of individuals, including headquarters staff and lay activists.[4]

Formal democracy in a trade union

Like all trade unions in the United Kingdom, the NIPSA suffered adverse circumstances during the 1980s and 1990s. Waves of economic recession and high unemployment caused a drop in union membership and profoundly weakened the bargaining power of unions. The period of continuous Conservative government between 1979 and 1997 compounded their disarray with economic policies that were ruthless in allowing weaker enterprises to founder and by imposing cuts and reorganisation on the public sector. The Tories also introduced a sequence of new laws favouring management at the expense of employees, curbing union rights and enforcing changes to their procedures.[5] Simultaneously the leadership of the Labour

Party distanced itself from the unions, reducing their historic influence on the party.

The Conservative measures aimed frankly to undermine the unions' legitimacy in the eyes of their members and the wider public. But some backfired. The requirement to seek the consent of members to deduction of union dues from salary, for example, while costly and cumbersome for the union, seems to have increased awareness of the benefits of membership. The threat to jobs through cuts and privatisation has had a plus side too, attracting new recruits to some branches. Against all the odds, NIPSA's membership increased by 1020 between 1995 and 1996 and the increase occurred disproportionately among women in the lower grades in the public services. Another unintended effect of the Conservative government's industrial relations laws was to prompt the union to replace its loosely federal make-up with a tighter, and thus more effective, structure.

NIPSA's constitution, redrafted between 1991 and 1993 to reflect the new alliance structure, is a thoughtful attempt to lay the foundation for a democratic polity.[6] Its key principle, as with other trade unions, is a separation of the making of policy from its execution. It lodges supreme decision-making authority in an annual general conference attended by delegates from workplace branches in numbers proportional to their size. It is the annual general conference that elects NIPSA's president, vice president and honorary treasurer and passes the motions that determine the direction the union will follow in the coming year. The general council is the union's principal executive body, responsible for carrying out conference decisions. It has a set of functional committees and carefully defined executive powers to act on behalf of the union between conferences.

The branch is the basic cell of NIPSA, on which all the regional and central structure of panels and committees is built. Branch procedures are designed to ensure democracy and openness. Each operates through its own annual general meeting and its annually elected committee and officers, whose responsibilities are defined by rule. In lodging motions, voting on motions, nominating candidates and selecting delegates, the branches operate as unities. That is to say discussion in the branch meeting produces a decision reflecting the majority of individual members' views (one person, one vote). It is then forwarded up the structure as a branch vote, weighted by membership size. There are two exceptions to this 'block vote' system, imposed by the Conservative government's industrial relations laws. The general council and the general secretary of the union must now be elected by individual secret postal ballot.

Axes of collective difference

NIPSA's members share an interest as state employees. But within that overarching similarity they are differentiated – and not just by personal idiosyncrasies and the specific nature of their workplaces and union branches. There is the matter of women in relation to men. And there is this scatter of other 'differences' patterning the membership that already assailed me when I started my stay in NIPSA by reading through past annual reports, and copies of *NIPSA News*. Inherent in all of them are inequalities: inequalities in the ability of members to influence union policy and practice, to be effective in and through the union, obtain their needs by collective bargaining, and to make real the promise of NIPSA's constitution, that 'any fully paid up member may take part in all the union's affairs'.

Employment group

The differentiation that has boldest expression in the structure and day-to-day life of NIPSA is that of the two major employment groups, the Civil Service Group (CSG) and the Public Officer Group (POG) (see Note 1). It goes back many decades and was originally embodied in the Alliance's constituent trade unions. It reflects the fact that the two kinds of public sector employment have different histories and different cultures. Negotiation to bring the various constituent unions into alliance without prejudicing their interests have absorbed energies for decades.

The union structure established in the 1993 reform is designed, while binding the CSG and the POG into a tighter alliance, to allow the two groups a degree of autonomy. (See Note 8.) Each group has its own constitution, and an annual delegate conference governing its specific affairs. There are CSG and POG executive committees and advisory subcommittees. A principle of 'minimum representation' has been introduced, whereby each group must be assured a given minimum of seats on the 25-strong general council.[7]

Despite these rather elaborate provisions for parity, tension between CSG and POG remains. The ethos and culture of the CSG is distinctive. Civil servants are viewed by many on the POG side as conservative 'establishment' types. The past perception of some senior civil servants' association with unionist dominance (and with male dominance too) lingers in some minds.[8] Some on the CSG side would retaliate that the POG are 'too militant', always ready for strike action. The CSG is undoubtedly relatively advantaged in the scope of its collective agreements and in being afforded more 'facility time' for union work. Whether, as many POG members complain, they also have more than their fair share of general council seats, public roles, NIPSA officials' attention, time off to attend training courses, and other assets, is hotly debated.

Religion/community

Another distinction of huge significance, but much lower visibility in NIPSA, is *perceived religion* – whether a person is identified as Catholic or Protestant. In Northern Ireland this is frequently termed a distinction of *community*.

NIPSA aspires to recruit and represent proportionally from among Catholic and Protestant civil servants and public officers. There are three problems in this. First, the very categories are contestable. The terms Catholic and Protestant relate to several differences at the same time. They speak of an ancient ethnic distinction, including differences of geographical origin, culture and language. They map strongly onto a political divergence: nationalist and republican versus unionist and loyalist. They refer to religious belief, while many on both sides are not in fact believers. And they resound with power difference: Protestant numerical and political dominance in Northern Ireland against Catholic minority status and political marginalisation.

Second, an individual's belonging is difficult to ascertain. For many good reasons, people are often reluctant to identify themselves. Many do not have a clear belonging, nor the wish for one. But this will not prevent others labelling them, rightly or wrongly. 'Perceived religion' as it is often called, is usually ascribed on the basis of primary school attended, of family or first name, or of neighbourhood of origin – none of them reliable indicators of a person's sense of self.

Third, the very act of trying to distinguish between Catholic and Protestant is for most purposes divisive and undesirable. The law, with the intention of compensating for Catholic employment disadvantage in Northern Ireland, requires employers to take a range of measures, including making annual returns on the perceived religion of their workforce.[9] NIPSA's return for 1996 reported that fair participation was being accorded to the two communities in junior grades, but, counter-intuitively perhaps, Protestants were still under-represented at executive officer level and above.

The law on religious monitoring does not however extend from a union's employment to its membership. In the absence of statistics, NIPSA relies on impressions. It is believed that the majority of NIPSA members are in fact Protestants, but Catholics are perceived to be a majority among activists and on NIPSA's governing bodies, including the general council, so that, in this sense, as one of my informants put it, 'there may be a view that we are a Catholic-oriented organization'.

Political disagreements between Catholic and Protestant in the membership create dissension from time to time. Some Catholic members resigned when they learned NIPSA had given a donation to the Ulster Defence Regiment Benevolent Fund. Conversely, some Protestants expressed outrage that NIPSA was supporting Amnesty International, an organisation that had pronounced the shooting of IRA suspects in Gibraltar by British security forces a human rights violation. But many people I spoke with were reluctant to discuss such matters. The religious/community axis of difference is of such overwhelming significance in Northern Ireland, and is associated with such violence, that they were unwilling to give it more prominence than was strictly necessary.

The constitution includes both 'religious belief' and 'ethnic and national origins' among the matters on which it guarantees not only equality but positive action to achieve it. But in this climate, and since disadvantage to either side is not a source of formalised complaint, it is not felt to be appropriate for the union to take steps concerning religious/community balance in representational structure and process. Monitoring the perceived religion of the membership would be a precondition. A report commissioned by NIPSA from consultants Jones & Cassidy did indeed recommend religious monitoring of the membership.[10] But it was the one recommendation the general council rejected. One NIPSA official said in interview that it 'would send out the wrong messages to the wrong people for the wrong reasons'.

Other dimensions of difference

Object 1.3(e) of NIPSA's Constitution deals with the promotion of 'equality' (NIPSA 1996a). In addition to gender, religious belief and 'origins' (already mentioned), the clause commits the union to develop positive policies for equality in terms of disability, colour, race, age, marital status, sexual orientation and political opinion. The implications of some of these differentiations, and indeed of two more, must be mentioned briefly if the full complexity of NIPSA's democracy project is to be graspable.

Where a protective law exists, as in the cases of disability (Disability Discrimination Act 1995) and marital status (Sex Discrimination Orders (NI) 1976 and 1988), the union publicly endorses the legislation and argues for its strengthening. It has regard to implementing it in its own affairs and presses for its observance by employers. For example, in the last return made by the union under the Fair Employment Act it was able to affirm that it employs three disabled people (4 per cent of the payroll). And while, in the bad old patriarchal days, the union supported the notorious ban on married women in civil service employment, today it not only defends the interests of women, married and unmarried alike, but campaigns tirelessly for workplace nurseries.

On the issue of racial discrimination, NIPSA has long campaigned for the British Race Relations Act 1976 to be extended to Northern Ireland (NIPSA 1996c:18).[11] Black, Asian and other visibly differentiated ethnic groups are a smaller minority of the workforce in Northern Ireland than in Britain. With a Race Relations Order for Northern Ireland imminent, NIPSA was planning to strengthen both its action on racial disadvantage in employment and its concern with the racial composition of its own membership.

In the cases of age and sexual orientation, the union lacks a legal instrument. Discrimination against young people and older people on account of their age, or against lesbians and gay men on account of their sexuality, is something to which negotiators are alert in dealings with employers. One NIPSA official believes it might at some stage prove appropriate to reserve seats on the union's executive bodies for young members. But because of the sensitivity involved in the issue of sexuality, the union finds it difficult to introduce positive action for homosexuals unless and until the need is voiced by a group of members wishing to identify themselves as such.

Political opinion is an anomalous 'difference'. NIPSA strongly asserts that it is 'non-political'. Unlike many unions in the UK, it has no political fund. Conference may debate human rights issues but not, for example, the question of the border separating North from South in Ireland.

The commitment to equal treatment regardless of political opinion may be in NIPSA's Constitution to reflect the opinions associated in Northern Ireland with religion/community. But it is, curiously, not this axis of political opinion so much as the left–right dimension that most taxes NIPSA's policy-makers and represents a challenge to democracy. Contesting political difference, of course, is carried on not through special structures ordained by union decision, but informally through mobilisation and lobbying. The broad left faction in the union, which, since the communists diverged, is effectively the Socialist Party, actively caucuses and runs a slate at elections. Its aim is, as a former adherent put it, 'to develop a left agenda and take the union along that road'. There is no matching faction of the right, although the left insist that right-wing organisation is carried on behind the scenes, especially as elections approach.

Finally, there are two axes of difference mentioned to me by members that are absent from the list of equality issues addressed in the union's constitution. One is the relation 'Belfast/periphery', that is, the relation between the 'capital' and the 'provinces' of Northern Ireland. I heard, at both first and second hand, of dissatisfaction among members in rural or small-town branches remote from Belfast who feel disadvantaged relative to members in the city, close to headquarters and its resources. 'There is this concept', said one rural member, 'that everything is done or based in Belfast and if they go beyond Lisburn these full-time officials become a wee bit lost.' One recent 'positive action' measure addressed to this dimension of difference has been the opening of a NIPSA office in Derry/Londonderry.

The second silent dimension of difference is class. NIPSA recruits its membership from the top to the bottom of the public sector employment grades. Its policy is to stress action to end low pay. I heard it mentioned that higher-grade members of NIPSA could thus feel that their interests are not prioritised. But, conversely, it is they who tend to put less energy into the union. As managers they are in an ambivalent position when workplace conflict arises. For this reason, one NIPSA official said, 'I have activists who don't feel their managers should be a member of our union, who won't give them copies of circulars.' But NIPSA's position on this is, the official stresses, that 'just because somebody's higher paid doesn't mean you shouldn't be looking for a pay rise for them'.

Women, disadvantage and change

The proportion of women in the membership of NIPSA has grown as the number of women joining the paid workforce has increased, and as the union more and more set out to attract women and look to their interests. By the 1990s, women were a majority of the membership. In 1991 their share was 58 per cent, by 1996 it had grown to 61 per cent. Although the percentage of women is characteristically higher on the public officer side (currently 71 per cent as against 53 per cent on the civil service side), their share in the increase has been similar.[12]

So today women are a majority in NIPSA. The question is, do they have equal influence in its affairs? For a group to be effective in a trade union is a matter of three things: (a) representation: having access to the union's decision-making structures; (b) fair employment: a fair share of paid officer jobs at all grades; and (c) bargaining: women's issues lodged equally on the agenda negotiated with the employer.

Representation: women's access to decision-making

By one measure, and a very public measure, NIPSA today is woman-led. In 1995 it became the first Irish union in history to have an all-woman leadership team of president, vice-president and treasurer (NIPSA 1996b). This achievement has been of great importance in encouraging women and giving their strengths a high profile.

But the prominence of a few women conceals a continuing overall sex/gender disadvantage. Women are still under-represented among those key decision-makers, the delegates at annual conference, and among lay representatives at branch level. While women were 61 per cent of total membership they were only 33 per cent of delegates to the 1996 NIPSA Annual Conference. They were 53 per cent of members of the Civil Service Group but only 29 per cent of delegates to the CSG annual conference; and with 71 per cent of POG membership, only 45 per cent at POG conference. These percentages had fluctuated up and down by 2 or 3 percentage points over 5 years without showing any significant improvement. In February 1997, women were only 23 per cent of branch chairpersons and 41 per cent of branch secretaries. (Cynics explain the difference here by the fact that secretaries do more work while chairs have more status.)

Being effective within a trade union can be a lever to playing an effective part in a wider society. NIPSA's records show that members fill perhaps sixty public roles, such as membership of industrial or social security tribunals and of various councils, commissions and boards. Mostly it is people with representative status within the union that represent it outside. Consequently, of these public roles, women fill only half those they would fill if they were to be represented in proportion to their share of union membership.

Many members express disappointment with these figures, given the 'positive action' the union has taken to improve women's participation. Motions had appeared on conference agendas on such matters as equal pay since the 1950s, leave for domestic purposes since the 1960s and workplace crèches since the 1970s. From the early 1980s, NIPSA, like other unions in Northern Ireland, was strongly encouraged along the path of equality policy by developments in the Irish Congress of Trade Unions.[13] A motion to conference in 1981 concerning participation of women in NIPSA began a process of discussion that resulted, in 1983, in the creation of a women's committee.[14] Around this time too, a decision was taken that each branch should have its women's officer and some departmental/ section committees and panels also now have their own women's committees.

NIPSA has never instituted a women's annual conference. On the other hand it has put real effort into monitoring sex ratios, consciousness-raising about gender relations and training for women. Gender statistics are reported and debated every three years. The union runs four-day courses on 'women's issues' through which at least five hundred women have passed in nine years. Equal opportunities is a subject addressed on all training courses for both sexes, and women are particularly encouraged to take up training opportunities. Annual seminars are held for branch women's officers, and a resource pack has been published to help them develop their role. A series of 'awareness seminars' was mounted in 1996, with women specially in mind, to encourage inexperienced members to stand for delegation to conference. For many years now a crèche has been provided at conference. And women now have a twice-yearly newsletter.

So NIPSA is, as one member put it, 'wide awake to women's issues'. It is all the more vexing, then, to those who have been backing these developments, that the statistics of women's membership of representative bodies in NIPSA have not shifted greatly. The current constitution's 'minimum representation' clauses, discussed above in relation to the CSG and POG, provide for women to fill at least 8 seats of the 25 on the general council, and 8 on the CSG and POG executive committees, respectively. But this has not prompted the swelling of nominations and elections that had been hoped for.

Disappointment is compounded with confusion by the one startling improvement there has been – in women's membership of the general council at the 1996 election. While there had been a steady improvement in women's share of council seats, from 12 per cent to 52 per cent over ten years, in 1996 women leapt into a majority (68 per cent) that surpassed their share of the membership (61 per cent). Since the CSG and the POG executive committees did not show similar changes in their gender composition, it was necessary to conclude that this shift in the general council was not due to the union's 'positive action' measures from branch level upwards. It was an effect of the government's introduction of the postal ballot.

To play a part in the higher representative structures of the union, women must first become effective in their branch. Both NIPSA and other unions, including the large public sector union UNISON, have found problems here (Cockburn 1991). Something may finally depend on men, as the story of Branch 523, organising in the education sector, illustrates. Two men had together held the posts of chair and secretary in this branch for some ten uninterrupted years. In 1992, feeling the time had come for new faces, they resigned. The officers elected in their place were also men. For a variety of reasons the branch then disintegrated. Dismayed, the two original branch officers looked around for alternative, particularly female, candidates. So the branch election of 1996 brought several women onto the committee, and resulted in a young, untried woman becoming branch secretary, with a team of three more women also in the roles of branch chair, vice-chair and treasurer. In addition to scant experience of trade union organisation, the chair and secretary both had young children claiming their attention at home. But with the advice and support of their practised male colleagues they turned around the branch, raised a petition of 120 000 signatures and political support across the spectrum, so as to reverse a government decision to annihilate the Western Education and Library Board.

The remaining impediments to women's activism debated in NIPSA today arise from women's circumstances in combination with union procedures. On the one hand, women's domestic responsibilities reduce the time they have available for activism and the fact that many women work part-time may make it difficult for them to attend all meetings or to deal with workplace problems arising when they are not there. On the other hand, the union has not yet considered providing for branch roles to be job-shared. Nor, for fear of losing the experienced activists it has, has it considered limiting the number of times a person may stand for re-election as branch chair or secretary. As Branch 523 shows, speeding up turnover is a move that can bring women through.

Women among the union's paid officials

NIPSA members and lay activists are supported by a team of paid officials. The organisational chart shows a pyramid, topped by the general secretary, descending by way of a deputy general secretary, two assistant general secretaries, seven assistant secretaries and seven higher executive officers to the broad base of middle and lower grades. At the time of our research, all 18 officials in the senior grades, from general secretary down to and including the 7 HEOs, were men. Below that line, of the 35 executive officers (EOs), personal secretaries, word processor operators and various categories of assistant within the administration, all except 4 were women. The tendency is for men to hold posts that involve them in being out and about in the country, attending meetings and committees. Consequently their faces are familiar to members and employers, and visible to the public, the media and the Northern Ireland administration. Characteristically, most women stay at their desks and do the essential support work, keeping records, taking dictation and answering the phone.

NIPSA has a second group of paid officials, members who are 'seconded' from their employment to work for the union as full-time convenors.[15] The position of secondee has a special importance in potentially enabling a transition from unpaid activism at branch level to full-time paid employment at HEO level in NIPSA headquarters. There are currently 24 such secondees, all but 4 in civil service branches (something cited as a source of disadvantage by POs). Only 9 are women, against 15 men.

The corps of senior male officials are troubled by the employment inequalities over which they preside – the tendency to Catholic advantage as well as to male advantage. A case against the union had recently been won in tribunal by an aggrieved (male) candidate for a seconded position who claimed the recruitment process had been biased against him. One member of the panel that had interviewed him for the job had previously taken a public position against his (left-wing) political opinions. This had prompted NIPSA to commission a thorough review of its recruitment and promotion procedures to ensure they were 'fair' on all dimensions of difference (Jones and Cassidy 1996, see Note 10).

But one problem seemed to defy solution. The crucial distinction in NIPSA employment is between senior jobs, which usually involve *negotiating with the employer* (normally HEO and above), and more junior jobs (normally EO and below), which usually do not. The former are almost always held by men. NIPSA's difficulty lies in enabling access to higher positions by promotion from EO, since experience up to and within that grade cannot normally furnish the necessary negotiating experience for promotion. Besides, there is a great deal of competition from secondees for the HEO posts that infrequently become vacant.

Rare women have broken through the EO/HEO barrier in the past. Women have held posts at assistant general secretary, assistant secretary and HEO levels. They, and several promising woman EOs too, have left the organisation for a variety of reasons, and NIPSA is disappointed in its failure to hold able women. The demands of the negotiating job and the culture that surrounds it are perceived by many as discordant with women's characteristic qualities and lives. It is not just in NIPSA that such jobs are seen as being stressful, and calling for toughness, an ability to stand your ground, to say 'no', not only to employers but sometimes to members (Cockburn 1991, Cunnison and Stageman 1993).

Women, of course, often decline to fulfil the 'non-combative' stereotype. An instance is the former woman HEO, now working for another employer, with whom I spoke at length. She had liked all aspects of the work and felt well equipped to do it, in the context of ready support from senior officials. But men do not as often step the other way and defy the masculine 'non-domestic' stereotype, sharing with their partners the caring roles at home so as to free them for demanding work in the union. And this former negotiating official said she certainly could not have combined the job with children and family ties.

NIPSA's approach to equal opportunities for women in their own employment has, so far, focused on *encouraging* women – for example to get negotiating experience by becoming an activist in the GMB's APEX branch that represents paid officials in NIPSA. 'Shadowing' of working negotiators has been agreed in principle but no way has yet been found to implement it. One current EO, an ex-secretary, was, unusually, being given some negotiating tasks in a positive move by management to help break the barrier between EO and HEO. But changing the nature of the negotiating job – introducing part-time, flexi-time and job-share possibilities at EO grade and above – had so far been considered only on an *ad hoc* basis.

Another way to break the barrier was discussed in response to the Jones & Cassidy recommendations: opening up a dual track promotion path, creating some senior job or jobs that are purely administrative and so accessible by EO. This would, for instance, assist a woman such as the training officer, who was feeling she would be unlikely to make it to HEO because she had come from the secretarial grades rather than from lay activism. It would not however remove the obstacles to women becoming negotiators, and arguably might harden the distinction between the two kinds of job.

Bargaining: including women's agenda in negotiation with employers

How well were women's interests represented on negotiating agendas? The main bargaining issues for NIPSA are pay and conditions; privatisation; and equal opportunities. On pay bargaining, there have been major changes in the Civil Service. Union interests were damaged by the Conservative government's move to replace the long-standing system of grades, scales and annual increments with individual performance-related pay. In addition in 1996 the Government ended national pay bargaining for the civil service. This resulted in NIPSA having to shift more resources to the separate pay negotiations involved in the Northern Ireland Civil Service. On the public officer side, performance-related pay has not yet prevailed, but decentralisation has gone further. For example, the once-central National Health Service bargaining system has disintegrated into 4 health boards and 20 trusts, so that NIPSA feels 'we've lost the initiative'.

There tends to be little movement or change from year to year in the negotiable content of pay bargaining. NIPSA have not taken the route of 'equal pay for work of equal value' cases, which they consider almost impossible to win. But they do have a strict 'no overtime' policy and they put emphasis on basic pay rather than bonus schemes. In this they avoid negotiating positions that further advantage men. They also stress higher increases for lower grades. This is intended by the union to be a measure to counter class, rather than gender, inequalities. But in practice it benefits more women than men.

NIPSA, like all unions organising in the sector, has been fighting to defend public employment against the Tories' privatisating moves. On the civil service side, large parts of departments have been split off and 'agentised'. Some functions, such as cleaning services and payroll operations, have been privatised. NIPSA's largely successful strategy in response to compulsory competitive tendering in the public service has been to assist local councils and other employing bodies to prepare bids and win in-house contracts.

This struggle against privatisation is recognised as having a gender dimension. In November 1995 the Northern Ireland Equal Opportunities Commission concluded a formal investigation into CCT by recommending the government to suspend the policy in health and education services because of 'clear evidence ... that competitive tendering has had a seriously damaging effect on the numbers of women employed and on their terms and conditions of employment. Women have been affected to a much greater extent than men' (Equal Opportunities Commission for Northern Ireland 1995a). NIPSA use this argument in negotiation, despite its rejection by the secretary of state, who placed 'the broader public interest' over 'the need to tackle inequalities' (Equal Opportunities Commission 1996).

The third important item on the bargaining agenda is equal opportunities. In so far as the civil service, local councils and other public services have adopted sound equality policies over the years, this has been largely the product of union pressure.[16] In every organisation where they are represented, NIPSA members press for action against discriminatory recruitment and promotion, against sexual harassment, for woman-friendly and family-friendly policies of all kinds, and, recently, for awareness on domestic violence. They have long campaigned for employer-assisted childcare, but are disappointed in the results.

Despite the disproportionate presence of men among NIPSA's negotiators, women and women's needs have been central to their negotiating agendas. In some cases the issues clearly specify 'women' and in others they refer to any employee with domestic responsibilities. In yet more, women's interests are served by serving other sets of interests, by virtue of the multiple identities women bear;

as people of a given class, religious grouping, employment group and so on. It is this multiplicity and its handling that gives NIPSA its particular relevance for discussions of democracy.

Equality, democracy, community

The arrangement you make for the deployment of power is the nature of the community you end up with. That, more or less, is the message of Nancy Hartsock's book *Money, Sex and Power* (1985). We always have a choice between shaping power as domination 'over' things and people, and shaping it as capacity, the capability 'to' and 'for'. Trade unionists sometimes feel uneasy discussing power relations among the union's own members and employees, thinking it is only outside, in relation to the employer and the state, that power is an issue. After all, 'we are all workers' and it is only a modest power, our labour power, we have available to us.

But there is no avoiding that a trade union is fissured by power relations, by virtue both of its search for effectiveness (it needs an authority structure and a division of labour to achieve its work) and the various axes of difference in the collectivity, which, as we have seen, have tendencies to advantage and disadvantage within them. Like it or not, a trade union is a polity. Questions like 'What are the powers of the general secretary?', 'Which is the more powerful, the annual conference or the general council?' and 'What power does the ordinary member have to shape the policy of the branch?' are meaningful ones. However, because NIPSA is already constituted as a democratic organisation, mostly power here expresses itself not as crude control but as relative effectiveness. And it is around this notion that much of the above discussion has circled. Are members, 'regardless of' (as the rule book puts it) sex/gender, employment sector, perceived religion, political opinion and so on, able to be equally effective in and through their union?

Those who are most involved in making policy for NIPSA have quite clearly struggled with the problem of ensuring that no member, whatever marks them as different from any other member, is prevented from being equally effective – being active in the representative structure, getting a job as a paid official, getting their interests dealt with through negotiation with the employer. The difficulty they have confronted is that *differences differ*. The sources of potential inequalities do not operate in the same way. In fact, in public sector employment and in NIPSA their severity and their effect are widely disparate. So the Alliance has been obliged to take quite divergent approaches in its attempt to secure its organisational democracy against the destabilising potentials of each.

For example, while Catholic–Protestant difference in the membership is allowed to remain largely invisible and is dealt with by voluntary sensitivity, CS–PO and man–woman differences are spotlighted and the compensatory measures, though dissimilar, are in each case highly structured. The interests of lesbians and gays may be watched over by union representatives in the workplace, but to set up a committee of general council for them, in the way it has been done for women, is well understood as likely to do more harm than good. Practical measures to assist mobility and communication, together with a fair recruitment procedure, are felt to be the appropriate strategy for empowering people with disabilities. As to left and right, it is not thought to be appropriate that they get formal recognition in NIPSA – unlike in Westminster where the Conservatives and Labour sit on opposing benches. But it is of concern that the political process be transparent enough to allow people of different political persuasions to contend safely for influence in the union.

Furthermore, dimensions of difference are not freestanding. They map onto each other in complicated ways. If we happen to be concerned with the potential effectiveness of 'women' we cannot avoid being concerned about other dimensions of inequality too. Grade groups like 'support' and 'typing' include disproportionate numbers of women. Part-timers are more likely to be women than men. Women, being less mobile than men, are more liable to feel the disadvantage of working in the rural areas, far from Belfast. There are more women in the Public Officer Group than in the Civil Service Group, so what happens to PO Group interests within NIPSA affects women slightly disproportionately. And, since Catholic women have worse chances in the labour market than Protestant women, greater union effectiveness on the part of Catholic trade unionists could be seen as differentially useful for women (Equal Opportunities Commission 1995b:46–7). And so on. A women is not a unitary subject but (inconveniently perhaps) will have an unpredictable and complex self-identity. If, in Chantal Mouffe's words, a woman is 'the articulation of an ensemble of subject positions ... always precariously and temporarily sutured at [their] intersection' (Mouffe 1992a:10), then a women's committee is always going to have a voice too singular to speak for her. And if it is not enough, should it be there at all?

NIPSA is, in fact, caught up in the tension between rival approaches to democracy that are widely debated in the literature. And if the union, struggling to achieve political community, sometimes seem indecisive or riven with dissension it is because, like most other polities large and small, it straddles the crack between the two.

Classical liberal democracy in its various forms, the legacy of the Enlightenment, confers citizenship on the individual, notionally free and equal with other citizens, with guaranteed rights and duties. But as some feminist writers have pointed out, in reality these citizens differ widely and some have less clout than others. Votes do not all weigh the same. Some citizens for instance are men and some are women, in a world where men control women's labour power and women's bodies (Pateman 1988). The shortcomings of liberal democracy have become more apparent with the development since World War II of new social movements – among them the women's movement, the gay movement, movements of black and other ethnic minorities in white western countries. These marchers and movers claim their group interests are not well served by existing democratic forms.

'The achievement of formal equality does not eliminate social differences, and rhetorical commitment to the sameness of persons makes it impossible even to name how those differences presently structure privilege and oppression', wrote Iris Marion Young (1990:164). She argues for affirmative action. A democracy, she says, 'should provide mechanisms for the effective recognition and representation of the distinct voices and perspectives of those of its constituent groups that are oppressed or disadvantaged' (Young 1990:184). This reasoning has legitimated the women's committees and all the other special structures and positive actions trade unions have experimented with since the 1970s. They are steps along the road to what Chantal Mouffe calls 'radical plural democracy', responding to the interests of complex social agents (Mouffe 1992a).

But doesn't this 'identity politics' deepen our divisions? Doesn't it reduce us to one-dimensional stereotypes? Or, alternatively, doesn't it oblige us to rush from one place to another to press our case (now the women's committee, now the public officers executive committee, next (perhaps) the forum for people with disabilities, or the left caucus)? We are talking here about not just double militancy but exhaustive militancy.

So perhaps there is something to be said for the original formula of liberal democracy: guarantee the rights of each citizen, considered as identical to the next, and you will have a well-governed polity. Hesitating between the two answers, Anne Philips says 'I do not want a world in which women have to speak continuously as women – or men are left to speak as men' (Phillips 1991:7). She looks forward to a time when special measures like women's committees become redundant, when people are no longer defined through their nature as women or men (or, we could add, their positioning as Protestants and Catholics). She wants to see 'a politics in which people will no longer be locked into their own specific or localised concerns, but will participate with other members of their community in reaching decisions that are mutually acceptable, on matters that are common to all' (Phillips 1991:8).

So it is not surprising that members and officials in NIPSA were beginning to discuss the merits and shortcomings of their pragmatic diversified approach. Was there not another way, one that would simply deliver 'justice' to every individual NIPSA member and public sector employee whatever their job, wherever they live, regardless of whether they run a mile before breakfast, whatever kind of church (if any) they attend on Sunday, or, indeed, on Friday or Saturday, whether they have children or not and whether they read Marx or Hayek?

Recently NIPSA had taken a step towards a unitary, general justice in the matter of harassment. Some years ago, as the union became more conscious of women's disadvantage, it had taken on board the concept of sexual harassment. Training courses were organised for NIPSA's lay representatives. Over the years, sexual harassment policies were negotiated with most employers. But both the Fair Employment (NI) legislation and the Policy and Fair Treatment (PAFT) Guidelines, a voluntary code of practice introduced by the Northern Ireland administration to end discrimination in public sector employment, also brought the questions of perceived religion and sex/gender together in a single frame of action. Why confront the two forms of harassment separately?

In NIPSA enthusiasm for sexual harassment training had been waning. Men, in particular, seemed apathetic. Taking their cue from FE and PAFT (and the imminent arrival of race relations legislation), the union redesigned the training course and their negotiating approach. Henceforth harassment would encompass all forms of persecution in the workplace, down to and including bullying, 'the persistent demeaning and downgrading of human beings through vicious words and cruel unseen acts which gradually undermine their confidence and self-esteem' (NIPSA 1996d). The new policy included reference to racial slurs, offensive attitudes to gay men and women, people with disabilities, and dismissive treatment of the older or younger worker.

In this vein, a non-specific 'Joint Declaration of Protection' had been signed between the Irish Congress of Trade Unions (ICTU) and the Confederation of British Industry, and by 1997 more and more employers and unions were signing agreements on this model, covering matters of perceived religion, political opinion, gender, race and all other dimensions of difference. In other words, the aim now was to chivvy each employer along the path towards making the workplace a caring, humane, just community, in which difference is neither ignored nor exploited, where diversity is acknowledged and valued.

But not everybody agrees the way to achieve that goal is to dump all affirmative actions into one pot. The women's committee had been involved in drafting the new guidelines, which had also been discussed with the Equal Opportunities Commission and Fair Employment Commission. But some women would agree with the comment of one I spoke with, that somehow now 'we've lost ownership of the harassment issue.'[17]

'Mainstreaming 'is a word in common usage in trade union circles these days. It has become part of ICTU's vocabulary (1993). It means completing the gender-transformation of unions by shifting gender issues out of a women's ghetto into the mainstream of policy making. But mainstreaming is difficult to do – often the mixed membership of general conferences and committees just do not have the expertise or the commitment to analyse and deal with gender differences and inequalities. And too often it is used as an excuse to close down the special structures developed for women.

In NIPSA, it has to be said, there are rumblings about converting the women's committee (on the precedent of the shift from 'sexual harassment' to 'harassment') into an equalities committee. Some of its members feel the time has come for such a change because 'it has lost impetus'. Some female lay officials do not support the continuation of 'reserved seats' for women under the minimum representation rule. A young executive officer I talked with says 'there's no such thing as women's issues any more'.

The thought that 'the women's committee has served its purpose' is given impetus by the recent success of women in the general council election. Women, it seems, can now do it on their own.

Look, it is said, they are putting themselves forward, using their vote. Male branch secretaries can no longer 'deliver' (manipulate?) the block vote of their branch. But another possible reading of re-action to this election result is that it is a male backlash at the first slender signs that women's bid for better representation is succeed-ing. In interview some men showed themselves already alarmed and resentful. 'The *overwhelming majority* on the council now are women.' 'Women are just going down the list and voting for women.' One man said, 'We need reserved seats for men now.' There are complaints about a decline in the calibre of these new untried rep-resentatives produced by the postal ballot. These women are 'inexperienced', 'unknowns', 'springing from nowhere'.

So the Alliance, fired by divergent motivations, was allowing itself for the moment to be guided by experience, letting each axis of difference suggest a different take on democracy. And the piece-meal arrangement they had made to embody power, to disperse it, to gather it together, was indeed defining the kind of community they were – a continually self-questioning one.

Notes

1 The major departments of the Northern Ireland Civil Service are the Northern Ireland Office, the Department of Finance and Personnel, the Department of Economic Development, the Department of the Environ-ment, the Department of Health and Social Services, the Department of Agriculture and the Department of Education. Other civil service agencies and units in which NIPSA organises include the Police Auth-ority for Northern Ireland, the Social Security Agency and the Child Support Agency. The main areas of public service employment are the Northern Ireland Housing Executive, the regional health and social service boards and education and library boards, and local authorities.

2 The literature on gender relations in trade unions is by now extensive and international in scope, including many studies of individual unions. Recent works in English include Cockburn (1991), Cunnison and Stageman (1993), and Briskin and McDermott (1993).

3 I use the term sex/gender to reflect the existence of a range of mean-ings my interview subjects implicitly gave to the terms 'man' and 'woman', sometimes emphasising biological differences, sometimes stressing more cultural differences, with interaction between the two.

4 For further details see Appendix 2.

5 Two policies pursued by successive Conservative governments during the 1980s and 1990s bore heavily on public sector trade unions in particular. One was the tightening of management control over public sector employment, involving expenditure curbs, the decentralising and privatising of many public sector institutions, and the trimming of workforces. The second was a policy of marginalising and deregulating

trade unions. The Employment Acts 1980, 1982, 1988, 1989 and 1990, and the Trade Union Acts 1984, 1992 and 1993 subjected industrial relations to 'a programme of change unparalleled in this century' (McIlroy 1995:226). Union density however has remained higher than in the private sector and 'some form of collective bargaining has remained the norm' (Bailey 1994:123). Many employers have lacked the capacity to overcome union resistance and fully implement Conservative intentions (Smith and Morton 1993).

6   During the 1970s and 1980s NIPSA had developed a federal structure linking formerly separate unions. Given trends in both public sector employment and industrial relations law, this was becoming increasingly costly in administrative time and resources. Following a decision by the annual conference of 1991, late that year NIPSA's branches, panels and committees were asked to consider a range of alternative arrangements set out in a document, *Options for Change*. Following this consultation, a second paper, *NIPSA in the Nineties: The Case for a Unified Organisation*, was prepared by the Alliance Council for Conference 1992. This too was debated throughout the union and a ballot of members and decision of Conference in 1993 resulted in the more integrated Alliance embodied in NIPSA's current Constitution (NIPSA 1996a).

7   The constitution provides separately for minimum representation on the Civil Service Group executive committee for members employed in a variety of specific sectors of employment. The Public Officers' Group executive committee similarly names minimum representation for subgroups. On the general council of NIPSA, minimum representation is constitutionally established for the Public Officers' Group (3 seats) and two sub-groups of the Civil Service: P&T (2 seats); and General Service, Typing, Secretarial and Support grades (3 seats). In addition, at least one seat must be filled by a female member of the POG and another by a female number of the CSG.

8   The firm KPMG Management Consulting, engaged by the Northern Ireland Civil Service to look into its organisational culture, found significant differences in men's and women's perceptions of each others' motivations, and in the two sexes' modes of communication. Women were encountering significant chill factors in the promotion process. (Summary of unpublished research by KPMG Management Consulting 1995).

9   This provision derives from the Fair Employment Act 1989, under which most employers in Northern Ireland must periodically review the religious and gender composition of their workforce, and the number of disabled people employed. They are also required to take positive action to correct any failure to achieve fair participation. NIPSA regularly makes such a 'Section 31' return after consultation with the branch of the union GMB/APEX that organises NIPSA employees. In recent years it has adjusted its advertising strategy in an attempt to increase the number of Protestants putting themselves forward as candidates for vacant posts.

10 In 1995 NIPSA was taken to a fair employment tribunal by a candidate for a secondment position, claiming NIPSA's recruitment procedure had been biased against him owing to his left-wing political opinions. On losing the case, the union appointed consultants to review its recruit-

ment procedures and practices and make recommendations for change. The report of the consultants, solicitors Beverley Jones and Fiona Cassidy, dealt with all dimensions of equality in relation not only to seconded trade union positions but also to appointments to NIPSA's own staff (Jones and Cassidy 1996).

11 Race relations legislation was introduced in Northern Ireland in 1997.

12 Figures in this and the subsequent paragraph are the product of NIPSA's regular monitoring.

13 ICTU adopted its first equality programme in 1982. At the time of our research it was in its third five-year equality programme, 1993–8, which stresses 'the need to mainstream equality issues on the trade union agenda and to ensure that women are represented at all levels in the trade union movement in proportion to their membership' (Irish Congress of Trade Unions 1993).

14 Control of selection of the women's committee's membership has shifted over time from the general council to the branches. Today 8 of the 12 seats are filled by election by branch delegates at Conference, 4 nominated by the general council. Responsibility for administration of sex equality policy is included in a line of responsibility from the general secretary down to an executive officer who services the committee. The committee meets for half a day, approximately five times a year. It elects its own chair and vice-chair. There is no limit to the times a member may seek re-election, either as a member of the committee or as an officer.

15 Secondment positions are 'trawled' internally among branch members and usually attract applications from branch officers who have previously been active on limited 'facility time' or in an entirely unpaid capacity. The selection is made by NIPSA, using standard recruitment procedures similar to those for headquarters officials. The secondee is paid by her or his original employer, though sometimes the salary is supplemented by NIPSA.

16 The Northern Ireland Civil Service, for example, has its own action plan for women in its employment (Department of Finance and Personnel 1993), produced in consultation with the trade union side on the principle negotiating body, the Central Whitley Council.

17 See Note 2, Chapter 1.

References

Bailey, Rachel (1994) 'Annual Review Article 1993: British Public Sector Industrial Relations', *British Journal of Industrial Relations*, 32(1), 113–35.

Briskin, Linda and McDermott, Patricia (eds) (1993) *Women Challenging Unions: feminism, democracy and militancy*, Toronto: University of Toronto Press.

Cockburn, Cynthia (1983) *Brothers: Male Dominance and Technological Change*, London: Pluto Press.

Cockburn, Cynthia (1991) *In the Way of Women: Men's Resistance to Sex Equality in Organizations*, London: Macmillan.

Cunnison, Sheila and Stageman, Jane (1993) *Feminizing the Unions: Challenging the Culture of Masculinity*, Aldershot: Avebury.

Department of Finance and Personnel (1993) *Action Plan on the Employment* of Women in the Northern Ireland Civil Service, Belfast: DFP.

Department of Finance and Personnel (1994) Fifth Report of the Northern Ireland Civil Service Equal Opportunities Unit, Belfast: DFP.

Equal Opportunities Commission for Northern Ireland (1995a) 'EOC Calls on Government to Suspend Competitive Tendering', Press Release, Belfast, 9 November.

Equal Opportunities Commission for Northern Ireland (1995b) Catholic and Protestant Women in the Northern Ireland Labour Market, Belfast: EOCNI.

Equal Opportunities Commission for Northern Ireland (1996) 'EOC Criticises Government Response to Competitive Tendering Investigation', Press Release, Belfast, 27 January.

Hartsock, Nancy C. M. (1983) Money, Sex and Power: Towards a Feminist Historical Materialism, New York and London: Longman.

Irish Congress of Trade Unions (1993) Mainstreaming Equality: 1993–98, Belfast.

Jones & Cassidy Solicitors (1996) Review of NIPSA's Selection Procedures and Practices for Appointment to Headquarter Staff and to Seconded Trade Union Positions, Belfast: Jones & Cassidy.

KPMG Management Consulting (1995) Summary of Research into Organisation Culture in the Senior Northern Ireland Civil Service: Equal Opportunities for Women, Belfast: KPMG.

McIlroy, John (1995) Trade Unions in Britain Today, Manchester and New York: Manchester University Press.

Mouffe, Chantal (1992a) 'Democratic Politics Today' in Mouffe (1992b) 1–14.

Mouffe, Chantal (1992b) Dimensions of Radical Democracy: Pluralism, Citizenship and Community, London: Verso.

Northern Ireland Public Service Alliance (1996a) Rule Book (revised June 1996), Belfast.

Northern Ireland Public Service Alliance (1996b) NIPSA News, March. Belfast.

Northern Ireland Public Service Alliance (1996c) Annual Report 1996, Belfast.

Northern Ireland Public Service Alliance (1996d) Tackling Harassment Course, Belfast.

Pateman, Carole (1988) The Sexual Contract, Cambridge: Polity Press.

Phillips, Anne (1991) Engendering Democracy, Cambridge: Polity Press.

Smith, Paul and Morton, Gary (1993) 'Union Exclusion and the Decollectivization of Industrial Relations in Contemporary Britain', British Journal of Industrial Relations, 31(1), 98–114.

Young, Iris Marion (1990) Justice and the Politics of Difference, Princeton, NJ: Princeton University Press.

6

Swimming against the mainstream: the Northern Ireland Women's Coalition

Kate Fearon and Monica McWilliams

The Northern Ireland Women's Coalition (NIWC) was created out of the frustrations and aspirations of women from a diverse range of backgrounds and affiliations. The majority of these women had been, for many years, concerned about the exclusion of women from mainstream politics in Northern Ireland. All of them hoped that the opportunity to create a lasting peace would not be wasted and believed that women had particular experiences and insights which could help to move the process forward. Within weeks of its foundation in April 1996 the Coalition had achieved an historic success: the election of two of its members to the Northern Ireland Peace Talks table. In this chapter, we describe the origins of this almost unique party and discuss the ways in which its distinctive and new values and methods of organising were constructed. Its interventions in the mainstream of politics will be discussed, as will some of the responses from the established parties. A central theme will be the dialogues among women from the unionist, nationalist and other traditions and affiliations within the Coalition.

The beginnings

The divisiveness of the constitutional issue had always confounded the women's movement in Northern Ireland (Loughran 1986, McWilliams 1995, Roulston 1997). As Chapter 1 of this book has argued, however, women in community organisations had managed, against the odds during the years of armed conflict and political stalemate, to work across the sectarian divide on common interests.

The declarations of cease-fires by the IRA and loyalist paramilitaries in September 1994 brought a new political climate. As the British and Irish governments began to prepare the ground for a new round of peace negotiations, some women began to see the possibility that political talks would start only to founder once again. They also identified the paucity of women from the major parties and mainstream politics as an issue of common concern. These themes, of women's desire to secure a peace settlement and to make space for women, were discussed in a series of conferences.[1]

Within months of the cease-fires being declared, the British and Irish governments published a Framework Document[2] outlining their views on how accountable government in Northern Ireland could be achieved as well as their views on North–South and East–West – or British–Irish – relations. The language adopted in the document reflected a new commitment to replacing outright solutions with an 'accommodation of the two traditions'. This language provided the buzz-words of the peace process: identity, diversity, parity of esteem, pluralism, respect and inclusive relationships. However, the document left many women's organisations sceptical about how such concepts might translate into practice. Monica McWilliams[3] convened a planning committee that organised a conference, supported by the Northern Ireland Office, to discuss women's hopes for the future and to ascertain their response to the governments' proposals in the Framework Document. The discussions and presentations at the conference, attended by a wide range of women from over two hundred organisations, and held in the Rural College in Draperstown in June 1995, brought the problem of women's political space sharply into focus. The conference report recommended that a broad commitment to improving the status of women in politics was no longer sufficient. A clear strategy for the support and development of women's participation should be devised, including the setting of targets for women at local, regional and parliamentary level. In particular, the conference concluded, specific 'mechanisms for women to become involved in Constitutional talks are needed' (Porter and McWilliams 1995). There were many allegiances and perspectives among the women at this and other conferences, but they shared a strong desire to see women making a decisive move into the political mainstream.

This hope became a possibility quite suddenly, and in ways not entirely welcome to many of the women involved. The Irish and British governments issued a Joint Communiqué on 28 February

1996, proposing that elections be held to choose the delegates at the forthcoming Peace Talks[4] and inviting parties to give their views on the electoral system. Voluntary organisations were not specifically invited to respond, but many did so, including the Northern Ireland Women's European Platform. In a paper circulated to other non-governmental organisations and political parties, the Northern Ireland Women's European Platform (NIWEP)[5] strongly advocated the adoption of an electoral system which would maximise the numbers of successful women candidates.[6] The paper also referred back to the emphasis placed in the Framework Document produced by the two governments on parity of esteem and inclusion. Women, NIWEP argued, wanted everyone fully involved in determining the future of Northern Ireland, but were 'particularly conscious that they have not been included to date and wish to have this injustice redressed' (1996a:4). The paper acknowledged that many women chose not to involve themselves in politics as currently arranged, but stressed that women did play active and key roles contributing to policy development, and that this civil society activism should be more clearly acknowledged by the mainstream party political process.

Over dinner one evening, Avila Kilmurray, a former trade union official and current director of the largest community foundation in Northern Ireland, got together with Monica McWilliams to brainstorm round this paper. The issue of women and the proposed Peace Talks process was the focus of that night's discussion. They needed to find a way in which women could be written into, rather than out of, the scripts that had been set in motion by the British and Irish governments on Northern Ireland's political future. They agreed that Monica would take to NIWEP's next management committee meeting the bold idea of a women's coalition contesting the election. From there, the idea was circulated to women's groups and other voluntary and community organisations, from whom the response was surprise, interest and, despite reservations, general approval.

On 21 March, having received responses from parties to the Joint Communiqué, the British government published proposals for the election[7] which recommended a hybrid, two-tiered list system of proportional representation[8] that would elect 110 delegates to a Forum for Political Dialogue (HMSO 1996a). The Forum parties would then send three (for the bigger parties) or two delegates to the All-Party Talks. If the Talks failed, the Forum would be wound up.

NIWEP were frustrated at the lack of response to its earlier paper. They sent a new response to the proposals (NIWEP 1996b), stressing the need for an inclusive process and questioning the proposed designation of parties eligible to contest the election. NIWEP felt that the government had failed to allow the entry of representative groups other than the established parties into the negotiation and consultation process. They pointed out again the serious absence of women in party politics, and argued that many women who had been active over the course of the Troubles had great difficulty in joining the existing parties. The suggestion that a women's network might contest the election was floated. Other organisations also spoke publicly about the government paper and the proposed elections. Derry Women's Centre, in a press statement, argued that a broader base was needed 'to allow independents, women, community leaders and trade unionists who are anxious to engage in solution focused talks'.

In the meantime, a partnership of organisations led by Bronagh Hinds, chair of NIWEP, issued invitations to over two hundred groups of women to attend a meeting in the Ulster People's College on 17 April.[9] The two NIWEP papers were enclosed to provide a starting-point for discussing what should be done to ensure women were represented at the Talks table. These documents were also circulated to the political parties, none of which responded. Over the course of the following week, NIWEP and others lobbied both governments furiously on the issue of a women's caucus or network contesting the election. Shortly before the People's College meeting, a fax was received from the Northern Ireland Office confirming that space had been reserved in the election for a women's party and asking for the party's full name. Bronagh rang her contact list asking 'what will we do here?' (Hinds, 1996, personal communication).[10] The consensus was to keep the options open by submitting a party name: the Northern Ireland Women's Coalition.

The campaign

At the first meeting, over a hundred women turned up. After much discussion, the decision to stand was taken, though the decision was not unanimous. Several women were uncomfortable with the idea of a gender-specific party. Some women spoke against a cross-community alliance, others against contesting this election. There were doubts about going ahead without a broader consensus among the wider 'activist' community. In the end, the majority agreed that there had to be balance between taking a decision quickly within the time constraints laid down by the government and consulting and building consensus with as many people as possible. The practice at this stage was not to have a vote, but to allow as much discussion as possible to take place. The sense of the meeting was that the vast majority of women attending had agreed to form the Northern Ireland Women's Coalition to fight the election. Some of the women activists who did not agree with the decision did not return to subsequent meetings. Their dilemma is reflected in a letter, signed by mainly republican women, to *Women's News* (a Belfast-based feminist magazine) in its Summer 1996 issue. The signatories stated:

> As feminists we agree with [the NIWC] that the proportion of women nominated by all the other parties is abysmally low, and we sympathise with their efforts ... The Women's Coalition is not agreed on a policy on future constitutional arrangements for this island. If one or more Women's Coalition candidates are successful they will necessarily have to take a position on the key constitutional issues under negotiation. Inevitably, they will not be able to represent the views of all the people who have voted for them ... the Women's Coalition's inability to agree on fundamental issues of policy reflects the inherent weakness of a women's political party.[11]

To ensure that everyone who might be interested would have the opportunity to inform the process of creating the Coalition, a team was formed to produce an information and consultation paper outlining the steps to the creation of the Coalition and setting out some protocols for the new party. Were the Coalition successful, it would mean sitting at both the Talks and the Forum. It was proposed that the NIWC would be created initially only for the duration of the Talks process, with a commitment to review its existence after two years (NIWC 1996a).

At a second meeting (on 23 April 1996), three core principles were identified around which the NIWC would build its policies. These were: support for inclusion, equality and human rights. Three papers setting out some fundamental policies were discussed in open meetings, of about sixty people, and other papers were circulated for comment. The paper on inclusion was debated first; without agreement to that, the new party would not survive. The proposal to support the inclusion of Sinn Féin in the Peace Talks, with or without a cease-fire by the IRA, was difficult for unionist women. Calling for a cease-fire was similarly unwelcome to some women from the republican tradition. Despite these difficulties, the positions were accepted. There was more difficulty over the human rights paper, especially over proposed support for the transfer of paramilitary prisoners from Britain to Northern Ireland. The earlier discussion on inclusion facilitated this debate. Prisoner transfers were put into the context of humanitarianism and the impact on families, and this paper was also approved. In all, fourteen policy and briefing papers were produced in the months April and May of 1996. Many policies produced by the NIWC in the pre-election period had their origins in the preparatory work carried out for the Northern Ireland delegation at the NGO Forum of the UN Fourth Conference on the status of Women in Beijing. The new party was in a very real sense a product of the solidarity of many organisations, including the trade unions.[12]

Meetings between the core organisers were convened almost continuously, with policy meetings held every Wednesday and campaign strategy meetings on Saturdays. A technical support team was created. At the first meeting of this team, advice from Sydney Elliot, a psephologist at Queen's University, that a threshold of some 10 000 votes would guarantee two seats was considered. Thinking of this figure in terms of a 'pyramid' selling scheme, whereby 100 women standing each had to get 100 votes, made the whole thing seem realisable. By the middle of the following week, a bank account (with no money) and election headquarters in Belfast, Enniskillen and Derry were opened and advertisements seeking candidates were published. Two criteria were set out: candidates should have ideas on issues and problems facing their community and should be willing to seek a political accommodation inclusive of all interests.

As the close of nominations approached, the numbers of women putting themselves forward as candidates crept up from 30 to 50, and finally, with three hours to go, to 70. It was not the target 100, but it was among the biggest candidate slate of any party. The candidates were 'Catholic and Protestant, Unionist and Nationalist, Republican and Loyalist. They work inside the home, and in business, in trade unionism, community voluntary and education sectors' (NIWC 1996b). Of the 10 women who stood on the regional list, 5 were perceived[13] to be Catholic, 5 Protestant; 2 had their own consultancy businesses, 1 worked in the home, 2 in trade unionism, 2 in further or higher education, 2 were community workers and 1 worked in the voluntary sector. Achieving this balance meant that some potential candidates had to show goodwill and step down.

The nomination papers were lucky to be lodged. After the frenetic task of getting names, addresses and constituencies in the right order, on the right papers, the car carrying them to the electoral office for 5 p.m. on 13 May got caught in rush hour traffic. Monica McWilliams called on the resourcefulness (and her former experience as a cross-country runner) that characterised many of the women in the NIWC. Abandoning the vehicle, she sprinted through the centre of Belfast to the electoral office, where May Blood, seeing her dishevelled shape, met her around a corner, away from the madding media crowd, so that they walked in together, calm and composed, ready to fight the first election. The only further hitch was that, in their confusion they mistook the doorman for Pat Bradley, the chief electoral officer, and had to start running again, up six flights of stairs, to beat the clock after relaxing on getting to the electoral office.

Once the candidates' names were safely lodged, the coalition was launched at a press conference. This was different from the usual party event. Party members and supporters sat behind the journalists, wildly applauding the platform speakers. The press were somewhat at sea, but over the weeks they got used to the new style.

Getting names on paper was, of course, only the first step. Planning and support teams were created to deal with policy, publicity and electoral information. Interested women were given basic political training, specifically in aspects such as public speaking, and dealing with the media. The policy team produced a manifesto (in the purple, green and white of the women's suffrage movement), passing policy ideas through unionist and nationalist filters. Underpinned by the three core principles, the manifesto set out the Coalition's five-point election plan, arranged by the acronym WOMEN: Working for a Solution; Offering Inclusion; Making Women Heard; Equity for All, and New Thinking. It centred around women as agents of change, pointing out that over the years of violence women had been effective in developing and maintaining contact across the various divides in Northern Ireland. Women could draw on their experience of exclusion in prioritising inclusion in negotiations. All parties should have access 'as of right' to the All-Party

Talks. The party also wanted to deflate some of the pomposity of mainstream politics. Cheeky election posters and cards with the slogan 'Wave goodbye to the dinosaurs!' with appropriate illustrations were produced.

In the campaign, the NIWC insisted that its strength lay in not taking a fixed position on the constitutional issue. This meant that the NIWC would be able to negotiate, accommodate and include views from all the participants in the process (and some outside it). It would listen to the views of others, and attempt to incorporate them, as opposed to merely stating its own position and expecting others to accept it. Candidates faced tough questions from journalists and other parties who could not comprehend how the gender issue could intersect with policies on 'the constitution'. Would the NIWC take part if some parties were excluded? Should Sinn Féin be allowed at the table without decommissioning? Will the NIWC attend the Forum if some parties do not attend? The NIWC guaranteed it would attend the Talks come what may. A solution would not be reached if any parties were kept out and the NIWC believed that the issue of dialogue must take priority over all other issues. The commitment to non-violence and to decommissioning was stressed, side by side with the view that inclusive dialogue was the best way to achieve these goals.

All over the country, clutches of women were to be found in shopping centres and swimming pools, post offices and petrol stations, crèches and convents, canvassing, cajoling and, sometimes, convincing others to support the NIWC. Posters were pasted onto waste cardboard gleaned from supermarket skips or from sympathetic management. Intrepid campaigners exchanged top tips on poster longevity: covering in clingfilm was a favourite. On the day after the election, it all became worthwhile. After six weeks of do-it-yourself campaigning, the NIWC secured 7731 votes, coming ninth among all the parties who contested the election, guaranteeing its two seats in the Forum for Political Dialogue and the right to send two delegates to the All-Party Talks.

Acknowledging difference, accepting diversity

The three principles of human rights, equality and inclusion were applied both when debate was conducted within the Coalition and in its relationships with other parties and groups. They formed an ethical framework for policy and positions on all issues. The primary motivation which led Coalition members to engage in politics was to achieve the inclusion of women. But the solidarity on gender politics would be effective only if members were confident that their strong feelings on other aspects of rights and justice were acknowledged and taken into account in the process of creating policies. The members of the NIWC, coming from many religious, cultural and political backgrounds, were to find that they disagreed profoundly with each other over the ways to resolve social and political problems. Therefore, most policies required long exchanges of ideas, hopes and often fears, followed by drafting and redrafting to calm anxieties. By constantly revisiting the three principles, the NIWC found itself equipped with the tools to benefit from the different perspectives within the party. Monthly meetings were held at which all the issues concerning members could be discussed. A team was assembled to advise the two elected delegates on all the matters being raised at the Peace Talks.

At the monthly meetings, usually attended by around forty people, the delegates at the Talks gave a summary of what was happening, and the membership asked questions and offered opinions and advice. The 'Talks team' would then distil all of these and use them to inform its position in the official process. There was a difficult line to tread at times, for several reasons. Confidentiality was a key issue at all times in the Talks, and one to which the NIWC delegation adhered. But there was also a commitment to demystifying the political process, which required giving explanations and information to the members. The problem was compounded by the fact that monthly meetings were still 'open' meetings – you did not have to be a member to attend. The Talks team tried to be as open and transparent as possible, and members respected the pressures they faced; there was never a moment when someone had to say 'I'm sorry, but I can't tell you that.' This elaborate process allowed members to trust each other's good faith and sometimes to accept policies they did not fully agree with, as the examples which follow will indicate.

One of the most contentious issues in recent years has arisen over the annual parades by the Orange Order.[14] Some members of the Coalition had personal or family connections with the order and expressed fears about the curtailment of the right to have parades. Other members argued that the parades were inherently sectarian and therefore could not be defended. To move beyond this point, a series of talks was arranged in which both the representatives of the loyal orders and the residents groups opposed to parades agreed to participate. After this, Coalition members exchanged their own views and positions on what they had heard.

In the end, the Coalition agreed to move away from absolute positions for or against the parades, and called for an independent commission which would encourage safe and constructive dialogue between residents and the Orange Order. The policy team also called for more creative use of legal powers to foster civic responsibility on the part of organisations arranging, supporting or sanctioning commemorative or celebratory marches. As a result of its facilitative, yet challenging, approach to this issue, the Coalition has been invited to engage in discussions with the Orange Order and local residents groups to find ways of resolving these ongoing disputes. In May 1999, Avila Kilmurray (the Coalition member experienced in trade union negotiations) was invited to mediate the talks between a local branch of the Apprentice Boys (one of the loyal orders) and a local group of residents. This is the first example in Northern Ireland where the two opposing sides on the parades issue have agreed to enter direct dialogue, using a local person whom they regarded as mutually acceptable.

Another issue which was potentially politically divisive but which was resolved successfully for the NIWC was the imprisonment on remand of Roisin McAliskey (the daughter of veteran political activist and former MP Bernadette Devlin McAliskey). She had been arrested in Northern Ireland, then imprisoned in a high-security wing of Belmarsh Jail, a men's prison, awaiting a hearing on extradition, on charges of participating in a plot to plant bombs at a British Army base in Germany. Roisin McAliskey was pregnant, and suffering from serious complications, which were exacerbated by stress. After much lobbying, she had been moved to a women's prison, but her medical condition worsened and there were fears for both her own and her baby's survival, so there continued to be a campaign for her release on bail.

There was little doubt among Coalition members about the humanitarian concerns, but many members were fearful of being associated with the republican sympathies that were extended to the McAliskey family. The NIWC was strongly committed to non-violence and wanted to find a distinctive and independent approach to this – and similar – issues. For two months in early 1997, Roisin McAliskey's case and its implications were discussed.

One of the reasons why this had become such a difficult issue for the NIWC was the opposition from the Democratic Unionist Party, led by Ian Paisley, which was using the Coalition's support for McAliskey to label the NIWC a pro-republican organisation. Some members, living in predominantly Protestant communities, were concerned that the campaign could lead them to being physically attacked, particularly since Roisin McAliskey's mother Bernadette was being portrayed as a hate figure within their areas.

The coalition decided that it needed to carve out its own clear message on the human rights aspects of the McAliskey case. At its monthly meeting in Newry, a decision was made to send one of its members, who was also a doctor, on a fact-finding mission to the prison. Press statements were then based on her report and it was agreed that, where possible, members of the Coalition who came from unionist backgrounds would become the public spokespersons for this campaign. The aim here was to discourage any public perception that it was only the nationalist members of the Coalition who felt strongly about human rights. In this way, the support for McAliskey was extended beyond the nationalist community, which is not an easy thing to do given the traditionally one-sided nature of political action in Northern Ireland. The Coalition was able to focus its political lobbying on the standard of care afforded to a seriously ill pregnant woman in prison as well as challenging the procedures which had led to her being held on remand throughout her pregnancy and the year following the birth of her baby. The human rights side of the story, rather than the political affiliations of her family, remained the Coalition's concern throughout the campaign.[15] The NIWC had worked to break the perception that human rights were the preserve of only one community. Even after a position had been reached there were still reservations. When one Protestant woman said 'I have a bad feeling about this in my gut', the time was taken to go over the ground again to try and make people as comfortable as possible, while making sure the issue was resolved without losing the principle.

There were often issues like this that needed a good deal of discussion, particularly where they could be seen to be lending support to the 'combatants' on one side or the other. At the meetings in February and March 1998, there were heated debates about the decision by the NIWC delegates to oppose a motion, by other parties in the talks, to expel the UDP (a loyalist party linked to the paramilitary Ulster Freedom Fighters). This was a very difficult choice, as the UFF had been conducting a random murder campaign since

December 1997, and there was real fear on the streets. The NIWC delegates, however, argued that the UDP was actively trying to dissuade the paramilitaries from engaging in acts of indiscriminate violence. Nationalist, unionist and other members of the Coalition found this hard to take, so the Coalition's delegates and advisory team at the negotiations were subjected to tough questions by the members over this decision. Because they had spent a lot of time in dialogue with the UDP delegation, they were able to convey the difficulties faced by that party and describe their efforts to end the violence. It was much easier, once this dialogue had taken place, for members to accept the NIWC position on a similar debate when Sinn Féin was excluded from the Talks in March.

These monthly meetings often led to the creation of smaller discussion groups of women of the same background, where they could exchange opinions with less fear of being misunderstood. In the Talks, the NIWC was a party that emphasised process, though not process so as to impede progress. In its own internal workings, the NIWC was careful to provide for a system of checks and balances – having strong principles to guide positions between meetings, and regular open meetings to refine any such positions taken. The principles provided a value base that explicitly recognised the conflict, and explicitly recognised difference among the women who comprised its membership. This can be especially challenging in Northern Ireland, where many people can choose to ignore the conflict and its pervasive effects. Often, for example, it can happen that, at cross-community events, people are encouraged to 'leave their baggage at the door' for fear of offending someone, and 'corrupting' a nice group dynamic. The NIWC, however, has, from the outset been careful to create space whereby members can feel able to express their opinions and hopes. They can have their anger and fears not accepted, but acknowledged as relevant to a solution. Consciously choosing *not* to ignore the conflict has paradoxically helped to keep conflict in check.

Working creatively in a hostile environment, the new party was not universally welcomed, and its attempts to promote accommodation often met hostility, misunderstanding and derision. In the Peace Talks, Senator George Mitchell and his colleagues Harry Holkeri and John de Chastelain were effective chairs, who listened without favour to whoever had the floor. Their attitudes encouraged other Talks delegates to do likewise. The Forum for Political Dialogue however, was not so effectively chaired and had poor rules for procedure. This was compounded by the fact that Sinn Féin never took their seats, and the SDLP withdrew in the midst of the Drumcree crisis during the summer of 1996. Women's Coalition delegates Monica McWilliams and Pearl Sagar often had to bear the brunt of a lot of unionist anger, which often took the form of gendered abuse.

The list of insults that were hurled across the floor of the elected chamber at the Women's Coalition included the more base-level comments that they were whingeing, whining, feckless women to the rather higher level of accusation that 'their chant' sounded like that of a Greek chorus of women. Roles more traditionally ascribed to women were invoked by members of the DUP in their admonishment to the Women's Coalition members that they should 'stand behind the loyal men of Ulster'. The jibes provided the Coalition with moments of humour as the two women began to sing *Stand By Your Man*, requesting that the men who had made the comments should join them since they were recorded gospel singers. In one exchange, Monica McWilliams and Pearl Sagar were told they should be at home, 'breeding children for Ulster'. In exposing the unacceptable nature of this political culture, the Coalition used the tactics of publicly naming and shaming those politicians who chose to engage in a dialogue that involved only the labelling and name-calling of others.[16]

So far success, what chance sustainability?

Despite many setbacks during 1997 and the increase in sectarian murders at the start of 1998, the multi-party Peace Talks eventually reached agreement on 10 April 1998. The Belfast Agreement, or the Good Friday Agreement as it is more familiarly known, has been widely publicised as an 'honourable accommodation', and the role of the Women's Coalition has been acknowledged in the achievement of the historic outcome (Mitchell 1999). The NIWC exercised its belief in the possibility of a successful outcome both inside and outside the Talks process. Constantly engaging in the bilateral and multilateral meetings with the British and Irish governments, the chairpersons of the Talks, the other participants and members of civic society, from grassroots community organisations to business and trade unionists, the NIWC was always well briefed as to what was, or might be, 'acceptable' on any given question. The Coalition actively negotiated the constitutional elements of the Agreement as well as on the 'conflict resolution' issues such as policing, prisoners, human rights, and equality.[17] It also succeeded in having its idea of a Civic Forum, to sit alongside the elected Assembly, included in the Agreement as well as clauses affirming the right of women to full and equal participation in political life. The inclusion of gender participation echoed the South African constitutional accord, while the language articulating it came from the Report of the UN Fourth Conference on the Status of Women, held in Beijing in 1996. The Coalition also ensured that the role of victims was not forgotten, enabling a basket of measures that addressed the human impact of the conflict to be written in during the final hours of negotiations. By paying attention to process, product and public involvement at every stage, the Coalition believed that this was the kind of peace treaty in which citizens could feel they had a stake. When McWilliams joined the Prime Minister and Taoiseach, alongside the other party leaders, to declare in favour of the Belfast Agreement on Good Friday 1998, the Women's Coalition had ensured that on this occasion women were present at an international peace declaration.

After campaigning hard to ensure a 'yes' vote in the referendum which confirmed the public endorsement of the deal in May 1998, the NIWC contested the election to the new Northern Ireland Assembly. The Coalition confounded its critics by gaining two seats in June of that year. Its success was built on its ability to draw on votes from both communities and in breaking the mould in Belfast by obtaining a substantial working-class endorsement from both loyalist and republican areas. When its two delegates entered the Assembly on 1 July 1998, they were required to formally designate themselves in the Members Roll Book as Nationalist, Unionist, or Other. This procedure had been introduced as a way of deciding whether motions before the Assembly carried cross-community support.[18] However, the Coalition refused to be boxed or labelled like this, arguing that this was yet another form of institutional sectarianism. They caused a furore on the first day when they both signed in as Nationalist-Other, Other-Unionist. Interestingly, one of the Coalition's elected representatives came from the unionist community while the other had a nationalist background. However, the presiding officer took legal advice and informed the Assembly that he could not permit 'Other' to be used alongside the stipulated designation of Unionist or Nationalist. An Assembly member had to be 'either/or', not 'both/and.' The Coalition had made its point and after lengthy discussions, its members were designated as

'Inclusive Others'. The debate was carried live on television and brought sharply into focus the difficulties of dealing with difference in the context of Northern Ireland's political parties.

It is still too early, perhaps, to draw up a balance sheet evaluating the performance of the NIWC. Clearly, getting Women's Coalition representatives elected to the Talks process, and two years later to the parliamentary Assembly, was a major success. Simply by contesting the election, the Coalition had demonstrated that women were available and able to compete, contrary to the myth purveyed by other political parties which claimed that they couldn't find any women who wanted to stand. In their manifesto, the NIWC highlighted the contribution that women had made and could make to peace, politics and progress in Northern Ireland. By showing the availability of skilled and committed women, the NIWC put pressure on political parties to select women candidates, and to address women's issues, although this brought responses which were more rhetorical than real.

Last, but not least, the election was an experience of action-based learning about, and training in, electoral politics for significant numbers of women, as the consolidation of support in the subsequent Assembly election shows. Women from both Protestant and Catholic communities who had crossed over into each other's territories had gained much from this experience. Women canvassed in difficult loyalist and nationalist areas. Given the segregated geographical terrain of Northern Ireland, it was often the first time that many women had entered 'the other's territory'. Some have commented that the men from their communities would have found this work highly dangerous because of the risk of being targeted by 'the other side'. The cross-over was not without its difficulties, with some women being subjected to taunts or obscene gestures. However, the issues of unemployment, low wages, domestic violence and sexual harassment had a special meaning for them. They knew that their citizenship was conditional, not just on religion, which is the main defining factor in Northern Ireland, but on their class background and sex. Their personal experience combined with the knowledge of the policy changes that they wanted to create made them effective canvassers on the doorstep.

As the women in the Coalition began to interact with each other, first climbing the nursery slopes of political activism and then acting as political agents, both they and the local electorate began to realise that they no longer had to depend on their elected, mostly male representatives, but could start to negotiate their own rights of citizenship. For its part, what the Coalition has still to work out is how best to match the demands of being a political party – however short-lived it might yet prove to be – with its desire to maintain organising strategies learned from years of women's community networking and interest group advocacy work. Essentially, this entails internalising the requirements of participatory democracy within the Coalition itself, and steering a path between the dangers of hierarchical decision-making and 'the tyranny of structurelessness'. To maintain its links with the wider women's movement, the Coalition has developed a report-back and consultative process by holding a series of public conferences. Although this has been constrained through lack of financial resources, it has managed to hold two consultative seminars with an open invitation list. The first looked at the issue of 'confidence-building measures' – including the decommissioning of arms – and some 100 women attended; while the second concentrated on 'influencing women's political power', with 155 in attendance. The concept behind these gatherings is to encourage a flow of ideas and views between the members of the Coalition and other women activists. The Coalition has engaged in this outreach work in the knowledge that if party politics is to become more participatory, it will have to find ways of becoming more inclusive of those outside of the electoral system. Unless this begins to happen, any 'new' forms of representative democracy will remain as sterile as before.

The NIWC had managed to do something that had eluded the women's movement in Northern Ireland for many years: unite and organise around an identity as women. In part the reason for this is practical, and in part political. Practically, the financial resources that came as a result of being elected enabled the NIWC delegates to operate as full participants in the process, and to have the time to meet with the membership or inform them by mail, on a regular basis. Politically, the application of the ethical framework grounded in principles and not ideologies allowed individuals within the NIWC to retain their own sense of identity within the group – not to have to deny their own allegiances – while simultaneously supporting the collective position. Additionally, the fact was that the prize on offer – peace in Northern Ireland – was so great that people were more prepared to submerge their own demands and desires for the collective good. Even at that, there has at times been a lack of clarity as to where responsibility for decision-making has been.

The question of sustainability remains open for debate. In the summer after the signing of the Agreement, and to date, attendance at the monthly meetings increased, as did NIWC membership. The monthly meetings have been incorporated into a constitution,[19] written in autumn 1998, and adopted at the NIWC's first party conference, held in Cookstown in November 1998. NIWC structures have evolved from and remained true to the organisational methods that developed from its inception. The writing of the constitution attempted to formalise the structures somewhat, clarifying internal decision-making processes, while maintaining the fluidity that served the NIWC well during the course of negotiations. The constitution now envisages a much longer life span for the NIWC than was initially planned – the duration of the negotiation process. That negotiation process continues, with many discussions about the way in which the Agreement is to be implemented. The Coalition still aims to 'promote the principles of inclusion, equality and human rights in every sphere of politics'[20] and this will continue to be the ethos that informs the methodology of the organisation.

As the political context changes, it is to be hoped that the objective of achieving and sustaining 'a balanced gender representation that reflects the eligible voting population, elected to the Northern Ireland Assembly and local government, Westminster and the European Parliament'[21] will become less necessary. The NIWC will no doubt lose some members from both the right and the left; the values at its core will continue to be tested. The experience of the NIWC undoubtedly suggests that a party based on strong values and principles can make a valuable contribution to a conflict resolution process. It is too soon to tell whether or not women's contributions will be valued in any post-conflict reconstruction which might emerge from the present, perilously poised reconciliation process.

What is becoming increasingly clear is that in entering the political process in Northern Ireland in such a sudden and dramatic manner, the Northern Ireland Women's Coalition moved beyond the comfort zone of lamenting and lobbying about the lack of women's involvement in decision-making. It entered the 'scene of the crime',[22] which brought with it an extensive range of responsibilities as well as opportunities. It is less interested in proving whether women are any better than men in resolving conflict than in being able to show how the process of peace-building can be done differently.

Notes

1 The republican and loyalist cease-fires in 1994 provided a catalyst for this change and encouraged women's organisations to further press their claim for greater political involvement. At a conference in Belfast in 1994, a group of republican women, Clár na mBan (A Woman's Agenda For Peace) argued for the increased participation of women in political negotiations relating to the future of the island and questioned the lack of accountability in the secret negotiations that has been taking place between John Hume and Gerry Adams. The European Women's Platform in Northern Ireland and the National Women's Council in the Republic articulated their concerns about being excluded from mainstream discussions in a conference held jointly between the two organisations in 1995. Miller *et al.* (1996) had completed a large-scale ESRC study on women and political participation in Northern Ireland which confirmed the lack of opportunities for women in mainstream decision-making. Rooney and Woods (1995) had also shown that women who were prepared to engage in community activism were much more reluctant to become involved in local government and of those who did, these women had encountered major obstacles in achieving even the most minimal political roles.

2 The Framework Document (HMSO 1995) was a key publication, jointly launched in Belfast by the prime minister, John Major, and the taoiseach, John Bruton. This signified that the two governments saw their proposals as the way ahead for Northern Ireland. The proposals dealt with the maintenance of the union with Great Britain, participatory government within Northern Ireland, north–south links between Northern Ireland and the Republic of Ireland, and east–west links between UK and the Republic. The proposals were built on previous declarations that Northern Ireland would stay part of the UK while a majority of its people desired it. If a majority voted against this at some future stage, it would become part of a united Ireland. The proposals also stipulated that any new administration in Northern Ireland would include Unionists and Nationalists and that north–south relations would be put on an intitutionalised footing through a new north–south body. The framework document was published in February 1995. When the peace talks commenced in June 1996, the negotiations were strongly focused on the two governments' proposals.

3 Monica McWilliams was at that time the course director for women's studies at the University of Ulster. Through the access and outreach programmes for women's studies alongside the well-established contacts with women's groups and community activists, a large database had been maintained which was utilised for women's conferences and events.

4 The proposal to hold elections was made by the British prime minister in January, 1996. It was sharply opposed by nationalists, republicans and, initially, the Irish government, and was viewed by many as the result of pressure by unionists on the weak conservative government. During the wrangling over this issue, the IRA ended its cease-fire on

9 February with a no-warning bomb at Canary Wharf in London. (For an excellent account of this and other aspects of the elections to the Peace Talks see Elliot 1997.)

5 This group is affiliated to the European Women's Lobby. It campaigns to raise awareness about EU policies on women and makes representations on women's issues in Northern Ireland to EU institutions. NIWEP's response was a paper entitled *Gender-Proofing the Electoral System and the Talks Fora* (1996a).

6 Ibid.:2 The paper recommended that if an index or list system was to be used, party lists should be published in advance of the election, so that the order in which candidates were placed could be made public. In the event of parties declaring that they were unable to persuade sufficient numbers of women to stand as candidates, women and men should be alternated until no women candidates remained.

   Should a multi-seat method be deployed, NIWEP felt (in common with the British Labour party) that party leaderships should give clear leadership and direction on equal opportunity selection to each constituency branch. Recommendations about a multi-seat STV system mirrored those of the list system – running equal numbers of men and women, for instance, or providing for equal access to safe seats for men and women candidates.

   Noting that parties themselves and the selection systems they use to identify candidates are key gatekeepers to how well women do in political life, NIWEP made additional comments on pre-election preparation. Parties should take an active role in recruiting women to put themselves forward, clear criteria for selection should be agreed and candidate selection committees or conventions should be trained in the process of selection, with attention being paid to equal opportunities guidelines. The paper drew attention to the 1996 case concerning women-only shortlists used by the Labour Party in Britain, in which a tribunal ruled that the selection of candidates for a shortlist is considered tantamount to an interview for employment. NIWEP cautioned parties that men-only lists might lead to a presumption that there had been discrimination.

7 Two further papers were issued: on 26 March *Methods of Allocating Seats* and on 1 April *Designation of Parties for Election*. The latter caused controversy. The government proposed to include, in the legislation setting up the elections, a list of 15 parties which it thought would encompass the widest possible range of political positions (HMSO 1996b). Many smaller and radical parties found this objectionable, and when the Bill was published on 17 April 30 parties were listed.

8 The system proposed was complex. 90 candidates were to be elected using constituency lists and 20 from a regional list. The Droop quota was used to determine the number of votes needed per seat in any constituency – by dividing the total number of valid votes cast by the number of seat plus one. Those who reached the quota or multiples of it were given seats. The D'Hondt method was then deployed to calculate seats in the event of portions of quotas over awarded seats, or under seats not awarded. By this method the total number of votes for each party was divided by the number of seats it attained, plus one.

The additional 20 seats were awarded to the ten parties which had accrued the largest number of votes across the region.

9 The signatories to the letter were Bronagh Hinds, NIWEP; Margaret Logue, Derry Women's Centre; May Blood, Shankill Women's Forum; Monica McWilliams, Centre for Research on Women, University of Ulster; Kathleen Feenan, Women's Information Group and Kate Fearon, Democratic Dialogue.

10 Personal communication from Bronagh Hinds to the authors.

11 *Women's News*, Belfast, June/July 1996 (*passim*) Some of those signed the letter subsequently qualified their position further (*Jacobson* 1997).

12 The papers were: *Inclusion and Accommodation, Human Rights, Equity, The Mitchell Commission, Conflict, Peace and Settlement, Women in Power Structures and Decision-Making, Employment, Education and Training, Poverty, Rural Areas, Violence against Women, Community Relations, Environment Strategy* and *Northern Ireland – Basic Facts*. Most were written by Bronagh Hinds; the paper on human rights was written by Christine Bell, then chair of the Campaign for the Administration of Justice, while Avila Kilmurray prepared the one on equity.

13 'Perceived religion' is a phrase used in Northern Ireland, particularly in employment recruitment, to identify a person's background, even if the person is not practising any religion, in order to monitor the backgrounds of job applicants and employees.

14 The Orange Order and the Apprentice Boys are the two main Protestant institutions responsible for organising parades which commemorate victorious battles. When these parades pass through predominantly Catholic areas, they become extremely contentious events. An independent body has been established by government to make decisions on disputed routes, but there are still many cases of riots, arson and clashes with police officers as a result of the antagonism between local residents who oppose the parades and members of the loyal orders who demand their right to march.

15 Roisin McAliskey was allowed to remain in hospital with her baby and when she was eventually released by the home secretary, almost a year later, the charges against her were dropped.

16 As a result of her public comments on their behaviour in the Assembly, Monica McWilliams has been issued with high-court writs from Ian Paisley and his son. The BBC has also been issued with writs.

17 See Fearon and McWilliams (1999).

18 This also has the effect of minimising the votes of those choosing to designate as 'Others'. In a cross-community vote 'Others' votes are not counted, since the procedure requires 40 per cent of Nationalists and Unionists only to be in favour of the motion for it to be passed.

19 It is interesting to note that one of the difficulties in the debate over the constitution was not just the wording of various clauses, but about the fact that it could have explicitly declared the NIWC did not want to be political party. Many women still, after two years of involvement in the NIWC, did not want to be associated with the term 'political party'. In the end 'organisation' was used to describe the NIWC in the constitution. In early 1999, though, there was much less objection to

the NIWC registering as a political party as required by new legislation, which it has done.
20 *Ibid.*
21 NIWC Constitution, November 1998.
22 This phrase comes from the poem *It's a Woman's World*, in which Eavan Boland wrote 'As far as history goes, we were never on the scene of the crime.'

References

Elliot, S. (1997) 'The Northern Ireland Forum/Entry to Negotiation', Elections 1996, *Irish Political Studies*, 12, 111–22.

Fearon, K. and McWilliams, M. (1999) 'The Good Friday Agreement: A Triumph of Substance Over Style', *Fordham International Law Journal*, 22(4), 1250–72.

HMSO (1995) *A New Framework For Agreement*, London: HMSO.

HMSO (1996a) *The Framework for a Broadly Acceptable Process Leading to All Party Negotiations*, London: HMSO, 21 March.

HMSO (1996b) *Designation of Parties for the Forthcoming election in Northern Ireland*, London: HMSO, 1 April.

Jacobson, R. (1997) *Whose Peace Process? Women's Organisations and Political Settlement in Northern Ireland, 1996–1997*, University of Bradford, Peace Studies Papers.

Loughran, C. (1986) 'Armagh and Feminist Strategy', *Feminist Review*, 23, 59–80.

McWilliams, M. (1995) 'Struggling Peace and Justice: Reflections on Women's Activism in Northern Ireland', *Journal of Women's History*, 6(4), 13–39.

Miller, R. L. Wilford, R. and Donaghue, F. (1996) *Women and Political Participation in Northern Ireland*, Aldershot: Avebury.

Mitchell, G. (1999) *Making Peace*, New York: Alfred Knopf.

NIWC (1996a) *NIWC Operation*, Belfast: NIWC Archive.

NIWC (1996b) *NIWC Synopsis*, Belfast: NIWC Archive.

NIWC (1998) *NIWC Constitution,* Belfast: NIWC Archive.

NIWEP (1996) *Gender-Proofing the Election System and the Talks*, Belfast: NIWEP, 19 March.

NIWEP (1996b) *Designation of Parties for the Forthcoming Election in Northern Ireland: A Response by NIWEP on Behalf of Women in Northern Ireland*, Belfast: NIWEP, 10 April.

Porter, E. McWilliams, M. (1995) *Women, Politics and Ways Forward*, Conference Report, Belfast: University of Ulster.

Rooney, E. and Woods, M. (1995) *Women Community and Politics in Northern Ireland: A Research Project with an Action Outcome*, Jordanstown: University of Ulster.

Roulston, C. (1997) 'Women on the Margin: The Women's Movement in Northern Ireland, 1973–1995', in West, 41–58.

West, Lois A. (ed.) (1997) *Feminist Nationalisms*, New York: Routledge.

Women's News (1996) 'Letter to NIWC', *Women's News* (Belfast), June/July.

Part III
Debate and Dialogue

7

Participatory Democracy and the Challenge of Dialogue across Difference

Elisabeth Porter

Women are active in democratic, participatory practices in Northern Ireland, as the case-studies outlined in the previous chapters testify. In this chapter, I explore what the diverse case-studies add to understandings of democratic processes. What hope do the studies present for a future of equal participation between diverse perspectives? To answer this question, I examine three major issues: public participation and pluralism, creating a dialogue across difference, and deliberative democracy and difference. Particularly with the first two issues, I build on the arguments outlined in Part I of this book to assess the implications of the case-studies for a feminist critique of gender, democracy and inclusion in Northern Ireland. I also draw extensively on feminist theorists to argue that what is often missing in political debate is a preparedness to change, a recognition of the partial and situated character of knowledge and identities, and an excitement about the possibilities that participatory dialogue can engender. The third section looks beyond the case-studies toward the emancipatory potential of deliberative democracy to foster dialogue across difference. As an Australian, living in Belfast, my interpretations are those of an insider–outsider.

Public participation and pluralism

Politics of participation

All of the case-studies in Part II of this book demonstrate an understanding of politics as an activity irreducible to representative government. The women involved in the women's centre, an inter-faith community, a trade union, as well as in political coalition, accept politics as a 'collective and participatory engagement of citizens in the determination of the affairs of their community' (Dietz 1992:75). Democracy is understood as the form of politics that enables people to come together as active citizens, the combination of speech and action is what makes us political agents, and it is the public space that makes the participation political.

Participatory democracy is based on the desire, indeed on the demand for political inclusion. Such demand for what Anne Phillips calls 'a political presence' often comes from groups which 'see themselves as marginalised or silenced or excluded' (1995:5). The need to express distinctive voices is strong. Participatory democracy requires participatory structures 'in which active people, with their geographic, ethnic, gender, and occupational differences, assert their perspectives on social issues within institutions that encourage the representation of their distinct voices' (Young 1990:116). In Northern Ireland, the very contested, conflictual nature of distinctiveness makes participatory democracy highly problematic in an everyday pragmatic sense. Later, I explore in more depth why this is so, and how feminists suggest some of the obstacles may be overcome. It is important to note, however, that not all political participation is positive. Although political activity can promote sectarianism or terrorism, the concern in this book is with democratic processes of inclusion.

Inclusive democratic participation is crucial, because when distinctive voices are suppressed, or differences are not recognised, or there is a compulsion toward consensus, the purposes of democratic participation are undermined, 'for the benefits of thinking things through together are lessened when some voices are not heard' (Bickford 1996:16). It is this collective participation of thought, discussion and activity that is central to democratic inclusiveness. Mary Dietz summarises the constructive possibilities of democratic citizenship as being threefold: 'its relation is that of civic peers; its guiding virtue is mutual respect; its primary principle is the "positive liberty" of democracy and self-government' (1992:75). That is, participation is carried out with other equal citizens, it presupposes a respect for all citizens and it promotes self-determination.

A consequence of the increased political presence of women (or other previously marginalised groups) who express their uniqueness through participatory democracy is a decided sense of empowerment. Empowerment to Marli Karl 'is a process of awareness and capacity building leading to greater participation, to greater decision-making and control, and to transformative action' (1995:14). The nature of these transformative processes is significant, both in a feminist sense and in breaking down destructive barriers within a conflict society. The sort of empowerment that emerges as women discover the importance of political participation 'breaks the boundaries between the public and the private domain' because the participation connects the personal, social, communal and political worlds (Yuval-Davis 1994:180). In refusing oppositions between the individual and community, knower and known, reason and emotion, society and nature, feminism offers an alternative framework.

However, barriers to feminist transformative political processes are immense and particularly so in a conflict society. Many women are still learning the skills of empowerment, while others seem comfortable with traditional femininity or are hostile to feminism. Empowered women become tired of the stresses involved in combining the triple load of paid work, domestic labour and child-rearing with always having to fight against patriarchal values and structures. Cynthia Cockburn (Chapter 5), in examining the Northern Ireland Public Service Alliance (NIPSA), maintains that the demands of negotiating and being part of the trade union culture are perceived by many women as discordant with their characteristic qualities and lives. The discord relates particularly to the need within trade unions for a ruthless toughness, a refusal to give in and an ability to stand one's ground. Similarly, Kate Fearon and Monica McWilliams (Chapter 6) from the Northern Ireland Women's Coalition (NIWC) outline the barriers feminist elected representatives face in a strongly patriarchal society in wanting to serve 'women's interests' without assuming that interests of childcare, welfare, care of the old and sick, education and housing are essentially 'women's interests' (see Porter 1998a). Carmel Roulston (Chapter 2) explains how further barriers in Northern Ireland relate to a culture that is resistant to compromise or accommodation, reluctant to abandon a sectarian zero-sum mentality where a gain for one is a loss for the others.

It is not that women cannot be politically tough, because they can and many are. It is rather that their prime nurturing roles, adopted through choice, coercion and/or socialisation require women to be flexible, accommodating and compassionate. Further, many women and men who are sympathetic to feminism and decent relationships value highly those traits traditionally associated with femininity, like cooperation, non-hierarchical modes of operating, adaptability and nurturance. An apt example of this valuation is both the women and men in Cornerstone (Chapter 4) who prefer a consensual form of discussion and decision-making and shy away from resolving conflicts through the exercise of power. The NIWC is unafraid to exercise power and combines its authority with the goal of inclusive, feminist modes of operating. The politics of participation is about maximising political inclusion, and the case-studies are examples of encouraging women to participate more actively and meaningfully.

Repoliticising the public

This emphasis on participation requires a certain notion of politics, and here Hannah Arendt's ideas are pertinent. Arendt's ideas reinforce the civic-republican tradition of politics which stresses active citizenship, civic engagement, political deliberation and responsibility (Weeks 1993:197). Civic republicanism repoliticises the public sphere (Phillips 1991:48). Maurizio Passerin d Entrevès highlights the significance Arendt gives to the public sphere, political agency and collective identity. First, the public sphere expands to encompass the sphere 'where citizens interact through the medium of speech and persuasion, disclose their unique identities, and decide through collective deliberation about matters of common concern' (d'Entrevès 1992:146). Second, whenever we engage in action and political discourse we are 'engaging in the constitution of our collective identity' (*ibid.*:158). It is through articulating one's position, no matter how confusing it is, through definition and redefinition, through negotiation and renegotiation, through defence and offence of competing conceptions of political legitimacy, culture and identity that individual agency is expressed and collective identity is cemented. Third, this collective identity allows what Nancy Fraser (1986:425–9) calls, 'the standpoint of the *collective concrete other*'. Through political deliberation and action with others, political agency is exercised and thus citizenship is reaffirmed because there is a lived experience of having a meaningful say in the conditions which define our socio-political lives.

The question of agency cannot be assumed for those women who struggle (both within themselves and against men or structures) to realise their potential. All women have political capacities; realising these through political agency leads to empowerment. Cockburn thus is right to draw attention to Nancy Hartsock's (1983) ideas on power, that people have the choice between shaping power as domination over people or shaping it as a capacity, a capability to exert influence. Certainly, there is no avoiding the fact that trade unions are fissured by power relations as axes of difference in collectivities and in search for effectiveness. We would expect individuals in trade unions to be confident in their capacities to be powerful. Also, for elected representatives, their entire work context is within a nexus of power struggles, wherein their efficacy as agents is tested daily. However, we cannot assume that all women have developed their capacities likewise, as the other case-studies suggest.

One key concern is to broaden the political sphere in ways that are inclusionary. Hence what is public 'is what is open and accessible. The public is in principle not exclusionary' (Young 1990:119). To cater for the fact that accessible public spaces should expect different voices whose experiences and perspectives are diverse, Young proposes that participatory democracy should promote 'the ideal of a heterogeneous public, in which persons stand forth with their differences acknowledged and respected' (1990:119). The ideal should translate into 'layers of heterogeneous publics that guarantee respect for the cultural specificity and needs of different groups' (Young 1993:142). What Young means by this notion of 'heterogeneous publics' is that social groups are differently placed in society, depending on their past history, gender, ethnicity, able-bodiment, class, national identity, and their specificity must be given a place within politics in order to promote just policies.

A good example of inclusivity is the commitment by Cornerstone to live in houses on the 'peace line', on the interface between Catholic and Protestant housing districts, as a stand against the narrow-mindedness perpetuated by residential segregation and as a commitment to those who have suffered some of the most violent effects of the troubles and where social deprivation and poverty dominates. Similarly, the Chrysalis Women's Centre, based in an area of socio-economic deprivation reaches to the diversity of local women who are Travellers, Vietnamese, Bengali, Irish and British, although this is a qualified inclusiveness where relatively few Protestant women attend. Questions have to be asked why this is so. The NIWC is inclusive in its community, class and regional membership as well as in its broad negotiating goals to encompass all democratic parties and viable political options. The active participatory nature of shared political endeavours must be compatible with democratic pluralism. As Chantal Mouffe explains, 'somebody who *acts* as a citizen, who conceives of herself as a participant in a collective undertaking [gains an] idea of politics as the realm where we can recognize ourselves as participants in a community' (1992:4–5).

Participation in communities

Participation in communities of family, work, social, leisure, church, neighbourhood networks and politics is fundamental to Northern Irish culture. The question is how to make our belonging to different communities 'compatible with our common belonging to a political community' (Mouffe 1993:80). This question is central to the conflict in Northern Ireland, the answer thus is crucial to democratic processes that promote reconciliation between plural citizens. Herein lie enormous difficulties. To survive, communities need to be sustained through common practices, symbols and activities that affirm identity and the uniqueness of communities. However, 'community' is often used to preserve and re-invent our differences, to protect our individual and collective diversity (Weeks 1993:200). Pressures toward accepting communal consensus preserve communal boundaries but suppress the voices of those with differing views. When identity and difference is fixed or closed, community is a focus of retreat for those with the same identity to return to. Closed communities are welcoming to their own who conform, and fiercely rejecting of those who dissent or are unlike them. While it is the supposed 'good of the community' which acts as a 'moral imperative', the tendency to see any change as a threat results in 'an extremely conservative ideology' (Yuval-Davis 1997:8).

While openness and inclusiveness are central norms of feminist moral and political discourse, Alison Jaggar (1998) gives some interesting examples of groups who limit discursive openness and restrict participation by excluding those who do not share basic commitments. Her examples include prostitute groups who maintain that middle-class feminists are ignorant of their real conditions, North African women who assert that western feminists do not understand the purpose of clitoridectomy in African culture and some lesbians who exclude heterosexual women from discussing lesbian practices. Jaggar perceptively notes that these groups struggle to maintain self-respect and cultural integrity, hence communities' resistance to outside scrutiny 'may be interpreted less as an attempt to limit the discursive autonomy of others than as a claim to discursive autonomy for themselves' (1998:10). I agree with Jaggar that endemic to closed communities are epistemological and moral dangers of repression, dogmatism, intellectual dishonesty and self-deception, therefore, 'in order to increase the degree to which their moral agreements are justified, communities ultimately must open their basic commitments to critical scrutiny from the outside' (1998:15).

The case-studies in this book are in stark contrast to this closed understanding of community. Indeed, the epistemic communities that have been discussed share fundamental interests in coming together in ways that are emancipatory, and allow for a range of identities. The Cornerstone community works with other local community groups, content to display a 'doctrine of difference' over those areas in which Christians can disagree and yet still work together. The Chrysalis Centre acknowledges diversity. Accepting variance is fundamental to the NIWC's creation of a politics of inclusion, but its support comes largely from community-based and voluntary organisations and educated women. However, the nature of all shared values remains renegotiable, subject to change, flux and variation. The debates needed to ascertain common goals are almost always fraught with tension and hence political communities must be amenable to working with conflict, division, even antagonism. There is a time for discursive affirmation as well as a time for engagement with the other. In different ways, the examples above create space for these varied times.

Creating a dialogue across difference

In order to foster inclusive pluralist participation, there are certain essential conditions that, when put in practice, foster those processes that create dialogue across difference. I suggest there are four conditions that ought to be accepted: equality and difference are compatible; identities are partial, multiple, contested and negotiable; solidarity is a product of political debate; and respect for diversity undergirds all creative dialogue across difference. I discuss each essential condition in turn, tying them into the practical instances of dialogue and democratic practice explored in earlier chapters.

Equality and difference

Feminist theory exposes the mythical nature of a natural equality as well as exploding the equality-versus-difference option. The distinction between equality and difference has played a significant part in the constitution of two separate spheres of society, 'a public, political sphere of equal citizens, and a private, non-political realm in which difference, including gender difference, may be recognized and expressed' (Bock and James 1992:8). This distinction strengthens public–private and male–female polarisations. A neutral equality neuters; it assumes that to be equal, one must be the same. Such a notion provides no space for specificity such as sexual difference. The equal versus difference option assumes that we cannot have both equality and difference, because, as Elizabeth Grosz maintains, 'difference is understood in terms of inequality, distinction, or opposition' (1994:91). Arguments defending a same and difference option are circular and cannot escape homogeneity. Post-modern feminists of difference like Grosz assume equality but emphasise 'the right to be and to act differently' (1994:91). Cockburn, in looking at how '*differences differ*' (Chapter 5:108) examines the blockages between equality as sameness and the relativism of difference that may reduce identity politics to a one-dimensional stereotype. Yet she notes that shifting gender issues into the mainstream of policy-making is often an excuse to close down special structures developed for women's differences.

In support of the first condition of accepting that equality *and* difference are compatible, the important question is one Phillips raises, namely, 'how can democracies deliver on equality while accommodating and indeed welcoming difference?' (1993:2). Jane Flax answers in terms of 'an ethics of multiplicity' (1998:153) whereby rather than renouncing '"difference" to open space for "other" forms of identity, all subjects are viewed as mutually and multiply constituted' (1998:145). However, I disagree with her advocacy of suspicion and distrust toward one's 'own wishes and a deep scepticism towards an innocence of any political or subject positions' (1998:153). It is important to keep asking critical questions about one's situation and goals and to contemplate the motives of others; however, in an intensely divided society, where deeply felt hatred and bitterness exists, anything that increases hostility or distrust is counter-productive *in dealing ethically with multiplicity*. One of the most positive contributions individuals, groups and institutions can make is to confront 'the other' without suspicion, in a spirit of open equality.

Davina Cooper also links equality and ethics when she talks of 'an ethics of "sustainable equality of empowerment", the belief that people should have an equal ability to impact upon society and achieve their preferences' (1995:3). She argues that this ethics goes

beyond 'equal respect' or any formal parity of respect to a meaningful 'equal capacity to *achieve* their notion of the good life and
to contribute to the ways in which civil and political society are
shaped' (1995:147). In her trade union case-study, Cockburn maintains that for a group to be effective in a trade union they need
access to decision-making, status to negotiate, and to have group
concerns lodged on bargaining agendas. In discussing Cornerstone,
Roulston refers to the importance cross-community groups give to
confidence-building and empowerment strategies given the prevail-
ing high social deprivation and unemployment, poverty and demoral-
isation. The translation of respect into achievement and contribution
is an admirable ideal. Equality and difference are compatible. In
Northern Ireland, however, the basic minimal equal respect is not
yet granted to all by all.

Identities as partial and multiple

Part of the reason why many individuals in Northern Ireland remain wary of difference and refuse to grant 'due recognition' (N.
Porter 1998:191) is their reluctance to accept, let alone embrace,
the second essential condition, that cultural, national and political
identities are multiple, negotiable and gloriously rich, not singular,
fixed and exceptionally limited. Too often, literature, media and
community organisations talk of identity as if it is polarised around
two options: one is from the Irish, Catholic, republican, nationalist community (or some combination of these dimensions), or one
is from the British, Protestant, loyalist, unionist community (or some
combination). Indeed, the terms 'two communities' or 'two traditions' are commonly used. Not only does this reduction ignore
cross-overs that occur through marriage, political belief or cultural
attraction; it also ignores individuals who defy categorisation, who
despise stereotypes, who have changed significantly, or who like
me, come from other national, ethnic and cultural heritages. However, the reality is that there is sound reason why language pivots
around 'two traditions': it signals a major conflict of interest, in
that there are cultural traditions that not only differ from each
other but also contain individuals who see 'the other' as wholly
alien, as enemy, or at least, as strange other. Communities like
Cornerstone encourage conversations that expose this, allowing doubts
and questions as well as ideals and principles to be open to public
scrutiny. The Chrysalis Women's Centre seeks to cope with the
diverse needs of women in the local area. The NIWC has achieved

a remarkable combination of membership from all types of backgrounds and openly negotiates with all political parties.

Perhaps it is because women, blacks and other ethnic minorities, and persons from what is now the Third World, have for so long been taken to represent 'the other', that feminist theorists, writers of colour and post-colonial authors present a wealth of material on reinterpreting differences and the complexity of the other. For example, Lata Mani describes the politics of location or 'the relation between experience and knowledge' as 'not one of correspondence, but fraught with history, contingency and struggle' (1992:308). That is, being born into a Protestant family in Northern Ireland ascribes an identity connected to the Protestant cultural tradition, but does not simplistically mean that this person wants to adopt the British baggage, while being born into a Catholic family might instil into one the pain of discrimination and national uncertainty.

To use another example, Cockburn approached NIPSA with questions of gender equity, and realised the multiplicity of issues related, like religion, class, political opinion, sector, locality, age, marital status, dis/ability, colour, race, ethnicity, nationality and sexuality. Each of these issues expresses, as Cockburn puts it, 'cross-cutting needs'. Cockburn draws attention to the problems in recruiting from both 'Catholic' and 'Protestant' workers. The terms are contestable, drawing on ancient ethnic distinctions, political divergences, religious beliefs that may not exist and power differences. They also falsely identify those who have neither a clear belonging nor a desire for one. Monitoring background is an important part of promoting equal opportunities in order to combat discrimination, but it may be divisive in always stressing distinctions. In a culture where religion permeates the public and private, even though individuals are not necessarily strong believers, interdenominational acts of worship, accepted elsewhere as important aspects of ecumenicism, are viewed by the majority as scandalous and outrageous. Therefore, the worship in Cornerstone constitutes a brave, necessary and powerful challenge to insular and sectarian beliefs. The past affects the present but does not dictate the future. We are who we are through our histories, but many of us strive to defy supposedly inevitable cultural certainties.

Subversion can be a positive response to the partiality of identities. It is not that identities are 'partial' in the sense of being immature or not formed, rather that they are constantly changing. Subversion thus need not be destructive, but ensures that we keep taking critical checks on where we are heading, why, what sort of person we are, and what are our goals for society. In an important sense, in Northern Ireland, interaction with women from the supposed 'other community' or 'other tradition' is crucial to demystify, expose the lies or truths of stereotypes, and to subvert fixed images of each other. 'A feminist orientation to the politics of difference means that we each recognize that any standpoint we take is necessarily partial and based on the way in which we are positioned in relation to class, race, education' (Pringle and Watson 1992:69), as well as to ethnicity, conflict, colonialism, police and security force harassment, national identity and political division. Identities are formed through the interaction of multiple discourses which confuse, conflict, contradict and shape the persons we are. The more varied the interaction with people from all types of background, the more partiality can produce a richness of identity.

One's specific location is bound up with individual, communal and national identity. Elsewhere, I argue that with reference to women in Northern Ireland, there are both positive and divisive aspects to identity politics (Porter 1997a, 1997b, 1998a, 1998b). In a positive way, identity politics can empower women who have been marginalised by giving expression to that which has been suppressed. Also, the partial nature of identity encourages alliances by concentrating on the common concerns of overlapping identities. However, identity politics are divisive when it is exclusionary or undermines others through insularity and closure. In a fundamental way, identity politics necessarily are exclusionary.

What then allows coalitions like the NIWC to recognise and value different identities? Coalitions cannot assume a perceived unity or homogeneity, but rather, 'transversal politics' are 'based on dialogues which give recognition to the specific positionings of those who participate in them as well as to the "unfinished knowledge" that each such situated positioning can offer' (Yuval-Davis 1994:194, also 1996:23). Being able simultaneously to remain 'rooted' in one's specificity while 'shifting' to try to understand the other is no easy task. It 'does not assume that the dialogue is boundariless, and that each conflict of interest is reconcilable' (1994:194). It does accept identity as a political category that is 'a partial, transitory and temporary position to promote change and alliance rather than enclosure and division' (Burman 1994:155).

Given partiality, I find the idea of 'transitional spaces' to be helpful in working toward democratic possibilities. Flax explains that transitional phenomena or practices help us to manage the frustration and aggression engendered by the inevitable gaps between our wishes and ways of resolving conflict and those of others. They enable us to make creative use of the difference of others and of different sorts of relations. (1993:124)

We cannot all have our wishes fulfilled, particularly in a culture accustomed to a win–lose mentality. Nevertheless, transitional spaces 'help us to play with, tolerate, appreciate, or imagine ways to re-make the variety of relations, authority, and rules we find present in the external world' (1993:125). Given life's complexities, these spaces enable us to move back and forth within multiple locations, as women, lovers, mothers, colleagues, activists, negotiators, community workers, church members, political participants, equal citizens of difference.

Transitional spaces should ward off the fear of ambiguity, uncertainty, ambivalence and difference. They should be seen as the locale of possible discoveries. Such opportunities existed in the time of the cease-fires, during the Multi-Party Peace Talks, and after signing the 1998 Good Friday Agreement. Those who have placed massive obstacles in the way of political progress are responsible for having stymied the welfare and well-being that could accompany devolution, the formation of the Executive, Assembly and cross-border bodies attending to citizens' everyday needs.

In this section, I have argued so far that in order to create dialogue across difference, equality and difference must be accepted as compatible, and that identities are multiply constituted. In order to prepare the ground further for exploring feminist theories of dialogue, I now turn to two further conditions to be accepted and put into practice, namely that solidarity is a product of political debate, and then to the need to respect diversity.

Solidarity through political discussion

Given the feminist value placed on difference, activists need no longer be plagued with any precondition for unity prior to forming alliances. As Martha Minow puts it, 'solidarity does not arise from understandings prior to politics, but instead politics permits its construction' (1997:145). I am not suggesting that unity is not important, because I believe it is. However, unity cannot be presumed, but where it does exist, it is a product of political discussion and struggle among people of diverse backgrounds, experiences and interests who are differently situated in matrices of power and privilege. The process of discussion and disagreement among feminists forges a common commitment to a politics against oppression that produces the identity 'woman' as a coalition. (Young 1997:21).

What is common is not individual identity but the collective coming together in political processes around a purpose. It is through the practice of solidarity that the uniqueness of difference is recognised (Jones 1996:90) as Sara Ruddick aptly expresses it, in 'particular situations of struggle' and suffering (1989:240).

It is thus the common interest that cements a commitment to solidarity, gives a coalition a group identity and has 'the potential to unite the fragments' (Lister 1997:80). In the women's centre, the interests concern developing women's capacities; in the religious community, there is the belief that Christian values should motivate reconciliatory practices; in trade unions, employment rights and active participation are central; and with the NIWC, common interests revolve around inclusion, equity and socio-economic well-being for all. As the Introduction informs the reader, all of these groups ensure that women's distinctiveness and diversity are incorporated into decision-making processes and structures. Identities shift. The boundaries of solidarity are rarely fixed. Coalitions are always negotiable. As Simona Sharoni, writing in the context of the Israel–Palestinian conflict puts it, the success of alliances hinges on constantly renegotiating the terms of solidarity (1995:141, 147). Accommodation and compromise discourage hostility. I agree with Judith Squires that a radical pluralism that embraces solidarity and difference should accept 'that dissent is inevitable, and yet also demand a grammar of conduct – a minimum shared sense of belonging as a basis for political co-existence' (1993:8).

Coalition and compromise are crucial. Roulston (Chapter 4) notes that, for religious communities, joint activities often pivot around issues which do not directly touch the national question. Groups share a desire to have a common bond (of faith, spiritual growth, or a desire to alleviate socio-economic distress) which may reduce the negative effects of discussion on political difference. However, even where discussion on controversy is limited, it is unavoidable. The example Roulston uses is the different attitudes of Cornerstone members to the 1980 hunger strikes by republican prisoners; the

Protestants regarded the idea that young men would die for a dream as an outrageous waste, whereas Catholics saw it as a heroic sacrifice. Despite real difference of view, the outcome was that 'In the end they agreed to disagree.' This is a mature response – it acknowledges fundamental, major differences, but it permits the continuation of a healthy working relationship within the framework of difference.

While alliances between Catholic–nationalist and Protestant–unionist women's groups have been successful on practical issues related to socio-economic reasons, the feminist movement has been fragmented as women have been pulled in different directions by the nationalist–unionist conflict. The formation of the NIWC presents the first major political coalition of women. Cockburn's definition is useful: the crux of an alliance is *'a creative structure of a relational space between collectivities marked by problematic differences'* (1998:211). Rather than requiring women to yield a set of allegiances or loyalties in the name of unified feminism, the NIWC attempts to include women as having multiple identities. Such inclusion requires complex processes including: meetings where disagreements over disarmament or oaths of allegiance are negotiated; information sessions; seminars and conferences held in various regions. What is key to this example is the emergent nature of solidarity whereby a pluralist politics of participation is being created.

Respect for diversity

To reiterate, dialogue across difference requires: equality, negotiable identities, solidarity, and respect. Respect is fundamental to appreciating diversity and the need for a meaningful interdependence. All polities thrive on the multivaried nature of human talent. Seyla Benhabib writes that what is shocking is not the inevitable dialectic of identity and difference, 'but rather the atavistic belief that identities can be maintained and secured only by eliminating difference and otherness' (1996:3). Differences are central to identity and 'it is not our differences which separate women, but our reluctance to recognize these differences and to deal effectively with the distortions which have resulted from the ignoring and misnaming of those differences' (Lorde 1992:53). Jodi Dean (1996) describes a way to develop solidarity whereby citizens accept themselves as strange and needing explanation and justification rather than viewing the stranger as peculiar other. We are all part of the richness of diversity.

'A creative handling of difference is central to democratic processes' (Cockburn 1998:214). Why? Minow answers succinctly: '[A] just politics should try to do justice to the differences among people' (1997:145). I am arguing along with Selma Sevenhuijsen that there is a moral obligation to respect diversity, and that this respect can strengthen democratic citizenship 'if we accept, in the spirit of Arendt (1958), that the most fundamental task of democratic societies is to find just ways of dealing with plurality' (Sevenhuijsen 1998:145–6). Linking a moral imperative to respect diversity with justice 'explicitly opens discursive space for deliberating about what constitutes *injustice*' (1998:145). The Cornerstone community appreciates that working-class or unemployed people face more pressures, which leads them to act in hostile ways, and that they have few opportunities to encounter their counterparts from the 'other community' in neutral arenas. Peace initiatives that focus on the needs of economically disadvantaged groups bring a concern for equality and social justice as important dimensions of peace-building and reconciliation.

All efforts to build peace are valuable, and peace-building should not be exclusively linked with women. Peace-building respects diversity and the possible alliances that common interests allow. The NIWC has developed key values which require that other traditions are respected. Respect for diversity underlies these values as well as a concern for justice, equity, open-ended inclusive dialogue, accommodation and workable solutions. The NIWC does not adopt an uncritical expression of difference. A 'position that respects diversity, makes space for different forms of individuality, and seeks grounds for commonality . . . adopts a *principled approach to the politics of difference*' (Porter 1997a:92). Any assertion of difference that harms, or may 'lead to victimization, intimidation or oppression is unjustified' (1997a:93). My argument is that a principled approach to difference affirms those differences that maintain a respect for others' differences.

To summarise the discussion so far, at the beginning I asserted the importance of public participation to permit plural voices. The public is heterogeneous, broadly defined to include all open accessible spaces, and participation in communities fosters civic engagement. Following this, I set out the processes necessary to create a dialogue across difference, namely that participatory democracy proceeds on the four moral assumptions that: persons are equal and different; identities are constituted in various socio-political situations; solidarity comes through political discussion; and a respect for diversity is foundational to dialogue across difference. In the final part of this chapter, I turn to examine suggestions feminist theorists make on the ideals underlying deliberative democracy, and conclude with explaining the challenge of listening as well as of speaking.

Deliberative democracy and difference

Language allows us to make sense of ourselves, and 'making sense of ourselves is what produces identity' (Spivak 1992:177) and therefore difference. In this final section, I explain why I consider a feminist understanding of deliberative democracy to be helpful in providing ideals to aspire toward. These understandings make selective use of Jürgen Habermas's concepts of communicative action, particularly his conditions of practical discourse (1990:89). Chambers summarises these conditions as follows: '[E]very actor affected by the norm may enter discourse; each participant must be allowed an equal opportunity to be heard; anything may be questioned, challenged and defended; no one may use force or deception to sway participants' (Chambers 1995:165). All forms of discussion can be challenged and need to be defended. Closure cannot be enforced unilaterally. Implementing domination-free communication may appear to be impossible; however I believe that ideals are worth defining and striving toward.

Additionally, as Jaggar notes, what makes a feminist conception of practical moral discourse distinctive 'is that it addresses directly issues of discursive equality and openness in situations inevitability structured by power' (1998:8). Providing sound reason in rational debate is constructive; it is in contrast to the destructive consequences of a refusal to engage, sanctions, preconditions, force and threats of terrorism that are typical in Northern Ireland. In articulating reasons in public, the individual has 'to think of what would count as a good reason for all others involved. One is thus forced to think from the standpoint of all involved for whose agreement one is "wooing"' (Benhabib 1996:71–2).

Deliberation and communication

Deliberative democracy is explicitly idealistic. The ideals start 'from the idea that each of us must be given access to and heard at the bar of informed ethical and political debate' (Frazer and Lacey 1993:203). An acceptance of the imperative to dialogue across difference provides the ethical impulse. The common core of deliberative or communicative democracy 'is that political engagement can change initial statements of preference and interest' (Phillips 1995:149). Phillips explains that 'deliberation matters only because there *is* difference' and that when dialogue is opened to difference, 'this is the point of closest contact with the politics of presence' (1995:150–51). Deliberation through communication accepts the complexity of difference, allows new positions to be formulated, accepts that not all conflicts can be resolved and makes possible new solutions by exposing protagonists to the widest spectrum of options. *Deliberative democracy relies on reciprocity*, the mutual respect which 'requires a favourable attitude toward, and constructive interaction with, the persons with whom one disagrees' (Gutmann and Thompson 1996:79).

Deliberation assumes that given the centrality of conflict in politics, it is essential to argue about interests and ends. Hence Susan Bickford contends that what makes adversarial communicative interaction possible is not consensus or even friendship, but 'a quality of *attention* inherent in the very practice of deliberation' (1996:25). Bickford stresses that this 'attention to the perceptions of one's fellow citizens' need not be warmly emotive, it 'can be strategic or grudging' (1996:41) but it keeps the conflict political rather than personalising it in the vindictive manner which the NIWC have had to face. While I accept Bickford's point about strategy, I think that where the attention is lacking in goodwill there can be no reconciliation. The goal of deliberative democracy is not to work through differences to an agreement; it is to attend to the variety of differences in order to formulate new possibilities and solutions. Reconciliation takes this goal further in that its spirit of acceptance is genuinely open to the other and to the changes this openness requires in our selves.

Young prefers to use the term 'communicative' rather than 'deliberative' in order 'to indicate an equal privileging of any forms of communicative interaction where people aim to reach understanding' (1996:125). Her notion of communicative democracy sees differences as resources for reaching understanding not as divisions that must be overcome (1996:120; also 1997). Communication of differences and conflicts as well as of shared goals facilitates the possibility that through the interaction of others' ideas with one's own ideas, practices might change. In addition to critical argument, Young offers three elements which maintain plurality (1997:70–4).

First, greetings like smiles, handshakes, hugs, the giving and taking of food and drink are important preliminaries that establish trust or respect. Media attention is given to the reluctance of mainstream Unionist MPs to shake the hands of Sinn Féin MPs. In the common rooms of parliament, informal intermingling is rare, and even basic courtesies taken for granted in other democracies are absent. Second, Young talks of rhetoric – that is, both a situatedness of the speaker's position in relation to the audience and a desire to please the audience through humour, wordplay, images and figures of speech. Good-natured rhetoric is foreign to most political discourse in Northern Ireland, except in debates on non-constitutional matters like farming or tourism, or the gold medal won in the Commonwealth games – for target shooting! Third, storytelling invites a narrative which fosters understanding across differences and demonstrates need and entitlement. Those differently situated cannot share a narrative, but some attempt to understand it is requisite to do justice to others. Women constantly share each other's life stories and the myriad of details that make up mundane ordinary lives, shared over the telephone, when walking the children to school, over coffee when borrowing a household item or clothes. Talking through our narratives with those who come from different traditions, communities and regions is crucial to break the barriers of distrust that too often are based on fear cultivated through ignorance.

Justice, care and dialogue

'Having access to knowledge of the other from the perspective of the other reflects feminist efforts to conjoin justice with care' as a model of judgement (Jones 1996:85). These words of Katherine Jones encapsulate three senses in which feminist theory makes a difference to ideas of participatory democracy and to the challenge of dialogue across difference. First, they refer to the importance of knowledge of the other from the other's perspective, the storytelling, listening and arguing that needs to occur for understanding to happen. Such an understanding requires wide participation and communities reassessing their positions as dealt with in the first section above. It also requires equal consideration of difference, the acceptance of the partiality and multiplicity of identities, the development of solidarity through political discussion and the need to respect diversity, as was dealt with in the following section.

Second, in conjoining justice with care, other interconnections are made explicit between cognition and emotional sensitivity, responses to the general rights and to the specific needs of others, formal equality and norms of equity. An 'emphasis on the dialogic characteristics of the practice of justice as communicative need interpretations has the advantage of supplanting the gaze of impartiality with the discourse of public speech' (Jones 1996:85). Just care requires an attention to difference as part of the political project. Just care adopts a responsibility to attend justly to the different needs people face; it makes it immoral to be emotionally distanced from people's needs. Just care attends to conflict through dialogue.

Third, the need for judgement in political dialogue is crucial. Sevenhuijsen argues that a principal task of collective citizenship is 'judging', distinguishing between good and bad and being accountable for the decisions that follow (1998:15). Sound judgements simultaneously recognise 'subjects' individuality and diversity while considering and treating others as equal (Porter 1999:87). Judgement assumes difference and conflict, but refuses the notion that disagreement must lead to antagonism and continual political blockage. Rather, through reasoned debate, and motivated by the urgency to deliver a resolution that is acceptable to all different parties, judgement allows citizens and political representatives to listen, talk, consider other's views and allow themselves to be persuaded of the need to change.

Participatory spaces: between speaking and listening

To accept the challenge of dialogue across difference is to maximise the participatory spaces for voices to be expressed and listened to, spaces where mutual respect permits profound disagreement without blocking the urgency to make workable decisions that are mutually acceptable. Listening is requisite for being attentive to differences. 'It requires an uncomfortable, shifting vision that is more difficult for the privileged than subordinates' (Flax 1998:151). Giving up the privileged position as speaker need not be disempowering; it is part of the reciprocity of democratic dialogue. I suggest that it involves a *quiet reflection* on the consequences of what one hears, that it is an intrinsic dimension to deliberation and sound judgement. Deliberation and listening provide the conditions for what Margaret Walker calls an 'expressive-collaborative model of morality' (1998:60–2), where people empowered to speak in their voices, together renegotiate the disputed and shared bases of moral discourse that provide the understandings of all the controversial issues that prolong conflict, such as blame, irresponsibility, injustice, lies and the refusal to forgive.

Let me contextualise Susan Bickford's helpful ideas on listening. She argues that it is precisely because of the dissonance of democracy that listening is so important. Given discord, what prevents us from facing ever-present conflict, anarchy, terrorism, war is the 'listening attention to one another' (1996:2). This attentiveness is driven by the exigencies of communicative relationships – the need to speak and listen together in the face of conflict and the urgency to make a judgement that will lead to sound participatory democratic practices. I am arguing that *politics requires the dynamic between speaking and listening*. Listening confronts 'the intersubjective character of politics' (Bickford 1996:4) and opens politics to difference. Communication acknowledges 'a separateness and a difference that may be the source of conflict, *and at the same time* foregrounds the possibility of bridging that gap by devising a means of relatedness' (1996:5). Listening thus is constitutive in the process of figuring out, in the face of conflict, what to do. Bickford stresses the interdependence of speaker and listener as 'different-but-equal participants' (1996:24), making *listening an active practice of citizenship*. Such a listening engages both agency and situatedness; it is akin to the rooting and shifting that is intrinsic to transversal politics. This involves a shifting back and forth, speaking and listening, equal participants of difference. The deliberative nature of the interaction is that through listening comes the strong probability 'that what we hear will require change from us' (Bickford 1996:149). The mere thought of this probability can be very frightening to citizens of Northern Ireland; the idea that one could learn from others is daunting – the prospect of changing one's position as a result can terrify. However, there are many examples of good practices in the case-studies examined in the previous chapters.

My strong argument is that *between speaking and listening lie the spaces wherein we accept the responsibility of the risk to dialogue across differences*. Spaces need to be created and recreated and utilised to the full. It is 'in structuring the space between us' that we are actually 'doing transversal politics' (Cockburn 1998:9). These spaces value participation because they nurture collective discourse and meet the challenge of dialogue across difference. 'Dialogue is the key to a reciprocal recognition of our diversity and our commonality' (Porter 1997a:83–4). This space between commonality and diversity depends on the interactive dynamic between speaking and listening, paying attention and being paid it, respecting differences and being respected. Reciprocity is imperative to this dynamic. Only when these open spaces are fully appreciated will old views be revised or discarded, and visions of change translate into inclusive practices. Taking on the responsibility to engage in participatory, deliberative democracy fosters dialogue across difference. The exciting possibilities these challenges entail deserve to be more fully grasped.

References

Arendt, Hannah (1958) *The Human Condition*, Chicago: University of Chicago Press.

Benhabib, Seyla (ed.) (1996) *Democracy and Difference. Contesting the Boundaries of the Political*, Princeton, NJ: Princeton University Press.

Bickford, Susan (1996) *The Dissonance of Democracy. Listening, Conflict, and Citizenship*, Ithaca, NY, and London: Cornell University Press.

Bock, Gisela and James, Susan (eds) (1992) *Beyond Equality and Difference. Citizenship, Feminist Politics and Female Subjectivity*, London: Routledge.

Burman, Erica (1994) 'Experience, Identities and Alliances: Jewish Feminism and Feminist Psychology', in Kum-Kum Bhavnani and Ann Phoenix (eds), *Shifting Identities. Shifting Racisms. A Feminism and Psychology Reader*, London: Sage, 155–78.

Chambers, Simone (1995) 'Feminist Discourse/Practical Discourse', in Johanna Meehan (ed.), *Feminists Read Habermas: Gendering the Subject of Discourse*, New York and London: Routledge, 163–79.

Cockburn, Cynthia (1998) *The Space Between Us: Negotiating Gender and National Identities in Conflict*, London and New York: Zed Books.

Cooper, Davina (1995) *Power in struggle: Feminism, Sexuality and the State*, Buckingham: Open University Press.

Dean, Jodi (1996) *'Solidarity of Strangers: Feminisms After Identity Politics*, Berkeley, CA: University of California Press.

d'Entrevès, Maurizio Passerin (1992) 'Hannah Arendt and the Idea of Citizenship', in Mouffe (1992), 145–68.

Dietz, Mary (1992) 'Context is All: Feminism and Theories of Citizenship', in Chantal Mouffe (ed.), *Dimensions of Radical Democracy*, London: Verso, 63–85.

Flax, Jane (1993) *Disputed Subjects. Essays on Psychoanalysis, Politics and Philosophy*, New York: Routledge.

Flax, Jane (1998) 'Displacing Woman. Toward an Ethics of Multiplicity', in Bat-Ami Bar On and Ann Ferguson (eds), *Daring to be Good: Essays in Feminist Ethico-Politics*, New York and London: Routledge, 143–55.

Fraser, Nancy (1986) 'Toward a Discourse Ethic of Solidarity', *Praxis International*, 5(4), 425–29.

Frazer, Elizabeth and Lacey, Nicola (1993) *The Politics of Community. A Feminist Critique of the Liberal-Communitarian Debate*, Toronto: University of Toronto Press.

Grosz, Elizabeth, 1994, 'Sexual Difference and the Problem of Essentialism', in Naomi Schor and Elizabeth Weed (eds), *The Essential Difference*, Bloomington: Indiana University Press, 82–97.

Gutmann, Amy and Thompson, Dennis (1996) *Democracy and Disagreement*, Cambridge, MA: Belknap Press.

Habermas, Jürgen (1990) *Moral Consciousness and Communicative Action*, Cambridge, MA: MIT Press.

Hartsock, Nancy (1983) *Money, Sex and Power. Toward a Feminist Historical Materialism*, New York and London: Longman.

Jaggar, Alison (1998) 'Globalizing Feminist Ethics', *Hypatia*, 13(2), 7–31.

Jones, Katherine (1996) 'What is Authority's Gender?', in Nancy J. Hirschmann and Christine Di Stefano (eds), *Revisioning the Political*, Boulder, CO: Westview Press, 75–93.

Karl, Marli (1995) *Women and Empowerment. Participation and Decision Making*, London: Zed Books.

Lister, Ruth (1997) *Citizenship. Feminist Perspectives*, London: Macmillan.

Lorde, Audre (1992) 'Age, Race, Class and Sex: Women Redefining Difference', in Helen Crowley and Susan Himmelweit (eds), *Knowing Women. Feminism and Knowledge*, Cambridge: Polity Press, 47–54.

Mani, Lata (1992) 'Multiple Mediations: Feminist Scholarship in the Age of Multinational Reception', in Helen Crowley and Susan Himmelweit (eds), *Knowing Women. Feminism and Knowledge*, Cambridge: Polity Press, 306–22.

Minow, Martha (1997) *Not Only for Myself. Identity, Politics and the Law*, New York: New Press.

Mouffe, Chantal (1992) 'Democratic Politics Today', in Chantal Mouffe (ed.), *Dimensions of Radical Democracy. Pluralism, Citizenship and Community*, London: Verso, 1–14.

Mouffe, Chantal (1993) 'Liberal Socialism and Pluralism: Which Citizenship?', in Judith Squires (ed.), *Principled Positions*, London: Lawrence & Wishart, 69–84.

Phillips, Anne (1991) *Engendering Democracy*, Cambridge: Polity Press.

Phillips, Anne (1993) *Democracy and Difference*, Cambridge: Polity Press.

Phillips, Anne (1995) *The Politics of Presence*, Oxford: Clarendon Press.

Porter, Elisabeth (1997a) 'Diversity and Commonality: Women, Politics, and Northern Ireland', *European Journal of Women's Studies*, 4(1), 83–100.

Porter, Elisabeth (1997b) 'Citizenship as Belonging: An Australian in Northern Ireland', *Australasian Political Studies 1997: Proceedings of the APSA 1997 Conference*, 3, 863–78.

Porter, Elisabeth (1998a) 'Political Representation of Women in Northern Ireland', *Politics*, 18(1), 25–32.

Porter, Elisabeth (1998b) 'Identity, Location, Plurality: Women, Nationalism and Northern Ireland', in Rick Wilford and Robert Miller (eds), *Women, Ethnicity and Nationalism: The Politics of Transition*, London and New York: Routledge, 36–61.

Porter, Elisabeth (1999) *Feminist Perspectives on Ethics*, London and New York: Longman.

Porter, Norman (1998) *Rethinking Unionism: An Alternative Vision for Northern Ireland*, 2nd edn, Belfast: Blackstaff Press.

Pringle, Rosemary and Watson, Sophie (1992) '"Women's Interests" and the Post-Structuralist State', in Michèle Barrett and Anne Phillips (eds), *Destabilising Theory. Contemporary Feminist Debates*, Cambridge: Polity Press, 53–73.

Ruddick, Sara (1989) '*Maternal Thinking: Towards a Politics of Peace*, Boston, MA: Beacon Press.

Sevenhuijsen, Selma (1998) *Citizenship and the Ethics of Care. Feminist Considerations on Justice, Morality and Politics*, London and New York: Routledge.

Sharoni, Simona (1995) *Gender and the Israel–Palestinian Conflict: The Politics of Women's Resistance*, New York: Syracuse University Press.

Spivak, Gayatri Chakravorty (1992) 'The Politics of Translation', in Michèle Barrett and Anne Phillips (eds), *Destabilizing Theory. Contemporary Feminist Debates*, Cambridge: Polity Press, 177–200.

Squires, Judith (ed.) (1993) *Principled Positions: Postmodernism and the Rediscovery of Value*, London: Lawrence & Wishart.

Weeks, Jeffrey (1993) 'Rediscovering Values', in Squires, 189–211.

Walker, Margaret, Urban (1998) *Moral Boundaries: A Political Argument for an Ethic of Care*, New York: Routledge.

Young, Iris Marion (1987) 'Impartiality and the Civic Public: Some Implications of Feminist Critiques of Moral and Political Theory', in Seyla Benhabib and Drucilla Cornell (eds), *Feminism as Critique*, Minneapolis: University of Minnesota Press: 57–76.

Young, Iris Marion (1990) *Justice and the Politics of Difference*, Princeton, NJ: Princeton University Press.

Young, Iris Marion (1993) 'Together in Difference: Transforming the Logic of Group Political Conflict', in Judith Squires (ed.), *Principled Positions. Postmodernism and the Rediscovery of value*, London: Lawrence & Wishart, 121–50.

Young, Iris Marion (1996) 'Communication and the Other: Beyond Deliberative Democracy', in Benhabib, 120–35.

Young, Iris Marion (1997) *Intersecting Voices. Dilemmas of Gender, Political Philosophy, and Policy*, Princeton, NJ: Princeton University Press.

Yuval-Davis, Nira (1994) 'Women, Ethnicity and Empowerment', in Kum-Kum Bhavnani and Anne Phoenix (eds), *Shifting Identities. Shifting Racisms. A Feminism and Psychology Reader*, London: Sage, 179–97.

Yuval-Davis, Nira (1996) 'Women and the Biological Reproduction of "the Nation"', *Women's Studies International Forum*, 19(1/2), 17–24.

Yuval-Davis, Nira (1997) 'Women, Citizenship and Difference', *Feminist Review*, 57, 4–27.

8
Women in Northern Irish Politics: Difference Matters

Eilish Rooney

This chapter is a series of critical reflections. It is driven by the effort to grasp, explain and understand further what women do and how gender works in the politically divided and sectarian society of the north of Ireland.[1] It offers a situated exploration: of women in conflict; of democracy and sectarianism; and of feminism and local feminist approaches to conflict and war. The chapter contends that the historically sedimented, asymmetrical power relationships between unionism and nationalism in the north of Ireland matter to women and men. These relationships shape political perspectives, experiences, behaviour and life chances. They are the relationships at the core of the efforts to reach a more just democracy contained in the provisions of the Good Friday Agreement.[2] Democracy, what it is, who has a purchase on it, and how it works in a divided society, are all issues of popular political debate here in the north of Ireland. They are also matters of keen debate in the context of devolution in Britain. The chapter provides an analysis of some of the contexts within which takes place the work of people involved in the case-study organisations discussed in Part II of the book.

This chapter is 'situated' in a number of senses. I was born into and am involved in the changing political landscape in the north of Ireland. To a person from here my name signals my Catholic background. The first endnote of this chapter, prising open the closure of 'Northern Ireland', would suggest to some that I am some form of nationalist. The most personalised, as well as the most public, words in the language here carry historical, sectarian weight. I accept, although I want to argue with, the assumptions made about me from my name. In this chapter I refer to unionist and loyalist women, to nationalist and republican women, and working-class and middle-class women. Many of these women will want to struggle out from under the crude, homogenising assumptions of the language. In the case-study organisations, women, and men, have devised valuable spaces where they challenge the history and shift the weight of sectarianism, as well as addressing the issues of gender.

The first section of this chapter underlines the importance of making women visible in the north of Ireland. It begins with where women are most highly visible, albeit for their relative absence – in electoral politics. It then tracks these presences back to where women slip from public and political view: into the home, neighbourhood, and contested histories and territories of unionism and nationalism. The second section examines some of the problems of democracy in the north of Ireland and how the Agreement institutionalises 'difference democracy'. The potential impacts of the Agreement on women are examined in the final section, where the focus turns to feminism and feminists in the north of Ireland. This ends with reflections on feminism and nationalism from Scotland and Britain. The intention of the chapter is to continue to raise questions and stimulate debate, to keep the conversations of the book going, to extend them to Scotland and Britain – as opposed to answering questions and closing debate.

Making absence visible

Citing the virtual absence of women prominent in politics in the north of Ireland is a powerful way of making visible the absence of women in elected arenas. Like many other workers in the fields of women and politics, I have cited the low numbers of women in elected arenas, and in decision-making civic spaces, in order to argue for strategies for more women in these places (Moreland and Rooney 1998, Rooney 1994, 1995a, 1995b, 1997). The figures are so stark that they appear to speak for themselves. None of the north of Ireland's 18 MPs elected to the Westminster parliament is a woman; none of the 3 members of the European Parliament is a woman; and only 14 of the 108 members of the Northern Ireland Assembly (NIA) are women (13 per cent). This is just below the 15 per cent of women councillors elected to the north of Ireland's 26 district councils. Thus, two tiers of the representative democratic process in the north of Ireland have no women elected (see Chapter 1).[3]

Citing the low numbers, or total absence, of women in representative politics is one shorthand way of arguing for change. It has been an effective attention-seeking tactic in public and media-driven debates, where the subtleties of arguments about 'representation' and gender essentialism are set aside in favour of counting heads. Yet arguments for more women in politics in the north of Ireland, if they are to be meaningful, need to be integrated into arguments for equality, social inclusion and human rights for all. Otherwise, 'women' become an 'added on' extra, a 'take it or leave it' separate issue rather than being integral to the causes of conflict, and integral to its resolution. Representative democracy, politics and gender in the north of Ireland are enmeshed within the hierarchies of power and inequality, which are differently experienced and differently understood by differently positioned women. Seeing women in politics in the north of Ireland simply as an excluded group fails to reflect the complexities of women's presences, absences and agency within the historically specific, politically and culturally sedimented hierarchies of sectarian politics which have shaped the state since its beginnings. Women's inclusions in and admissions to or exclusions from party politics (or socio-economic and cultural influence) are not *the same* for Catholic women as they are for Protestant women.[4] They are not the same for working-class republican women as for middle-class nationalist women, for working class-loyalist women as for middle-class unionist women. The language of the Agreement goes further. The political parties who signed the Agreement affirmed therein (p. 16): 'the right to equal opportunity in all social and economic activity, regardless of class, creed, disability, gender or ethnicity'. An indication of some of the problems in realising these commitments may be grasped from the following outline of women in the parties.

Each of the political parties in the north of Ireland has its particular organisational history in relation to Irish and British politics (Rooney and Woods 1995). Each political party also has a particular history of debate and specific developments in relation to women's participation. These developments are linked to the party's ideological and political position in relation to the state and to the history of political conflict and political reform on the island of Ireland.[5] Each party's class and geographical constituency, and the religious make-up of voters, are formative features that have shaped women's access to political representation and party decision-making. Thus, Sinn Féin, as well as other left-wing parties not elected to the NIA, including the Workers' Party and the Communist Party of Ireland, have a history of women's involvement in electoral politics on the party agenda going back to the 1970s.[6] The SDLP and Alliance have had women on their party conference agendas since the 1980s. The UUP and the DUP have had formal inputs to party conferences on the issue of women's representation in the party since the 1990s.

So, where are the women elected to the NIA and what is significant about the gender make-up in the contemporary political context? Of the 108 members elected to the NIA, June 1998, 14 are women. The proportions by party are suggestive of interesting ideological and political cleavages, of party histories, and of different forms of gender participation (Table 8.1).

The low numbers of women elected make any analyses, of necessity, tentative. The numbers indicate a broad pattern of lower political representation presence for unionist women across unionist parties; and a relatively higher presence of nationalist women, in particular of republican women within SF. This affirms other findings and work on women within unionism and in nationalism and republicanism (Moore 1995, Rooney and Woods 1995, Rooney 1995b). Unionist parties, taken together, hold 58 seats, of which 3 are held by women (5 per cent). Of the 42 SDLP and SF seats, 8 are held by women (19 per cent). It might be tempting to see the emergence of the NIWC as one organic outcome of this 'creeping' awareness of the issue of women in politics. The story is more complex, more effortful, and linked to developments within the voting system and the existing networks of women's groups across the north of Ireland (see Chapter 6). Geographic location, as well as gender, class, and political persuasion are crucial determinants of people's experiences

Table 8.1 Northern Ireland Assembly: Party and Gender, June 1998

Party[7]	Members in Assembly	Women in Assembly	% Women
UUP	28	2	7
SDLP	24	3	13
DUP	20	1	5
SF	18	5	28
Alliance	6	1	17
UKU	5	0	0
PUP	2	0	0
NIWC	2	2	100
Ind. U	3	0	
Totals	108	14	13

of conflict, and of the choices available to them in the neighbourhood contexts within which they become political and social actors.[8] The formative political faultlines of unionism and nationalism in Ireland have shaped the history and practice of politics on both sides of the border. Some of the different dilemmas of women supportive of the union and of women opposed to the union are discussed below.

Women for the union

It cannot be assumed that unionist women are any less interested in or involved in party politics than are nationalist women. Unionist women have a lengthy history of active involvement in party politics and, in particular, of defending the union in times of crisis. Historically, this 'defence of the union' crosses class and gender boundaries. In 1912, the exclusively male Ulster Covenant had its women's equivalent supported by 234 046 unionist women (Ward 1983:90). Recently, loyalist women have supported the men of the Orange Order in their stand at Drumcree by making application for a women's march down Garvaghy Road. Loyalist women, with their children, were to the fore in roadblocks in support of the men at Drumcree in 1998. Gender-inscribed forms of political agency are an ideological and political resource within unionism and within nationalism, and are utilised by all political parties in the north of Ireland. The notion that women's active participation in politics is necessarily or essentially progressive or emancipatory for women *qua* women is fallacious. Women evidently see their political activity as valuable in promoting the interests of their collectivity.

Ruth Moore (1995) argues that the concepts of 'otherness' and 'difference' are useful in understanding Protestant women's sense of who they are. Protestant women as a group are clearly not homogenous. There is much diversity within such a group, structured not only by religious denomination but primarily by class, sexual identity, ability, etc., the extent of which, I think, has yet to be realised.[9] She says that Protestant women are themselves silenced within Protestantism and this is linked to 'sectarian patriarchal relations of ruling . . . it is associated with imperialist and colonialist power, which never has to explain itself' (*ibid.*). Writing of contemporary Protestant women, Moore sees the differences between unionist, Protestant women and nationalist, Catholic women as integral to the legacy of 'a Protestant state for a Protestant people' (*ibid.*). Given this legacy, 'Catholic women are the most significant other . . . Protestant women, particularly middle-class women, have been historically positioned and placed within the state which has mobilised and maintained the sectarian power relations which has enabled the majority Protestant population to have an unequal access to power' (*ibid.*). This unequal access to power is class- and gender-based and under material duress from global and local socio-economic developments, which have led to reduced workforces in the once secure sources of Protestant employment: the shipyard and manufacturing industries. It is also challenged by local fair employment legislation, albeit this legislation has not made the differences needed to reduce sectarianised levels of Catholic under-employment.[10]

The silence of and about Protestant women and their access to and exercise of various forms of 'power' is beginning to break down, at least at the level of discourse and in interactions in networks of local women's groups. The 1990s have seen the emergence of 'women' taken up as an issue harnessed for party political benefits, in annual unionist party conferences. For the first time in 1991, Rhonda Paisley, daughter of DUP leader Ian Paisley, used her allotted five-minute address to the party's annual conference to raise the issue of women in the party and to argue for more time to be allotted to the issue in the next annual conference. In 1998, at the UUP annual party conference, one commentator noted that the most energised contribution was from a woman party member who spoke on the issue of the low number of women representatives in the party. Before the conference, the party leader, David Trimble, was expected to have a tough time from his party's right-wing opposition to the Agreement. Raising the issue of women's virtual invisibility in elected positions in the party was regarded as a media-friendly issue at the conference.[11] Whether or not this activity will result in more women gaining access to elected and decision-making positions within unionism remains to be seen. Furthermore, what differences more unionist women in these positions will make will be worth watching, in terms similar to the ongoing scrutiny of Labour women in Westminster.

Perhaps the key here is that the issue of women in unionist parties, as packaged at the party conferences, is addressed as an issue that can be beneficial *for the party*. In 1999, unionist women's voices are being mobilised by victims' organisations and by wives and relatives of the Royal Ulster Constabulary, the future of which was the subject of a formal enquiry.[12] Gender 'scripts' are a powerful resource in social processes that protect and justify socio-economic, cultural and political stratification and closure.[13] Unionist women's roles are, so far, relatively hidden – but crucial – resources within unionism. They are integral to the asymmetrical, historicised power relations between Catholic and Protestant women in the north of Ireland today.

Women against the union

What Moore (1995) says of Protestant and unionist women may also be said of Catholic nationalist women – they are clearly not homogeneous, but are structured by class and other materially and culturally weighted 'differences'. As Table 8.1 has shown, there are more nationalist and republican than unionist women in the NIA. The higher level presences of nationalist women indicate significantly different, rather than greater, forms of political participation than unionist women. In her study of feminism and nationalism, Carol Coulter (1993:5) notes that:

> The involvement of women is a common feature of nationalist movements. From India to Egypt to Africa to Ireland, the upsurge of nationalism was accompanied by the emergence of women onto the streets in public protest and into public life as organisers, leaders and shock troops. The fact that these societies were often criticised by the imperialist power as repressive of their women, keeping them in thrall to religious and cultural practices redolent of a benighted past, makes this involvement all the more interesting and significant.

These general observations have validity in the north of Ireland. Women members of the SDLP are likely to have backgrounds in civil rights, student activist politics or social reform activities. Women in SF are likely to have experienced political crisis and communal political mobilisation en route to party membership (Rooney and Woods 1995). Nationalist and Republican women draw on historic and heroic role models (Catholic, Protestant, middle- and working-class women) who have held leadership and prominent positions in nationalist and suffragist political struggles. They also have examples from history where women's gains were undermined in the subsequent settlement. Women's part in the national struggle in Ireland was short-lived and overtaken by the counter-revolution. After partition, women were consigned to a secondary role and subjected to a series of repressive pieces of legislation, culminating in the 1937

Irish constitution which relegated Irish women to a 'special' (well-known) place in the family (see Cullen Owens 1984, MacCurtain 1985 and Ward 1995).

The teachings, practices and resources of the Catholic Church in the north of Ireland have come to shape everyday life, according particular and different meanings to women's and men's lives. By the late 1960s, the Catholic Church provided an (almost) parallel social world to that of the unionist state: 'the state culture was privileged and the state culture was unionist; nationalist culture was relegated to the margins' (Rolston 1998:27). A key challenge to Catholic Church hegemony came from the 'hearth' of Catholic teaching, the working-class home; and from those who weave moral teaching and church practices into the fabric of family life – the women. Some of the women who dressed their children with green ribbons for the St Patrick's Day Parade in areas of Belfast and Derry in 1968 were among the women to take to the streets in their thousands in anti-internment protests in 1971. For each man interned without trial, three, four or more women would be involved in his welfare; and their women friends and relations would be aware of the costs to a family, and often be supportive. Women made public appeals to the Catholic hierarchy in the newspaper columns; and then organised protests at the residence of the cardinal (Aretxaga 1997:65). By that time, the masculine face of the unionist 'state', in the form of the British army and the Royal Ulster Constabulary, had invaded, for search, arrest and harassment purposes, thousands of nationalist-Catholic homes in working-class neighbourhoods.[14] In the early days, the home, in these communities, was both billet and armoury. The 'private' space of the home – the so-called women's domain – became, in many cases, a site of political resistance and refuge.[15]

It was a combination of personal experience, political analyses and these lessons from history that motivated a group of republican feminist community and political activists to organise Clár na mBan (Women's Agenda for Peace) in 1994 in response to what was seen as the marginalisation of women in the emerging peace process. The conference platform called on unionist women to organise to have their perspectives included in the peace process. The conference report draws on the example of nationalist women's roles in Irish history (especially in the struggle for Independence) and contends: '[D]espite the efforts and achievements of these notable women, as well as those of countless others, whose names we may never learn, the lesson of history is that our voices are rarely heard' (Clár na mBan 1994:4; see also Hackett 1995). The women who organised the Clár na mBan conference subsequently made radical proposals to the Forum for Peace and Reconciliation, convened in 1994 by the Irish government. They called for: a demilitarised society; economic equality; children's rights; and for an end to discrimination against disabled people and lesbians.[16] Most of these women come from Catholic backgrounds. Their positions seem light years away from the social, political and moral teaching of the Catholic Church. In understanding the tectonic shift in nationalist women's roles and agency in politics in the north of Ireland, it is vital to understand the changing roles of women within and in relation to the Catholic Church. In particular, the time between the establishment of the state, the outbreak of the conflict in 1968 (and subsequent communal and political developments) and the responses to these of the Catholic hierarchy are important.

Thus, the ideological, political, socio-economic and religious differences, and different experiences of the conflict, between nationalist and unionist women matter. These differences have material and life chance meanings. They are powerful resources mobilised differently at different historical moments 'in the protection and justification of social stratification and social closure' (Brewer 1998:1).[17] Unionist numerical and political dominance within the north of Ireland has never been 'secured' in the sense of reaching stability. In this, it resembles the dynamics of other gendered relationships of dominance. What do these different gendered histories of struggle mean for the operation of contemporary democratic institutions and for women's participation in them in the north of Ireland?

Democratic difference

Anne Phillips (1992) explains the feminist challenge to liberal democracy as one that contests the concept of the undifferentiated individual as the basic unit in democratic life. Liberal democracy posits that differences should not count. Phillips argues:

> At its best, this is a statement of profound egalitarianism that offers all citizens the same legal and political rights, regardless of their wealth, status, race or sex. At its worst, it refuses the pertinence of continuing difference and inequality, pretending

for the purposes of argument that we are all of us basically the same. (p. 77)

Historically, in the north of Ireland 'democracy' has worked and continues to 'work' – theoretically and practically – on the basis of the 'difference' the individual brings with her into the polling booth. The unattached, undifferentiated individual of liberal democracy is not the basic unit of 'democratic' life in the north of Ireland. Here, democracy *admits* and, to use Phillips's phrasing, is defined by 'the pertinence of continuing difference and inequality' in the voter's allegiance to, and relationship with the state. Either the 'individual' supports the union of Northern Ireland with Great Britain, within the United Kingdom, and has various combinations of ideological, religious, cultural, historical, political, affective, and materially ad-vantageous reasons and experiences for doing so; or the 'individual' opposes the union and aspires to some form of Irish unitary state – and has a similar range of rational and affective sources of group collectivity, with contrary outcomes. There is nothing inevitable about history. It is conceivable that the state in the north of Ireland could have developed differently, even though the historical dice were loaded in favour of continuing sectarian conflict. The 'gendered' vote that Phillips explores is revealed in the north of Ireland to be a historically weighted vote.

The Good Friday Agreement is founded on a recognition that 'liberal democracy', within a context where the subordination of one group by another is historically and 'democratically' sedimented into the socio-economic, cultural, political and gender structures, requires radical change. The language of the agreement admits and safeguards *difference* in the operations of democracy within the new assembly. Each vote is of equal worth in returning members. How-ever, requirements for parallel consent and weighted majorities, provisions for petitions of concern (brought by 30 of the 108 mem-bers) within the Assembly, and commitments to human rights and equality, comprise negotiated efforts, and Irish and British govern-ment pressure, to make *difference* democracy work to bring about equality of participation in decision-making. Human rights, in the language of the Agreement, include the right of women to full and equal political participation. The Agreement is also a milestone in the resolution of the British–Irish–northern-Irish history of violent, political conflict.

One of the challenges of the present peace process, identified by Jennifer Todd (1994), is, 'to move from a zero-sum ideological position to an egalitarian and emancipatory one'.[18] Todd defines this as reaching a negotiating situation where considerations and compromises are focused on 'a series of choices between less good and better outcomes' (*ibid.*).

Among the difficulties tackled by Todd, and tackled differently by the political actors in the north of Ireland, is that reaching negotiation whereby 'less good and better outcomes' are the consideration, requires a tectonic shift in political culture and in political leadership. I. M. Young's ideas on communicative democracy, already discussed earlier in this volume, may be helpful. She argues that it is the task of communicative democracy to reach beyond 'difference' and, 'to locate or create common interests that all can share' (Young 1996:126). However, in these endeavours, Young cautions:

[W]hen discussion participants aim at unity, in the appeal to a common good in which they are all supposed to leave behind their particular experience and interests, the perspectives of the privileged are likely to dominate the definition of that common good. The less privileged are asked to put aside the expression of their experience, which may require a different idiom, or their claims of entitlement or interest must be put aside for the sake of a common good whose definition is biased against them. (Ibid.)

Arguably, the nationalist–republican acceptance of the principle of consent within the contrived 'democracy' of the north of Ireland is a 'setting aside' of a 'claim of entitlement or interest', to use Young's terms. This explains the significance attached by nationalists and republicans to the legitimacy of the aspiration to a unitary Irish state which is contained in the agreement. Young's analysis may also be applied to the claims of the most marginalised people within unionism and nationalism; arguably, these are working-class women. The people in these groups have borne the brunt of the conflict; they have also been the combatants. Men and women have paid different costs – men with their lives – over 90 per cent of the deaths are male – and women with their lives in the sense of living with the griefs and holding family lives together. The middle and professional classes of each collectivity live in areas materially unaffected by the conflict. They have generally had a hand-washing, hand-wringing or 'hands-off' approach. The material benefits of the conflict have generally been appropriated by the middle classes (Rolston 1993). There are, of course, remarkable exceptions to this generalisation.

Many unionists, perhaps all, would dispute my analysis of democracy up to this point. The local property franchise, which facilitated local government 'gerrymandering' in the north of Ireland, was withdrawn in 1969.[19] Unionists argue that the north of Ireland is a modern democracy, but Jennifer Todd (1994:72) argues otherwise:

> Unionists, as the majority in Northern Ireland, are at once in a better position to form parliamentary alliances with minority British governments, and morally able to present unionism as simple democratic choice. Protestants have the advantage in demographic and military power resources. Culturally, the state and the public world in Northern Ireland is structured in accordance with British-centred, unionist and Protestant meanings.

These meanings, and the dominance of unionism, are constantly challenged on a number of fronts. Todd argues that '[I]n each sphere . . . Catholic power resources have increased relative to Protestant' (*ibid.*).[20] Brewer further traces the current civil unrest to its roots, beyond partition, arguing that it

> reaches back to plantation when inequality between Catholics and Protestants was made government policy; inequality effortlessly reproduced itself in the eighteenth and nineteenth centuries once it became embedded in the social structure and affected politics, the economy, education, housing and employment. It worsened in the twentieth century with partition only because discrimination was enhanced by Protestant control of the state. (Brewer 1998:115).

The language of the Agreement alone does not dismantle the relations of power and inequality within the north of Ireland. That work is primarily the responsibility of government. Influencing that responsibility, living with, and making the consequences work, is the shared responsibility of all of the people of the north of Ireland. The language is one vital, tactical beginning.[21]

Women in conflict

Can the language and commitments of the Agreement improve the lot of women in the north of Ireland? Noam Chomsky's conclusion on another agreement (the Multilateral Agreement on Investment) is insightful in this regard. He avers that the outcomes of agreements 'are not determined by words, but by the power relations that impose their interpretations' (Chomsky 1998:26). Women and men are differently entangled in these power relations within and between nationalism and unionism. They experience differentiated benefits and oppressions as a result. The dominance of masculinity, and masculine meanings and material power and advantages over women, are not on the mainstream negotiating agenda in the north of Ireland. They are undoubtedly on the agendas of some women within the political parties. The NIWC may prove a vital witness to the unchanging gender status quo in the political arena of NIA and within northern Irish society.

Differences between women are integral to the brutal, bitter, grief-strewn story of conflict about democracy in the north of Ireland, the Republic of Ireland and Great Britain. In public media and state discourse on the situation, women have often been characterised as 'apart from' the conflict; they have frequently been shown as victims belonging to an 'innocent space' apart from the 'evil men' who have perpetrated the violence. This politically constructed, 'innocent', woman-only space has certain conditions of entry to which some women may have access, at some times. The emergence of hundreds of women's groups and dozens of network organisations is among the community development success stories of the north of Ireland in the course of the conflict. Many of the groups, in working-class loyalist and republican neighbourhoods, collaborate on a range of issues of mutual interest. And yet, these successes are contradictory.

In the late 1970s and early 1980s, some socialist feminists who identified the core problem as one where the poorest women were divided on the basis of masculinist, nationalist, identity politics, the resolution of which would not benefit women, acted to set this aside and worked to build alliances across identity and material differences. The analysis of these decisions and actions within the small but growing women's movement in the north of Ireland remains contentious for the women who were involved. Mainstream unionists blamed, and continue to blame, the political conflict on militant republicanism. The British government's criminalisation policy treated IRA violence as pathological, and the 'cause' of the civil unrest. By decoupling the political causes of the conflict from the lived political experiences and analyses of women in the most deprived and militarised working-class Catholic neighbourhoods, some feminist organisations inevitably met with opposition. The position was under volatile pressure, linked to ongoing political develop- ments, which appeared to lurch from crisis to crisis. Effectively, 'unity' feminist organisations were disabled from participation in campaigns against human rights abuses. Bitter disputes, for example, resulted from the refusal of some local feminist organisations to support the anti-strip-searching campaigns conducted by republi- can and unaligned feminists in the 1980s.[22] Feminist organisations refusing to support human rights issues were understood, and pol- itically constructed by republicans, as supporting an oppressive state which was often under scrutiny from international human rights courts and organisations. Individual feminists, aligned to 'unity' organisations, frequently supported campaigns on an individual basis. Such activism ruptured simplistic homogenising constructions.

There is nothing new in local disputes and competition for re- sources, for a foothold in political debate between varieties of feminists and differently aligned women. In practice, in working-class com- munities in the north of Ireland, some women say they have left politics 'at home', in order to mobilise within neighbourhoods and across opposed political positions and experiences to utilise resources for their mutual benefit.[23] When these alliances came under overt sectarian threat by unionist politicians, who signalled withdrawal of local council support, the local women's centres successfully mounted protests (see Chapter 1). Some women experienced these as transformative acts, whereby women acted in their gender, local group and collective interests, at particular moments. They have limited resonance beyond the women involved and do not neces- sarily translate into other, similar testing circumstances.[24] This is why I reluctantly doubt Todd's assertion that the 'increasing promi- nence of women and women's organisations is important [because] women – excluded from male-centred rituals of loyalist politics – may be better able to move beyond loyalist ideology' (Todd 1994:74). Her claim that the proximity in conditions of working-class Catho- lic and Protestant women, as opposed to those of Protestant and Catholic men, will lead to progressive developments within transi- tional loyalist politics remains in the realm of wishful analysis. The material conditions of women are inextricably linked to the employability and incomes of men, to say nothing of shared culture, history and politics. Social attitudes surveys indicate women's political attitudes are, if anything, less 'optimistic' than those of men.[25] Todd is on firmer ground when she realistically reflects that: '[H]ope for the present must thus be tempered with a consciousness of the structural limits to change: otherwise bottom-up attempts to transcend ideological oppositions will founder on the polarising experiences produced at wider levels' (Todd 1994:69). Women and men experience these 'polarising influences' differently, but they experience them as members of collectivities and neighbourhoods that share stored memories and hard-won belief systems, interwoven with socio-economic status and culture. Women are as prepared as men are to defend these 'sites of power'. They utilise gendered expectations of motherhood, presumed weakness and innocence to further the political goals of their collectivity.[26]

Feminists seeking to mobilise women on the basis of their common interests face particular problems in the north of Ireland. The problems contain echoes of feminist debates about the unencumbered, disembodied individual of western liberal democratic thought who turns out, on closer inspection, to be 'loaded' with concealed masculinities and other historicised, situated, 'privileges' of class and race.[27] The embodied femininities to be counted *in* to this political concept (*and practice*), within the northern Irish context, include the experiences of Protestant, unionist, loyalist, working- and middle-class women; and those of Catholic, nationalist, republican, working- and middle-class women.

Neighbouring national feminisms

'Nationalism' is a problematic 'difference' for various feminists and for feminisms – unlike, say, generalisable differences of race or class. It is not that feminists agree as to the problematics of race and class, but they more or less agree as to what is under discussion. It is a paradox of nationalism that it is both a universal socio-cultural concept and distinctive in each of its manifestations (Anderson 1983:13). Seen from a distance, nationalisms are messy 'differences'. They generally come into public or international view via war and conflict (*ibid.*). Within a stable democracy, this universal socio-cultural concept is invisible – so invisible that the 'nationalism' of a next-door neighbour, which is a manifestation of 'neighbourly' colonial histories, is written out of consciousness in the language. This is the case argued by Breitenbach *et al.* (1999) in relation to Scotland. They see the 'United' in the 'United Kingdom' as ironic: 'the apparent unity of Britain is a false imposition that works to marginalize, among others, women in Scotland' (Breitenbach *et al.* 1999:50). Scottish feminists are marginalised within homogenising British mainstream feminism, which presumes to 'speak for all' (*ibid.*). Like other nationalisms, the Scottish variety is generally regarded, they argue, as a masculinist and misogynist project. To speak out and defend the Scottish nationalist project is to risk, at the very least, being misunderstood. Breitenbach *et al.* see as narrow and arrogant the dismissal of Scottish nationalism: 'at the roots of this debate about the state and constitution are arguments about democracy, civil rights and the rule of law (that is to say, a system of justice that commands respect)' (Breitenbach *et al.* 1999:58). These same issues are at the core of the political conflict in the north of Ireland.

The Scottish Constitutional Convention debated, but did not adopt, the proposal for two-person constituencies – one female and one male. In one stroke, the Scottish Parliament could have become the most gender-representative in the world. However, the signals from Westminster, indicating the differences that more women representatives in government might make, are not encouraging. In a Labour government, with such a majority, with long experience of being powerless in opposition, and with a likelihood of being in power for a second term, other factors come into play in shaping the political behaviour of serving politicians; perhaps in particular in the behaviour of new and ambitious women politicians. To date, many Labour politicians who are women have not acted to 'represent' the interests of their sex (that is, of the most marginalised women). I am adapting I. M. Young's approach here. She argues that feminist coalition politics should organise on the basis of the situation of the poorest women. Not all theorists and perhaps not many female politicians would agree that they should, or could, represent the interests of the most marginalised women. The new politicians have not yet indicated that they can make the differences that are hoped for; and in particular not those hoped for by some feminist political scientists.[28] In the decision to cut lone-parent benefit premiums, just 9 of the 101 women Labour MPs signed an early-day motion in protest. Male signatories outnumbered women 8 to 1. It is too soon to reach conclusions about the increase of women in party politics in Westminster, but the story so far would suggest that other developments might prove to be more decisive for gender fairness.

Devolution may prove to be more significant for developments within British democracy, for democratic accountability, for constitutional change and for the devolution of power from the south-east 'centre' to places where 'other' people live. Breitenbach *et al.* (1998) note that debate on 'the establishment and composition of a Scottish Parliament has generated an active interest from women and women's groups throughout Scotland in the 1980s and 1990s, and widespread support for equal representation' (*ibid.* 58–9).[29]

I relate these recent British developments to show that highlighting the low numbers of women representatives within a parliament may successfully, and importantly, contribute to changing the terms of the public political debate. It may also result in strengthening the hand of some women in different political parties in their bids to get elected.[30] In British politics much of the debate and activism around this issue has emerged from within the Labour Party. The contest between positive action initiatives and the 'merit principle' is played out, in the main, between Labour (with affirmative initiatives such as 'Emily's List') and Conservative (the best person for the job). Hence the hopes and the disappointments registered by some English and Scottish feminist political scientists at a Political Studies Association seminar with women politicians in Westminster.[31]

There is no doubt that drawing attention to the women-friendly rhetoric, and indeed using women-inclusive language in public debate, has sensitised party politicians, and their listening electorates, to the male dominance of political life in these islands. Language is one 'site of power'.[32] Some rhetorical sleight of hand, however, is involved in using women-inclusive language in discussing the local political situation in the north of Ireland. The assumption is allowed to be floated, and is sometimes articulated, that more women in representative politics would make things 'better'. Recent developments in Westminster would suggest that this assumption has been given short shrift. The more subtle and serious assumption is that all women in the north of Ireland are equally excluded, or excluded for the same reasons, from political representation (for being women). This chapter argues that this assumption is seriously flawed within the context of the north of Ireland's history and politics.

Conclusion

What people do, from wherever they are positioned, in the north of Ireland, matters and makes differences. The choices are rarely straightforward. The distances between seeing, understanding, and acting, within a conflict situation, where personal safety is an issue, are fraught with hard decisions, which lack the clarity of either theoretical or ethical sanction, or the certainties of historical hindsight. Feminists, and many other women, have learned of these distances, made decisions and acted to make a difference. The difference made may not be the difference intended. This goes for the choices made by each political actor in the north of Ireland. The difference made may be the difference intended. The ability to imagine a future where sectarianism and political violence are disputed in language alone is where, I hope, our conversations are leading. Understanding how gender 'works' in the politically divided and sectarian society of the north of Ireland is central to understanding how politics and power work. Hopefully, this book is one contribution to that understanding. Acts of hope can count as actions.

Notes

1 Northern Ireland is a contested designation: '[E]very name has its politics' (Crick, 1993, p. 72). Many nationalists, republicans, socialists and human rights activists use 'the north of Ireland', or 'the six counties' in order to keep open questions otherwise ostensibly closed by 'Northern Ireland', namely, the legitimacy of the state and the linked questions of political equality between unionists and nationalists.

2 This refers to the Agreement reached in the multi-party negotiations, on Good Friday 1998. Henceforth referred to as 'the Agreement'.

3 For the case of the north of Ireland, there is also the matter of direct rule, often described as government by appointed agency.

4 In these regards, the constitutional aims of the NIWC are a model of inclusiveness and commitments to equality and human rights. However, the constitution uses the language of inclusion without 'naming' the disparities between Protestant and Catholic women. This strategy enables some women with different political perspectives, and experiences, to aspire to and work for an inclusive polity that treats all citizens equally.

5 For more on women's participation in party politics in the Republic of Ireland, see Coulter (1993), also Smyth (1993).

6 Sinn Féin operates a 25 per cent quota for women in the Ard Comhairle (Executive Committee), has a women's department and provides crèche facilities for party workers; the Social Democratic and Labour Party operates a 40 per cent quota in its governing body and has a women's group; Alliance puts forward the highest percentage of women for local council elections.

7 Ulster Unionist Party (UUP); Social Democratic and Labour Party (SDLP); Democratic Unionist Party (DUP); Sinn Féin (SF); United Kingdom Unionist Party (UKU); Progressive Unionist Party (PUP); Northern Ireland Women's Coalition (NIWC); Independent Unionist Party (Ind.U).

8 The neighbourhoods which have endured the highest levels of violence are among the most disadvantaged in these islands. For a study of the costs of the conflict calculated by electoral ward see Fay *et al.* (1997).

9 Ruth Moore's work has not been published and the cited paper has no pagination. Her Master's dissertation: *Proper Wives, Orange Maidens or Disloyal Subjects: Situating the Equality Concerns of Protestant Women in Northern Ireland* is lodged in the Linenhall Library, Belfast. See a report of her work by Ann McKay (1994).

10 For an analysis of implementation, or lack of implementation of NIO measures designed to address social need, see McCormack and McCormack (1995). Currently, 16 per cent of Catholic males are unemployed. The figure for Protestant males is 6 per cent. Robbie McVeigh argues that too little attention has been paid to the religious/class nexus. Geographic location could also be added; 10 per cent of all unemployment in the north of Ireland is in West Belfast (McVeigh 1999). For a study of differences and similarities between Catholic and Protestant women in the labour market, see Davies *et al.* (1995).

11 This may be an instance of what Anne Phillips (1994) sees as political actors being ahead of the political theorists. It may also be tokenism, but it is effective tokenism for unionist women in that it gets the debate going and challenges the hegemony of masculinity in the established unionist parties. Once attention was drawn to the presence of nationalist women in the Brooke and Mayhew talks (notably SDLP's Brid Rogers; SF was not a participant) and to the absence of unionist women, the inclusion of unionist women in delegations become routine (Rooney and Woods 1995:26–7). SF delegations are noticeably gender mixed. The urban loyalist PUP has virtually mounted a campaign in recent years to get more women into the party.

12 Chaired by Sir Chris Patton.

13 John Brewer's (1998) important study of processes of social closure, in relation to theology as a resource in anti-Catholicism in Northern Ireland, leaves out, or does not see, gender within the frame.

14 In a statement to the NI Assembly, in 1973, John Hume reported that one in 25 homes in minority communities had been searched (Wilson 1999:65). This figure could be refined in the light of the fact that searches were largely confined to working-class urban areas of Belfast and Derry. For analyses of how the home in conflict situations may become a site of resistance, see Hassim (1993), Sharoni (1995). Abu Zneid (1977) discusses the home as a site of oppression in Israel, where Palestinian homes are destroyed. Also see Cockburn's (1998) study of women in conflict situations. The 'home', like every other site of power, is a place with shifting and contested boundaries.

15 These mobilisations may be seen as 'foundation events' for women in these neighbourhoods. The concept is applied to major political events by the inter-churches Faith and Politics Group (1998:3). For her investigation

into the possibilities and limitations of feminist transformations in the Northern Ireland situation see Aretxaga (1997). She examines transformative political experiences and uses de Certeau's (1984) work on 'oppositional practices of everyday life' (Aretxaga 1997:19).

16 At the Sinn Féin Ard Fheis, 1996, a radical policy document on lesbian, gay and bisexual rights was adopted. See Mairead Farrell Cumann (1996).

17 Social closure refers to 'the processes by which groups protect their access to scarce socio-economic and political resources, and close off access to less powerful groups' (Brewer 1998:232, fn. 1).

18 Jennifer Todd (1994) specifically considers changes to be encouraged within the current loyalist leadership.

19 'Gerrymandering' refers to unionist manipulations of the local government property franchise whereby Catholics were excluded from local power by unionist-controlled housing allocations. The current conflict erupted in street demonstrations over this issue.

20 Todd provides no detailed data to substantiate this assertion other than indicating general trends – like demographic trends, nationalists' international alliances the Anglo-Irish Agreement and so on. (Todd 1994:75). Arguably, each of these 'advances' for Catholics could be deconstructed and the Ulster Unionists' leadership's implementation of the Agreement could be seen as a self-servingly astute, if short-sighted and minimalist response to these pressures.

21 For a discussion of the sociological role of language in 'both representing and reproducing sectarian experiences in Northern Irish society', see Brewer (1998:216).

22 Various feminist organisations in Britain sent delegations to the north of Ireland on International Women's Day, in support of the prison protests of women in Armagh Jail. For other examples of 'feminist fallout' see Rooney (1995a).

23 These resources include: funding initiatives that 'reward' what is termed 'cross-community' work; educational and servicing resources of feminist and women's network organisations; and resources in the form of organisational recognition within the growing community-based organisational frameworks.

24 The instance I have in mind, which supports this conclusion, remains too sensitive to identify here. Sometime in the future, women involved may tell their own stories.

25 Valerie Morgan (1992) suggests that this may be because women are more realistic than men; and that they have fewer educational or workplace opportunities to develop more optimistic views of future relations between Catholics and Protestants.

26 The north of Ireland's political history is peppered with examples. The loyalistwomen with their children in prams blocking roads in 1998 is a recent instance of women politically exploiting gendered expectations of how women should behave; naked republican women wrapped in 'prisoner' blankets and protesting support for the hunger strikers is an example from the 1980s.

27 As Chapters 2 and 7 have argued, feminists have challenged the construction of the 'individual' – equal before the law, and casting a vote

of equal worth in the democratic polity. Feminist, liberal and social-democratic debate has employed the 'equality principle' promised by 'democracy' to critique its shortcomings in practice (Held 1992:16–17). Models of deliberative and communicative democracy have been developed to include those otherwise excluded or marginalised; critiques of deliberative democracy have led to proposals for communicative democracy (Young 1996). Frazer's (1995) contribution to problems of identity and difference and political, cultural and social inclusion and participation involves widening the concept of politics to include material matters of recognition as well as redistribution.

28   Coulter makes a similar observation on the increased proportion of women elected to the Irish Dáil. The increase in the number of women has had no 'bearing on its legislative programme as all the women there are bound by their respective party's disciplines'. They are unlikely to do so 'unless they leave their parties, and that equals political death' (Coulter 1993:57).

29   This has also been the case for women and women's groups in the North. See Annual Reports of the group Women into Politics, Belfast, and of The Women's Support Network, Belfast, also Annual Reports of the Equal Opportunities Commission for NI. All were given a fillip by the prospect of a locally elected and accountable NIA.

30   The Northern Ireland Women's Coalition (NIWC) initially and effectively mobilised women on the issue of voting for a women's presence and making women's voices heard at the Talks table.

31   Political Studies Association Women in Politics Group seminar: 'One Year of a New Government: Women in Power?' held in Westminster on 30 June 1998.

32   Note that Foucault (cited in Parpart 1993:440) argues that language is the key site: the ability to control knowledge and meaning, not only through writing, but also through disciplinary and professional institutions, and in social relations, is the key to understanding power relations in society. Power is diffused through society rather than located in the state, and thus has to be understood in this much broader context.

References

Abu Zneid, Jihad (1997) 'Women, Children and Housing Rights: The Case of the Occupied Palestinian Territories', *Women and the Politics of Peace: Contributions to a Culture of Women's Resistance*, Zagreb: Centre for Women's Studies, 57–63.

Anderson, Benedict (1983) *Imagined Communities: Reflections on the Origin and Spread of Nationalism*, London: Verso.

Aretxaga, Begona (1997) *Shattering Silence: Women, Nationalism and Political Subjectivity in Northern Ireland*, Princeton and Chichester: Princeton University Press.

Breitenbach, Esther Brown, Alice and Myers, Fiona (1999) 'Understanding Women in Scotland', *Feminist Review*, 58 (Spring), 44–65.

Brewer, John and Higgins, Gareth I. (1998), *Anti-Catholicism in Northern Ireland, 1600–1998: The Mote and the Beam*, Basingstoke: Macmillan.

Chomsky, Noam (1998) 'Power in the Global Arena', *New Left Review*, 230, (July/August), 3–27.

Clár na mBan (1994) *A Woman's Agenda for Peace*, conference report, Belfast.

Cockburn, Cynthia (1998) *The Space Between Us: Negotiating Gender and National Identities in Conflict*, London and New York: Zed Books.

Coulter, Carol (1993) *The Hidden Tradition: Feminism, Women and Nationalism in Ireland*, Cork: Cork University Press.

Crick, B. (1993) 'Essay on Britishness', *Scottish Affairs*, 2 (Winter), 71–83.

Cullen Owens, Rosemary (1984) *Smashing Times: A History of the Irish Women's Suffrage Movement 1889–1992*, Dublin: Attic Press.

Davies, Celia, Heaton, Norma, Robinson, Gillian and McWilliams, Monica (1995) *A Matter of Small Importance? Catholic and Protestant Women in the Northern Ireland Labour Market*, Belfast: Equal Opportunities Commission for Northern Ireland.

de Certeau, Michael (1994) *The Practice of Everyday Life* (Steven F. Randall (translator) Berkeley, CA: University of California Press.

Faith and Politics Group (1998) *Remembrance and Forgetting*, Belfast.

Fay, M. T. Morrissey, Mike and Smyth, Marie (1997) *The Cost of The Troubles: Mapping the Troubles-Related Deaths in Northern Ireland: 1969–1994*, Derry/Londonderry: INCORE.

Frazer, N. (1995) 'From Redistribution to Recognition? Dilemmas of Justice in a "Post-Socialist" Age', *New Left Review*, 212, 68–93.

Hackett, Claire (1995) 'Self-determination: The Republican Feminist Agenda', *Feminist Review*, 50: 11–18.

Hassim, Shireen (1993) 'Family, Motherhood and Zulu Nationalism: The Politics of the Inkatha Women's Brigade', *Feminist Review*, 43 (Spring), 1–25.

Held, David (1992) 'Democracy: From City-States to a Cosmopolitan Order?', *Political Studies*, XL, Special Issue, 10–39.

McCormack, Inez and McCormack, Vincent (1995), 'More Bangs For Your Buck: Once For Jobs and Once For Justice', *Irish Reporter*, 43(17), 9–10.

MacCurtain, Margaret (1985) 'The Historical Image', in Ni Chuilleanain, Eilean (ed.) *Irish Women: Image and Achievement*, Dublin, Arlen House: 37–50.

McKay, Ann (1994) 'Report on Ruth Moore', *Women's News*, Belfast, June/July 69, 13.

McVeigh, Robbie (1999) 'Economic Inactivity and Inequality', *Economic Bulletin*, 6 (3, April/May), 8–16.

Mairead Farrell Cumann (1996) *Moving On: A Policy for Lesbian, Gay and Bisexual Equality*, Dublin.

Moore, Ruth (1995) 'An Exploration of the Impact of Sectarianism and Gender on the Experiences and Identities of Protestant Women in Northern Ireland', unpublished paper presented at Queen's University, Belfast, 17–18 February 1995.

Moreland, Rosemary and Rooney, Eilish (1998) 'Women and Participation: Empowering Communities', in Lovett, T. and Rooney, E. (eds), *Community Development, Democracy and Citizenship: Conference Report*, Jordanstown: University of Ulster, 27–33.

Morgan, Valerie (1992) 'Bridging the Divide: Women and Political and Community Issues', in Stringer, P. and Robinson, G. (eds), *Social Attitudes in Northern Ireland: The Second Report*, Belfast: Blackstaff, 135–48.

Parpart, Jane L. (1993) 'A Post-Modern Feminist Critique of Women and Development Theory and Practice', *Development and Change*, 24(3), 439–64.

Phillips, Anne (1992) 'Must Feminists Give Up on Liberal Democracy?', *Political Studies*, XL, Special Issue, 68–82.

Phillips, Anne (1994) *Why Should the Sex of the Representative Matter?*, paper presented at 'Women and Public Policy: The Shifting Boundaries Between the Public and Private Domains', Erasmus University.

Rolston, Bill (1993) 'The Contented Classes', *Irish Reporter*, 9, 7–9.

Rolston, Bill (1998) 'Culture as a Battlefield: Political Identity and the State in the North of Ireland', *Race & Class*, 39(4), 23–35.

Rooney, Eilish (1994) 'Excluded Voices', *Fortnight*, 332 October 31.

Rooney, Eilish (1995a) 'Political Division, Practical Alliance: Problems for Women in Conflict', *Journal of Women's History*, 6 (4)/7(1), 40–8.

Rooney, Eilish (1995b) 'Women in Political Conflict', *Race & Class*, 37, 51–6.

Rooney, Eilish (1996) 'Framing the Future, *Power, Politics, Positionings: Democratic Dialogue Report No. 4*', Belfast: Democratic Dialogue: 33–41.

Rooney, Eilish (1997) 'Women in Party Politics and Local Groups: Findings From Belfast', in Byrne, A. and Leonard, M. (eds) *Women in Irish Society: A Sociological Reader*, Belfast: Beyond the Pale Publications, 535–51.

Rooney, Eilish and Woods, Margaret (1995) *Women, Community and Politics In Northern Ireland: A Belfast Study*, Jordanstown: University of Ulster.

Sharoni, Simona (1995) *Gender and the Israeli-Palestinian Conflict: The Politics of Women's Resistance*, Syracuse, NY: Laurence Hill Books.

Smyth, Ailbhe (ed.) (1993) *Irish Women's Studies Reader*, Dublin: Attic Press.

Todd, Jennifer (1994) 'History and Structure in Loyalist Ideology: The Possibilities of Ideological Change', *Irish Journal of Sociology*, 4: 67–79.

Ward, Margaret (1983) *Unmanageable Revolutionaries: Women in Irish Nationalism*, London: Pluto Press.

Ward, Margaret (ed.) (1986), *A Dangerous, Difficult Honesty: 10 Years of Feminism in Northern Ireland*, Belfast: Women's Book Collective.

Ward, Margaret (1995) 'Finding a Place: Women and the Irish Peace Process', *Race & Class*, 37 (July–September), 41–50.

Wilson, Desmond (1999) *The Chaplain's Affair*, Springhill Community House, Belfast: Glandore Publications.

Young, I. M. (1996) 'Communication and the Other: Beyond Deliberative Democracy', in Benhabib, S. (ed.), *Democracy and Difference*, Princeton, NJ: Princeton University Press: 120–35.

Appendix 1: Northern Ireland: A Chronology of Key Events

1920 The Government of Ireland Act devolved powers to parliaments in Dublin and Belfast.

1921 The first Northern Ireland parliament opened.

1922 The government of the Irish Free State confirmed the 1920 border with Northern Ireland.

1929 The electoral system was changed: proportional representation was replaced by the first-past-the-post system for elections to the Northern Ireland parliament.

1937 The new constitution of the Irish Free State claimed sovereignty over Northern Ireland, gave a special place to the Catholic Church, and emphasised the importance of women's duties in the family.

1949 The Irish Free State became a republic. The new Government of Ireland Act guaranteed that Northern Ireland would stay part of the UK (as long as a majority of its citizens wished). Dehra Parker became minister of health in the Northern Ireland government (the first and only female cabinet minister).

1953 The first woman was elected from Northern Ireland to Westminster (Patricia Ford, Ulster Unionist). She held her seat until 1955, when the second woman MP was elected (Patricia McLaughlin, Ulster Unionist).

1961 The first Liberal MP (Sheelagh Murnaghan) was elected to Stormont.

1967 The Northern Ireland Civil Rights Association (NICRA) was formed.

1968 **(June)** Protests took place over the housing allocation policy of Dungannon Rural District Council.

(August) The first civil rights march was held (to Dungannon).

(October) A civil rights march took place in Derry. The Stormont minister of home affairs ordered a change of route; the march was broken up by baton-wielding police. The presence of television cameras and Labour MPs from Westminister resulted in widespread outrage at the violent methods used by the RUC.

(November) The Northern Ireland government (Unionist) announced a reform plan to meet NICRA demands.

(December) The Unionist Party began to split over reforms.

1969 **(March)** The RUC was rearmed (having been disarmed in 1965). The first explosions took place – caused by loyalist groups.

(April) Bernadette Devlin was elected to Westminister for the Mid-Ulster constituency as a Unity (Nationalist) candidate.

1969 **(August)** Serious rioting occurred in Belfast and Derry. The NI prime minister requested assistance from the British army to maintain order.

(December) The IRA split over the 'reformist' tactics of the leadership. The Provisional IRA was formed.

1970 **(January)** Sinn Féin split into two factions. Two other new parties
were created that year, the Social-Democratic and Labour Party, which
superceded the old Nationalist Party, and the Alliance Party, a cross-
community party.
(June) In the UK general election the Rev. Ian Paisley won a seat at
Westminister (North Antrim) from the Unionist Party.
From June onwards the Provisional IRA military campaign escalated.
The Equal Pay Act was adopted in Northern Ireland.
(November) *Women Together* was formed as a cross-community peace
movement.

1971 The Labour Party at Westminister revealed that a draft bill for direct
rule existed.
(August) Imprisonment without trial (internment) of suspected IRA
members was introduced.
(September) Further splits took place in the Unionist Party over talks
involving the Westminister and Dublin governments.
(October) The Democratic Unionist Party was formed (leader the
Rev. Ian Paisley).

1972 **(January)** The Paratroop Regiment fired on civil rights rally in Derry,
resulting in fourteen deaths (Bloody Sunday).
(March) The Stormont parliament was suspended and direct rule
from Westminster introduced.

1973 The UK and the Republic of Ireland joined the EEC.
(June) A new assembly was elected.
(December) The Sunningdale Conference on Northern Ireland took
place, attended by the British and Irish governments and the Northern Ireland power-sharing executive.

1974 **(May)** The Loyalist Ulster Worker's Council called a general strike
against the Sunningdale Agreement. The executive collapsed and direct
rule was resumed.

1975 In the International Year of Women the Northern Ireland Women's
Rights Movement was formed.

1976 Internment was ended.
(August) Three children from the Maguire family were killed during
a gun battle between troops and IRA members. The children's aunt
(Mairead Corrigan) and a neighbour (Betty Williams) called a dem-
onstration for peace, which led to the creation of a women's peace
movement (later the Peace People).
The Sex Discrimination Order became law in Northern Ireland; the
Equal Opportunities Commission, Northern Ireland, was created. The
Fair Employment Act was passed; the Fair Employment Commission
was set up.

1977 Betty Williams and Mairead Corrigan received the Nobel Peace Prize.

1981 **(March)** Republican prisoners went on hunger strike for political status.
(October) The hunger strike ended after ten prisoners had died. Among
those who died was Bobby Sands, elected during the hunger strike
as Sinn Féin MP for Fermanagh and South Tyrone. The European
Court of Human Rights ruled that the Northern Ireland law banning male homosexual acts was in breach of the European Convention.

1983 The government of the Irish Republic created an all-Ireland forum (the New Ireland Forum) to discuss ways of settling the Northern Ireland conflict.

1984 **(November)** The New Ireland Forum recommendations were firmly rejected by the UK prime minister Margaret Thatcher in the House of Commons.

1985 The SDLP leader John Hume agreed to discuss ways of ending the conflict with the Provisional IRA leadership.

(November) The British and Irish governments signed the Anglo-Irish Agreement, containing some of the policies recommended by the New Ireland Forum. The Unionist parties expressed outrage at the concessions to the principle of British–Irish joint sovereignty.

1986 **(March)** Women police officers in the RUC won a landmark sex discrimination case against the chief constable.

The Standing Advisory Commission on Human Rights report argued that under the Fair Employment Act the law failed to deal with inequality between Protestants and Catholics.

(September) The Ulster Unionist Party ended its boycott of meetings with British ministers over the Anglo-Irish Agreement.

(November) An IRA bomb at the Rememberance Day service in Enniskillen killed 11 people.

1987 All Northern Ireland MPs at Westminister voted in favour of David Alton's bill to reduce the legal limit for abortions to eighteen weeks of pregnancy.

SDLP and Sinn Féin began talks about possible settlements of NI conflict.

1990 A new Fair Employment Act was passed. The Community Relations Council was created.

Mary Robinson became the president of the Irish Republic.

1992 The Northern Ireland Office launched a new round of talks with NI parties.

(February) President Robinson visited women's groups in Belfast at the invitation of the Equal Opportunites Commission for Northern Ireland.

Secretary of State Patrick Mayhew announced that Sinn Féin would be included in political talks if the campaign of violence was ended.

1993 SDLP and Sinn Féin leaders resumed discussions on a political settlement.

The British government acknowledged that secret negotiations with Sinn Féin had been taking place.

The British and Irish prime ministers issued the Downing Street Declaration which upheld the principle that Northern Ireland would remain part of the UK as long as a majority of the electorate supported this; that a negotiated settlement would require respect for diverse traditions and that it must be achieved through peaceful means.

1994 The first woman (junior) minister in the Northern Ireland Office, Baroness Denton, was appointed.

(September) IRA and loyalist cease-fires began.

The Irish government convened an all-Ireland Forum for Peace and Reconciliation. The unionist parties boycotted the Forum.

1995   The British and Irish governments launched the *Frameworks for the Future* document setting out principles for political talks.

The Forum for Peace and Reconciliation issued a report accepting that constitutional change must be based on consent. Sinn Féin dissented from this report.

1996   **(January)** An international body chaired by Senator George Mitchell (USA) proposed six principles of democracy and non-violence to be observed by all parties to any negotiation.

The UK government decided that the composition of the Talks parties should be decided by election to a Northern Ireland Forum.

(February) The IRA ceasefire ended with the Canary Wharf bombing in London.

(April) The Northern Ireland Women's Coalition was created to contest elections and highlight the lack of women in major parties.

(30 May) Elections toook place to the Northern Ireland Forum for Political Dialogue. The Northern Ireland Women's Coalition won enough votes to send delegates to the peace Talks.

(10 June) The All-Party Peace Talks opened. Sinn Féin was refused entry because of its abandonment of its cease-fire.

1997   **(May)** Following the UK general election, the first woman secretary of state (Dr Marjorie Mowlam) was appointed.

A new IRA cease-fire was announced; Sinn Féin was admitted to the All-Party talks.

(July/August) Serious disturbances occurred because of the Orange parades issue.

1998   **(April, Good Friday)** The eight parties remaining in the Talks signed the Belfast Agreement.

(May) The Agreement was endorsed in a referendum by 71 per cent of voters (among unionist voters there was a slender pro-Agreement majority.)

(June) Elections to the Northern Ireland Assembly produced a narrow majority for pro-Agreement candidates among unionist voters. The Northern Ireland Women's Coalition won two seats.

(July) Serious rioting took place over the banning of an Orange Order parade in Portadown. Three Catholic children died in a sectarian arson attack on their home in Ballymoney, Co. Antrim.

(August) The anti-Agreement Real IRA placed a bomb in Omagh in which 27 people were killed. The Real IRA declared a cease-fire shortly afterwards.

1999   **(June–July)** The parties in the Assembly fail to create a new executive as Sinn Féin and the unionists disagreed over the process for decommissioning paramilitary weapons.

(September) George Mitchell opened a review of the implementation of the Agreement.

Women Together held a demonstration appealing for the parties to try to reach agreement.

Appendix 2: A Note on Methodology

Most of the material for the case-studies set out in Part II of this book was collected as part of an ESRC-funded study under the title 'Democracy, Gender, and the Politics of Women's Inclusion: Case Studies from Northern Ireland' (R000236224). While the NIWC was not formally included in this study at the design stage, the growing involvement of one team member (Monica McWilliams), and the clear relevance of this experience to the overall project, meant that updates and discussions became a regular part of the project team meetings. The decision was then taken to replace one of the original case-studies with an account of the NIWC.

The initial research design envisaged case-studies of four organisations selected in such a way that each would display a different tradition in terms of its thinking about being a democratic organisation, and that each would differ in terms of how it conceptualised the individual and of how its members would be likely to think in terms of rights and obligations. A detailed list of criteria was drawn up. The plan was to work closely with each of the organisations selected, involving them actively in the research process, utilising an action research methodology and giving extensive feedback.

A shortlist of organisations was drawn up and exploratory interviews were carried out both to inform the team about the fit of potential case-study sites with the criteria and to assess the extent to which cooperation and interest would be likely to be forthcoming. A short project summary and a protocol for the research, prepared with reference to the BSA Code of Ethics, was made available for discussion before the research began. This latter covered questions of access and confidentiality, as well as the rights and obligations of both parties, and gave undertakings about the ways in which the work would be carried out.

Each of the case studies employed a multi-method approach to data collection, which included observation, interviews and documentary analysis. Fieldwork in the first case-study, Chrysalis, began in October 1995 with an intensive period of interviewing and documentary analysis. 20 interviews were carried out over a period of approximately 6 weeks, together with attendance at as many management committee and other meetings as was feasible. Classes offered by the Centre and other events were attended. A programme of management training for staff was monitored. One of the researchers (Margaret Whittock) then continued to attend the Centre's regular meetings for the next six months. Occasional contact with the Centre was retained for the duration of the project.

A similar approach was taken with Cornerstone. The main fieldwork took place between January and April 1996, and included an examination of records and 20 interviews in all, some of which were with members who had left and representatives of bodies who had had close contact with Cornerstone. The relationship continued after the fieldwork stage. One of the researchers (Carmel Roulston) accompanied by another team member (Eilish Rooney), took part in an organisation review later in the year and offered, on request, a seminar on themes of women and politics. After preliminary work, the NIPSA case-study was completed in a three-month period between January and April 1997. Here there was more extensive documentary record and a much larger and complex organisation to be understood. Once again, there was a mix of documentary analysis, interviews and observations. A total of eighteen interviews was completed, balancing these between headquarters and branch level and between officials and lay activists.

Interviews were semi-structured, lasting mostly for around an hour, though on a few occasions interviews were of a longer duration. The researchers used a mix of tape-recording and note-taking. Material was then transcribed for later use and case-study summaries were discussed at regular team meetings throughout the project. Each of the case-study organisations was given feedback and furnished with a copy of a case-study report. Members of all the case-study organisations were invited to a one-day feedback workshop where overall themes and comparisons were drawn out. At this point, a formal decision was taken to lift the undertaking in the protocol to maintain the confidentiality of the organisations in the final report to funders and in subsequent publications. There had been preliminary discussion with each organisation individually on this matter and it was agreed that anonymity would be almost impossible to preserve in a small community such as Northern Ireland. It was also apparent by this time that that the accounts were not such as to cause problems for the organisations, and indeed feedback suggested that participants had had found them useful in thinking through their strategies for the future. Each case-study organisation was given a further opportunity to comment on the relevant draft chapter as it was being prepared for this book.

Index